D0277484

Latex and Lingerie

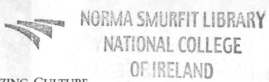

MATERIALIZING CULTURE

· ·

Series Editors: Paul Gilroy, Michael Herzfeld and Danny Miller

Barbara Bender, *Stonehenge: Making Space*

Gen Doy, *Materializing Art History*

Laura Rival (ed.), *The Social Life of Trees: Anthropological Perspectives on Tree Symbolism*

Victor Buchli, *An Archaeology of Socialism*

Marius Kwint, Christopher Breward and Jeremy Aynsley (eds), *Material Memories: Design and Evocation*

Penny Van Esterik, *Materializing Thailand*

Michael Bull, *Sounding Out the City: Personal Stereos and the Management of Everyday Life*

Anne Massey, *Hollywood Beyond the Screen: Design and Material Culture*

Wendy Joy Darby, *Landscape and Identity: Geographies of Nation and Class in England*

Joy Hendry, *The Orient Strikes Back: A Global View of Cultural Display*

Judy Attfield, *Wild Things: The Material Culture of Everyday Life*

Daniel Miller (ed.), *Car Cultures*

Elizabeth Edwards, *Raw Histories: Photographs, Anthropology and Museums*

David E. Sutton, *Remembrance of Repasts: An Anthropology of Food and Memory*

Eleana Yalouri, *The Acropolis: Global Fame, Local Claim*

Elizabeth Hallam and Jenny Hockey, *Death, Memory and Material Culture*

Sharon Macdonald, *Behind the Scenes at the Science Museum*

Elaine Lally, *At Home With Computers*

Susanne Küchler, *Malanggan: Art, Memory and Sacrifice*

Nicky Gregson and Louise Crewe, *Second-Hand Cultures*

Latex and Lingerie

Shopping for Pleasure at Ann Summers

MERL STORR

Oxford • New York

First published in 2003 by
Berg *(handwritten)* £23.71
Editorial offices:
1st Floor, 81 St Clements Street, Oxford, OX4 1AW, UK
838 Broadway, Third Floor, New York, NY 10003-4812, USA

© Merl Storr 2003

Berg is the imprint of Oxford International Publishers Ltd.

Library of Congress Cataloging-in-Publication Data

Storr, Merl, 1966–
     Latex and lingerie : shopping for pleasure at Ann Summers / Merl
Storr. – 1st ed.
          p. cm. – (Materializing culture series, ISSN 1460-3349)
Includes bibliographical references and index.
     ISBN 1-85973-693-9 (Cloth) – ISBN 1-85973-698-X (Paper)
   1. Ann Summers Limited. 2. Direct selling–Great Britain–Case studies.
3. Home-based businesses–Great Britain–Case studies. 4. Lingerie industry–
Great Britain–Case studies. I. Title. II. Series: Materializing culture.

   HF5439.L37S86 2003
   381'.45687'0820941–dc21

                                                            2003004505

British Library Cataloguing-in-Publication Data

A catalogue record for this book is available from the British Library.

ISBN 1 85973 693 9 (Cloth)
           1 85973 698 X (Paper)

Typeset by JS Typesetting Ltd, Wellingborough, Northants.
Printed in the United Kingdom by Biddles Ltd, King's Lynn.

www.bergpublishers.com

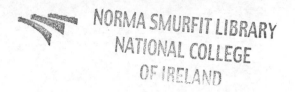
To Nicky and Hazel, with love

Contents

List of Figures   ix

Acknowledgements   xi

1   Introducing Ann Summers   1
The Ann Summers Party Plan   3
Ann Summers – a typical party plan?   4
Researching Ann Summers   12
Liquorice allsorts   14
'The No 1 Fun Company'   21
Personality, skill and emotional labour   22
'Young mums'   26
Ann Summers as post-feminist fun   30
Hidden depths   34
About this book   35

2   'The Ultimate Girls' Night In'   37
Conceptualising Homosociality   39
Male homosociality   39
Female homosociality   47
Ann Summers and Female Homosociality   54
Helping women to serve the interests of men   56
Being one of the girls   62
Lesbophobia   72
Summary and Conclusion   81

3   Objects of Desire   83
Ann Summers Parties for Men?   84
She Likes Men   90
Feeling sexy   90

Men in uniform – 'hello boys!'   97
'All That's Missing is the Man!'   103
The penis and the phallus   107
Pass my penis   110
Feel it, believe it!   114
Summary and Conclusion   121

4   Feminine Bodies, Feminine Pleasures   123
The Heterosexual Female Erogenous Body at
    Ann Summers Parties   130
Technique and interior zones   133
Technique and exterior zones   145
Erogenous functions   147
The Female Homosocial Body at Ann Summers Parties   149
The homosocial body's oral pleasures   150
The homosocial body's vocal pleasures   158
The homosocial body's tactile pleasures   164
The homosocial body's visual pleasures   168
Summary and Conclusion   175

5   Classy Lingerie   177
Peeling the Lemon   177
Homosocial Underwear   185
The girls go shopping   187
Luxury/utility   191
Sleaze/respectability   201
Eroticism/domesticity   213
Summary and Conclusion   216

6   Conclusion   219

References   223

Index   231

List of Figures

1.1 Ann Summers catalogue autumn/winter 1999   5

1.2 Structure of Ann Summers party plan. Shaded levels are those which are women-only and based on commission rather than a salary   7

1.3 Profiles of the fifteen interviewees, arranged by length of time with Ann Summers   15

2.1 The male homosocial-homosexual continuum (extrapolated from Sedgwick 1985)   45

2.2 The female homosocial-homosexual continuum   50

3.1 Goddess bra, from the Ann Summers catalogue autumn/winter 1999   94

3.2 Dreammen in Uniform calendar 2000, from the Ann Summers catalogue Christmas supplement 1999   98

3.3 (L–R) Discovery, Flower Power, Reelfeel, Dynamite and Light Up Vibrators, from the Ann Summers catalogue autumn/winter 1999   99

3.4 Jelly Willy Stress Buster, from the Ann Summers catalogue autumn/winter 1999   106

4.1 Cockerel Pouch, from the Ann Summers catalogue autumn/winter 1999   134

4.2 (Top R) Bath Massage Ball and (bottom L-R) Climax Creator, Little Beaver and Vibromatic Ring vibrators, from the Ann Summers catalogue autumn/winter 1999   137

4.3 (L–R) Jiggle Balls and Heart Throbber, from the Ann Summers catalogue autumn/winter 1999   138

4.4 Siren dress, from the Ann Summers catalogue autumn/winter 1999   171

5.1 Wild lingerie set, from the Ann Summers catalogue autumn/winter 1999   188

5.2 Vamp lingerie set, from the Ann Summers catalogue autumn/winter 1999   189

5.3   Fever basque, from the Ann Summers catalogue
      autumn/winter 1999   196
5.4   Fur Love Cuffs, from the Ann Summers catalogue
      autumn/winter 1999   208
5.5   Bondage Starter Kit, from the Ann Summers catalogue
      Christmas supplement 1999   208
5.6   Fifi maid's outfit, from the Ann Summers catalogue
      autumn/winter 1999   215

Acknowledgements

All photographic images in this book are taken from Ann Summers catalogues for 1999. Copyright on all these images is held by Ann Summers Ltd and they are reproduced here by permission. Some of the products shown in this book have since been discontinued from the Ann Summers range: for up-to-date details of the current Ann Summers product range, visit www.annsummers.com.

For their support, encouragement and indulgence during the writing of this book, I thank Ann Kaloski, Barbara Harrison, David Hansen-Miller, Diane Ball, Hazel Storr, Iris Stevens, Jenny Howell, Joan Friend, Joseph Bristow, Kate Beaton, Kathryn Earle, Lucy Bland, Mary Maynard, Nicky Storr, Paul Day, Paula Black, Ray Walmsley, Samantha Jackson, Sharon Morris, Sylvie Hudson, Terry Eaton, Tilly Storr, Tim Butler, Wendy Rickard, and the inter-library loan staff at the University of East London's Barking campus.

For their comments on previous versions of this work, I thank Amal Treacher, Ann Phoenix, Clare Hemmings, Derek McGhee, Helen Crowley, Kaeren Harrison, Kerry Hamilton, Lyn Thomas, Nirmal Puwar, Rachel Falmagne, and Ros Gill. Most of all I thank Stephen Maddison, who heroically read the entire manuscript – some of it several times – and made many invaluable contributions. If there are any good ideas in this book, Stephen probably thought of them first.

I thank the Ann Summers Press Office, particularly Delia Bourne, Kevin Barnes, Louise Hearn and Rebecca Franklin, for their assistance and co-operation. Above all, for their generous participation in this research project, I thank Carol O'Brien, Chantel Benefield, Joanne May, Lisa Agius, Lynda Lowe, Lynn, Natalie Daines, Nicola Hards, Samantha Hughes, Sandra Evans, Sharon Collier, Sharon Potter, Sue Covington, Susan Beeson, Wendy Donaldson, and the many other women who welcomed me into Ann Summers parties and meetings, talked to me, bought me drinks, gave me lifts, and tolerated my inquisitive presence.

Parts of Chapter 5 were previously published in *Feminist Review* 71 (2002).

Introducing Ann Summers

Girls just want to have **fun**!
We offer the most **sensual** lingerie, designed for sizes 10–24, plus our
exciting **new** supplement, **sexy** outerwear designed by Ann Summers.
We also give you a **wide range** of personal products and fun novelty
items for every occasion.
JUST INVITE YOUR FRIENDS & WE WILL DO THE REST! [. . .]
HAVE FUN WHILE YOU EARN! with the No. 1 Party Plan
Hold your own party and . . . BE THE **HOSTESS** WITH
THE **MOSTESS**!
FANTASTIC benefits and rewards for the Hostess based on
total party sales.
Become a party organiser and join in the fun with Ann Summers.
- **EARN £50 – £100+ PER WEEK**
- **BE YOUR OWN BOSS**
- **UNBELIEVABLE REWARDS**
- **ACHIEVE A COMPANY CAR**
TOO GOOD TO BE TRUE?
CALL today and discover that we mean business!
(Ann Summers publicity flyer, autumn/winter 1999)

This enticing flyer offers the opportunity to hold an Ann Summers
home shopping party in your own living room. You invite your friends
and provide alcohol and other refreshments; the Ann Summers party
organiser comes to your home, supplies catalogues and order forms, and
passes around some of the products for you to see and touch, including
lingerie, evening wear, sex toys, 'lotions and potions' from massage oils
to Banana Dick Lick, sex manuals and erotic fiction, and a range of saucy
novelties and accessories such as edible panties, penis-shaped soap and
the famous Ann Summers pink fake-fur handcuffs. There will be not
just catalogues and product demonstrations but also party games, a

raffle, probably some dressing up, and certainly a lot of laughter. Ten per cent of the money spent at your party will come back to you then and there as your 'hostess commission' for you to spend on Ann Summers products, and you may also receive a free gift. And if you do decide to 'join in the fun' and become a party organiser yourself, you only have to ask: there are no entry qualifications, no interview or selection process, no experience required; if you want it, the job is yours. There are just two conditions: to participate in Ann Summers, whether as a party organiser, a party guest or a 'hostess with the mostess', you must be aged eighteen or over, and you must be female.

Ann Summers home shopping parties are only available in the UK and, as British readers will know, 'Ann Summers' is an instantly recognisable brand name. According to the company's own figures, around 4,000 Ann Summers parties take place in the UK every week, and around 7,500 British women work as party organisers. The extraordinary success of Ann Summers Ltd, and the huge popularity of the parties in particular, make the company a significant force in the everyday construction of many British women's sexuality. Quite apart from the fascinating nature of parties as such, the sheer numbers of women involved seem to suggest that scholars of gender and sexuality should be taking Ann Summers rather seriously. But although Ann Summers has a high profile and receives a great deal of media attention in the UK, I have been able to find no previous scholarly or academic work on the subject.[1] This lack of attention to Ann Summers is surprising. Not only are party-goers buying sex toys and erotic lingerie in large numbers, but party organisers and party-goers alike are regularly talking about, representing and experiencing their own sexuality in highly specific settings – parties and meetings – which operate according to specific rules, structures and repertoires of meaning. The purpose of this book is to uncover those rules, structures and repertoires, and to consider their significance. In particular this book argues that the fun and laughter of Ann Summers parties involve not just pleasure and play, but also intense power struggles over heterosexual femininity, racked by identifications, exclusions, hierarchies and (self-)policing. This book is about those power struggles between women, and about the specific forms of heterosexual femininity at stake in them.

1. By contrast, the well known erotic lingerie retailer Victoria's Secret, which is based in the US and sells its products in high-street stores, by mail order and through its website (www.VictoriasSecret.com), has received some attention from feminist academics (e.g. Faludi 1991, Workman 1996, Juffer 1998, Wilson-Kovacs 2001).

This first chapter sketches the arena in which these struggles take place. The first part of the chapter gives an outline of the Ann Summers party plan, including information on the women who work as party organisers and the structure of the party plan organisation. It then introduces the research on which this book as a whole is based and the women who participated in it, before moving on to discuss some of the ways party organisers perceive themselves, both as women and as workers. The final section of this chapter sketches the book's main argument and maps the course of the chapters that follow.

The Ann Summers Party Plan

Home shopping parties are a well-known type of retailing, the best known purveyors of which world-wide include multinational companies such as Tupperware, Amway and Mary Kay. These organisations are known as 'party plan' organisations, although in some cases (including Ann Summers) the company may also use other retail strategies such as mail order, e-commerce and high-street shops as well as its party plan. Home shopping parties involve a salesperson (usually referred to as a 'demonstrator' or 'party organiser') coming to the private home of a customer (usually referred to as a 'host' or, more often, a 'hostess') to display and demonstrate products to a group of people invited by the customer. The party-goers are able to see, handle and in some cases try out the products for themselves before they buy. The party is a hybrid shopping and social event, with refreshments usually provided by the host(ess), and in some cases with party games, raffles and other diversions provided by the demonstrator.

Party plan as such is a form of direct selling. The UK's Direct Selling Association (DSA) describes direct selling as a marketing and retail method in which 'independent salespeople call on consumers, mainly in their homes, to show and often demonstrate products and obtain orders' (Direct Selling Association UK 2000). DSA figures show that direct selling has a 14 per cent share of the UK home shopping market and that 'it is a growing sector [. . .] with annual sales exceeding £1.2 billion' (Direct Selling Association UK 2000). (Other sectors of the home shopping market include mail order and internet shopping.) Direct selling retail sales for 2000 in the US exceeded $25.5 billion (Direct Selling Association USA 2001). Direct sales companies world-wide offer a broad range of products, including food, clothes, cosmetics and jewellery, household goods, children's books and toys and many other items.

Party plan is one of the two main types of direct selling. The second is what the DSA calls 'person-to-person' selling, epitomised by the door-to-door salesperson, which constituted 88 per cent of direct sales in the UK in 1999 and 70.3 per cent of direct sales in the USA in 2000 (Direct Selling Association UK 2000, Direct Selling Association USA 2001).

The Ann Summers party plan is just one element in the Ann Summers retail strategy, which achieves an average turnover of £64 million per year. All of the company's retail outlets offer the same product range of lingerie, outerwear, sex toys (especially vibrators), books, novelties and other 'personal' (i.e. sex-related) products.[2] There is a large and increasingly successful retail website (www.annsummers.com), and customers are able to use the Ann Summers catalogue, which appears twice a year, for mail order (Figure 1.1). In March 2002 there were fifty-five Ann Summers high-street shops in the UK, the turnover from which roughly equalled that generated through the party plan. But when my fieldwork began in autumn 1999 there were many fewer high street shops – the company opened around forty new shops between summer 1999 and summer 2002 – and party plan was by far the most profitable retail strategy for Ann Summers Ltd in the UK, representing around 70 per cent of the company's sales. Indeed, from the perspective of party organisers (though not necessarily of customers), the party plan operated largely independently of the shops and website. The party organisers who participated in my research rarely if ever spoke of visiting Ann Summers shops, and I never heard a single reference to the website during the entire research project. As far as party organisers themselves are con-cerned, Ann Summers *is* the party plan.

Ann Summers – a typical party plan?

Ann Summers Ltd was founded in 1970 by Kim Caborn-Waterfield, who reportedly decided to open 'Britain's first sex supermarket' after being inspired by the Beate Uhse chain of sex shops in mainland Europe (Gold 1995: 50). The company was acquired by the Gold Group in 1971 after going into voluntary liquidation. The Gold Group, owned by the brothers David and Ralph Gold, has diverse business interests including puzzle magazines, an airline, and Birmingham City Football Club, but it is probably best known for its ownership of a number of soft porn-ographic magazines. After 1971 Ann Summers Ltd continued to trade

---

2. Ann Summers Ltd also owns the Knickerbox chain of high-street lingerie stores. This chain stocks its own product range rather than that found in the Ann Summers shops.

through its shops and mail order, and in 1981 the Ann Summers party plan was launched by David Gold's daughter Jacqueline. Jacqueline Gold took direct inspiration from the Pippa Dee party plan, which sells clothing at home shopping parties in the UK. In many ways Ann Summers is a typical plan, sharing many of the organisational structures and motivational strategies common to party plan companies in the UK and elsewhere (Peven 1968; Davis 1973; Taylor 1978; Crawford and Garland 1988; Biggart 1989; Prus and Frisby 1990; Gainer & Fischer 1991; O'Neill 1993; Clarke 1999).

Ann Summers party organisers, like all party plan salespeople, are self-employed: they are not the company's employees but its customers. Party organisers make their money through commission from each party. Party-goers place their orders with the party organiser, who in turn orders the goods from Ann Summers. The party organiser then receives the goods from Ann Summers and passes them on to the hostess. It is the hostess who finally distributes the goods to her guests.

Figure 1.1 Ann Summers catalogue autumn/winter 1999

All items are delivered to the hostess wrapped in opaque plastic so that she cannot see what her friends have bought: in this way the privacy of each customer is assured (a particular consideration for customers buying sex toys). The process usually takes one or two weeks from the date of the party to guests' receipt of the goods.

Party organisers receive a 33 per cent discount on the price listed in the catalogue for Ann Summers items. Ten per cent goes to the hostess as her 'commission', to be spent on her own order rather than received as cash. The remaining 23 per cent is the party organiser's commission. The company sets 'standard' figures for party organisers which act as a minimum target to be achieved at each party; during the period of my research this figure was £180-worth of sales per party (plus two bookings for future parties from among the guests present). A party organiser achieving this standard would therefore receive £41.40 commission. However this figure does not represent simple profit, because the party organiser must pay for her own supplies, including items for her 'kit' to demonstrate at parties, stationery such as order forms and party invitations, items to give as prizes for party games and/or the raffle held at each party, and the stock of sweets, balloons and other sundries she may need for her party games. She will also of course be paying her 'overheads' such as travel expenses, lighting, heating and so on because she works from home: telephone bills can be a particular expense for party organisers, who are instructed to telephone every hostess at least three times before every party as well as having to telephone their managers, and the head office's Orderline to place all their orders. It should also be borne in mind that her working hours considerably exceed the two or three hours she will probably spend at the party itself, because of the time she also spends preparing for parties, placing orders and completing other kinds of paperwork, travelling, and attending Ann Summers meetings which usually take at least two hours per month and are both compulsory and unpaid. Although nominally self-employed, in practice it is unlikely that many (if any) party organisers officially register as such or pay tax or National Insurance on their income. Indeed one party organiser initially expressed reservations about participating in my research for fear that 'the taxman would find out' about her earnings, and only decided to do so after strenuous assurances of anonymity and confidentiality.

Ann Summers' party plan sales force is divided into a number of geographical 'areas', each headed by an area manager. Each area is in turn divided into 'units' headed by a 'unit organiser' who is also herself an active party plan saleswoman. All of the area managers are former

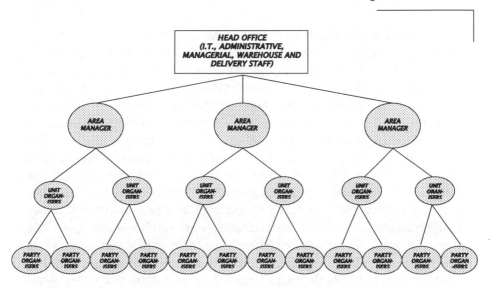

Figure 1.2 Structure of Ann Summers party plan. Shaded levels are those which are women-only and based on commission rather than a salary

unit organisers; all of the unit organisers are former party organisers and remain active party plan saleswomen in their own right. Consequently all three levels in the organisation are women-only; men are only employed at head office, either (in small numbers) as I.T., administrative or managerial staff or (in larger numbers) in the goods warehouse and as delivery drivers (Figure 1.2). This hierarchical structure allows information to flow up and down the chain between the company's head office and individual party organisers. Area managers hold monthly meetings for their unit organisers, and unit organisers hold monthly meetings for their party organisers, to ensure that accurate, up-to-date information is passed down about the product range, product promotions, prices and other facets of the party plan. This process of dissemination is known within Ann Summers as 'downlining'. Area managers and unit managers also hold occasional extra meetings for party organisers for training and/or motivational purposes. Party organisers pass their weekly sales figures up to their unit organisers (usually by telephone during designated timeslots during the week) and unit organisers pass their total weekly figures up to their area managers. This hierarchical organisational structure is also a pay structure. Unit organisers earn extra commission, known as 'override', on the income of their unit members and recruits, and area managers in turn earn override on the income of their unit organisers.

Area managers routinely promote competition and rivalry between the units and the party organisers in their charge by offering prizes for various achievements such as highest sales figures or greatest number of parties held. Some of these competitions and prizes are 'officially' set up by Ann Summers, while others are the brainchildren of area managers themselves. Unit organisers similarly offer a mixture of company and independent competitions and prizes to their party organisers. The most coveted prizes are the 'bars' which party organisers and unit organisers are awarded for achieving specific sales and recruitment targets, and which are proudly worn on Ann Summers badges. The sheer number, variety and complexity of competitions, prize draws and raffles being held every month is often dazzling and even bewildering. At unit meetings I observed it was by no means uncommon for party organisers to win prizes without realising it – indeed, sometimes without realising that the competition they had won was even taking place. My head would often be spinning by the end of one of these prize-giving sessions. The largest prize-giving session of all, and the highlight of every Ann Summers party organiser's calendar, is the 'catalogue launch'. This event is held twice a year to coincide (as its name suggests) with the publication of the new sales catalogue, and is attended by area managers, unit organisers and party organisers. (There are several regional launches rather than a single nationwide event.) Each catalogue launch has a different fancy dress 'theme', and is usually held in a large local venue with music and a bar, with stage performances by sales executives from head office, live modelling of the new clothes and lingerie, and male strippers as well as formal presentations of bars, prizes, company cars and other awards on stage. The tone of the catalogue launch is celebratory and highly emotional.

As Biggart (1989) points out, the formally hierarchical and competitive structure of direct selling organisations belies the more relaxed, personal style of interactions and relationships which take place within that structure. Unit organisers are not just providers of information and monitors of sales figures, but also act as sources of encouragement, support, help and advice to their party organisers, and area managers do the same for their unit organisers. Just as party hostesses provide refreshments for their party guests, so unit organisers often provide drinks and even cakes, sweets and crisps for party organisers during meetings, turning the meetings into quasi-social events. All of the units I observed during my research also held Christmas parties, arranged by the unit organisers for their party organisers. Alongside all the competitiveness and aspirational drive, party plans encourage a spirit of co-operation and mutual support amongst party organisers. Unit organisers will often set aside time during unit meetings specifically for party organisers to talk amongst themselves, share ideas and simply enjoy each other's company. While unit meetings are undoubtedly serious business, they are always also full of laughing, chatting and joking between the women. Indeed even the bars and other prizes awarded to individuals are often recognitions of *group* achievements: in particular, the company cars which can be 'won' (the women always talk about 'winning' company cars rather than 'earning' them) by a unit organiser are based on the income generated not just by her as an individual but by her unit as a whole. A sense of mutuality and even of 'family' is fostered by the use of language within the party plan, particularly in the words used to describe the relationships between party organisers and unit organisers. A unit organiser usually refers to the members of her unit as 'my girls'; if one of her 'girls' is herself promoted and becomes a unit organiser in her own right, she is referred to as the former's 'baby', and the former is her 'mother unit organiser'. Some unit organisers spoke of having not just 'babies' but 'grandchildren' in this way, and prestige is attached to unit organisers who have large numbers of babies.

This emphasis on emotion, mutuality and familial-style relationships is highlighted by Biggart (1989) as a common feature of direct selling organisations and as a core component of their appeal to women. Direct selling in general is a female-dominated sector: the UK Direct Selling Association (2000) estimates that 66 per cent of British direct sellers were women in 1998, with a further 16.5 per cent operating as husband-and-wife teams[3]. In fact in this respect Ann Summers is unusual in that it is explicit company policy to allow *only* women (aged eighteen or over) to operate as party organisers, and to allow only women (aged eighteen or over) to attend Ann Summers parties. Although I did occasionally hear of Ann Summers parties to which men and/or transvestites were invited, these were usually revelations by disaffected former party organisers or tales told to me by people who were not party organisers themselves. I neither witnessed any such party myself nor heard that any of my research participants had conducted such a party. On the contrary, the party organisers I encountered during this research were adamant that they would never breach this rule: not only would it result

3. Some party plan companies actively recruit husband-and-wife teams; in such cases the husband usually acts as salesman while the wife takes care of book-keeping and administration (Biggart 1989). The best known of these companies is probably Amway, which sells cosmetics, jewellery and household products.

in the 'instant dismissal' – meaning closure of a party organiser's account with Ann Summers – but it was also, party organisers assured me, actually *illegal* for a man to be present at an Ann Summers party, although none of them was ever able to inform me exactly which law (if any) it infringed.

Ann Summers parties themselves are just as typical of party plan selling as is the organisational structure of the sales force. Although individual party organisers generally develop their own styles and routines as they become more experienced, all parties share the same basic elements: the variation between party organisers mainly lies in the order in which the elements are completed and the relative time and emphasis devoted to each. These basic elements are the sales presentation; the kit demonstration, which is in turn subdivided into a lingerie demonstration, a vibrator demonstration, and a demonstration of massage oils and other sundries; the party games; the raffle; a period of catalogue browsing, and sometimes of trying on items of clothing or lingerie; and the placing of orders. Placing of orders is almost always the last segment of the party, and the sales presentation is usually (though by no means always) the first. Party organisers give their sales presentation with the aid of a 'Party Presenter Pack' provided by the company which gives information on payment methods, current promotions and prize draws, as well as information for potential recruits.

There are no entry requirements, qualifications or selection processes involved in joining the Ann Summers party plan: membership is formally open to any adult woman. Training offered to new recruits is similarly informal. On joining the party plan, party organisers receive a Party Organiser Training Manual – an A4 booklet just over thirty pages in length – and a book of party games. Some unit organisers supplement these with training material of their own devising: for example, two unit organisers I met during my research provided their new recruits with a book of jokes which they had compiled and produced themselves. Recruits are usually taken by their unit organiser to a 'training party' before their first party booking. In some cases this training party is specially organised as such and held in the recruit's own home with her own friends as guests; but more often it is simply one of the unit organiser's ordinary party bookings, and the recruit just goes along to observe. For most party organisers the Training Manual, book of games and training party constitute all of their induction and training, although unit organisers and area managers strive continuously to advise, motivate and inspire their party organisers at meetings.

Unit organisers in particular are always on the look-out for new recruits to join Ann Summers: as with all party plan organisations, turnover of party organisers is high, and unit organisers are constantly seeking to replace unit members who have left or become inactive. As well as making recruitment bids at parties, unit organisers will also gain new members from advertisements in local newspapers, personal recommendations from existing unit members, and indeed their own friends and family. This use of personal networks is another typical feature of party plan organisations. Party organisers and unit organisers draw on such networks not just to find new recruits but also to gain party bookings. New recruits themselves usually begin their party plan careers by persuading female friends or relatives to host parties for them; it is common, for example, for a party organiser's first Ann Summers party to be hosted by her mother. Party organisers routinely solicit bookings from the guests at every party, as well as seeking bookings through advertising in local newspapers and/or shop windows, canvassing in the high street or door-to-door in their local area, and sometimes even cold-calling local pubs for 'pub parties' (parties held in private function rooms of pubs, advertised in advance in the pub itself, from which landlords/ladies stand to profit through the extra bar sales). They also make deliberate efforts to stay in touch with hostesses of previous parties in the hope of repeat bookings: 'regular' hostesses who can be relied upon for repeat bookings are particularly prized. Party organisers sometimes also hold parties in their own homes, known as 'home parties', which if successful can boost both their income (they get to keep all of the 33 per cent commission for themselves rather than having to share it with a hostess) and their bookings from guests. The quest for party bookings is never-ending: the absence of party bookings is the most common reason why party organisers leave or become inactive. Unit organisers constantly stress that getting party bookings is both the most difficult and the most crucial aspect of party organising.

All of this may suggest that Ann Summers is a typical and perhaps even unremarkable party plan, albeit a highly successful one. What marks Ann Summers as a special case is of course its product range. The products themselves are explicitly erotic in orientation, and consequently the games, prizes, jokes and conversations at parties also tend to revolve around sex, either explicitly or by innuendo. Jacqueline Gold has suggested that 'Perhaps it is the slightly giggly, rather ribald attitude to sex in Britain that makes Ann Summers so successful' (Gold 1995: 75). I am not sure whether it really constitutes a national characteristic, but 'giggly ribaldry' neatly sums up the atmosphere at many of the Ann Summers parties I attended during my research.

Researching Ann Summers

My research was conducted in the autumn and winter of 1999–2000 in London and urban Essex. I made my initial approach during the summer of 1999 to Ann Summers head office in Surrey; after considering and agreeing to my research proposal, Ann Summers press office invited me to attend an area meeting, where I made a short presentation about my research and requested volunteers to participate. Several of the unit organisers present immediately offered to take me to parties and meetings with them, and from that point onwards it was relatively easy to find willing participants. Many party organisers were eager to help me write my book on Ann Summers: they were tired of having their work dismissed and trivialised by 'sleazy' media reports about Ann Summers parties, and in particular of being represented as 'bimbos' with no brains and overactive sex drives.

I used two main methods of data collection: participant observation and semi-structured interviews. I also of course collected Ann Summers party plan literature, press cuttings and the like, and remained in touch with the Ann Summers press office who kindly provided me with a great deal of background information. All of the research was conducted with the full knowledge and co-operation of Ann Summers Ltd, but without their interference. The press office and I made a written agreement that they would be able to read and comment on first drafts of any publications arising from the research, but that they would not attempt to influence my findings. Apart from factual information supplied by the press office, none of the findings in this book is endorsed or sponsored by Ann Summers Ltd.

Participant observation was intensively carried out over a period of five months at meetings and parties. During this period I focused on three unit organisers and their 'girls', many of whom also took me to one or more of their parties. I also attended a few parties organised by women from other units in the area, and attended a catalogue launch in December 1999. All of the area managers, unit organisers and party organisers I encountered at meetings knew who I was and why I was there, and I distributed brief written details of my research plan. However, when it came to parties I left it up to the party organiser to decide how, if at all, to explain my presence to the party-goers. Since each party is not just a social occasion but a source of livelihood for a party organiser, it seemed only right that this decision should be hers. Some party organisers informed the party hostess and/or her guests that I was a researcher, and in such cases I would always offer to leave the party if anyone felt uncomfortable with my presence: no-one ever did so, and indeed many party-goers were interested in the research and keen to co-operate. Other party organisers presented me to their hostesses as a trainee or simply did not offer an explanation of my presence at all. I took brief written notes during meetings and some-times (where I had been presented as a trainee) at parties, but never made any recordings in either setting for fear that this would be too intrusive.

After the first few months of participant observation I began to supplement my findings with formal interviews. These were all with unit organisers and party organisers rather than with hostesses or party guests. My criterion for selecting potential interviewees was simply that they should have organised at least one party before the interview – thus excluding only the newest of new recruits. Again it was relatively easy to find willing interviewees; one unit organiser even took it upon herself to recruit interviewees for me from her personal network of Ann Summers friends, so that there was one interviewee whom I had not met before the day I interviewed her. All but two of the interviews were conducted in the interviewees' own homes: the two exceptions were Diane, who was interviewed in the home of her elderly mother, and Melanie, who preferred to be interviewed in a local café. Many of the party organisers with pre-school age children were interviewed with those children in the room, or sometimes while the children were being looked after in another room in the house. Diane's elderly mother and pre-school age granddaughter (both of whom she was caring for on the day of the interview) were in the room while the interview took place, and Melanie brought a female friend to the café with her. The inter-viewees were all offered the opportunity to read and comment upon first drafts of this and other publications arising from the research, although in practice only a few chose to do so.

The interviews were semi-structured and covered broad topics such as recent parties they had attended, how they joined Ann Summers, their likes and dislikes about the party plan and the product range, and the attitudes of friends, family, customers and acquaintances towards their participation in Ann Summers. Each interviewee was also asked a short standard list of questions at the end of the interview to collect basic information about their age, length of time with Ann Summers, employment and housing status and so on; this included requests for self-descriptions in terms of class, 'race' or ethnicity, and sexuality. Four unit organisers and eleven party organisers were interviewed, and quotes from their interview transcripts appear throughout this book. A brief profile of each interviewee, including some direct interview quotes,[4] appears in table form in Figure 1.3: all of their names have been changed to preserve their anonymity and confidentiality. (Other men or women named during interviews have also been disguised in the transcripts as MX or FX respectively.) Such a small number of interviews is not of course intended to be 'representative' of the Ann Summers party plan sales force as a whole, nor even of the party plan at a specific time and geographical location: the interviewees 'represent' only themselves. But their accounts of everyday life as a party organiser or unit organiser provide many insights into the meanings and structures of Ann Summers from an 'insider' perspective.

Liquorice allsorts

At the first Ann Summers meeting I ever attended, the area manager came and sat next to me to have a cup of coffee and a cigarette before the meeting began. She turned to me and said 'I always say that Ann Summers ladies are like liquorice allsorts, because it takes all sorts to do this job, and we meet all sorts while we're doing it'. During the weeks and months that followed, the image of liquorice allsorts was repeated to me by party organisers and their managers alike. One party organiser even took bags of liquorice allsorts to her parties with her: she would refer to them during her presentation when canvassing for recruits to join Ann Summers. Her bag of liquorice allsorts was intended to represent not just the diversity of Ann Summers party organisers and their customers – 'it takes all sorts' – but the accessibility of the job to all who were interested – 'anyone can do it'.

Although party organisers regard themselves as 'liquorice allsorts', to me they appeared remarkably homogeneous. Of course I was not able to observe all party organisers everywhere, and even if I had done so the high turnover rate would make it impossible to produce an accurate picture of the entire Ann Summers sales force at any one time. But during the period of my fieldwork, in my particular geographical location, Ann Summers saleswomen were universally heterosexual, almost entirely working class or lower middle class, mostly in their twenties and thirties, and overwhelmingly white. The ethnic homogeneity of the sales force was particularly surprising, given the great

4. In this table, and throughout this book, an ellipsis enclosed in square brackets [. . .] indicates my editing of the quote for purposes of brevity or clarity. An ellipsis without square brackets indicates that the speaker left the thought unsaid and/or unfinished.

Name	Vanessa	Cherry	Helen	Donna	Trish	Diane	Melanie	Sarah	Joy	Beth	Cathy	Laura	Dawn	Lucy	Justine
Age	34	24	27	26	33	47	26	31	29	30	35	29	29	29	27
Status	Party organiser	Party organiser	Party organiser	Party organiser	Party organiser	Party organiser	Party organiser	Party organiser	Party organiser	Unit organiser	Unit organiser	Party organiser	Unit organiser	Unit organiser	Party organiser
Time with Ann Summers	3 weeks	1 month	7 weeks	9 weeks	10 weeks	3 months	8 months	9 months	10 months	11 months (4 months as unit organiser)	2 years (10 months as unit organiser)	2 years	3 years (18 months as unit organiser)	3 years (8 months as unit organiser)	5 years (incl. 4 month period as unit organiser)
Method of recruitment to Ann Summers	Newspaper advertisement	Newspaper advertisement	At party	Recruited by acquaintance	No data	Called local unit organiser at daughter's suggestion	At party	Newspaper advertisement	By friend	Recruited by friend	Newspaper advertisement	At party	Newspaper advertisement	By friend	At party
Other current paid employment	Hairdresser	None	Manageress in women's clothing shop	None	None	None	None	None	Works for subscription company (office work)	None	None	None	None	Secretary	Secretary
Marital status	Married	Married	Single (but has boyfriend)	Married	Cohabits with male partner	Married	Cohabits with male partner	Married	Cohabits with male partner	Married	Married	Cohabits with male partner	Separated	Cohabits with male partner	Single (but has boyfriend)
Children	2, aged 12 and 5	2, one of pre-school age	0	3, one of pre-school age	2, aged 12 and 10	3 adults, 4 grand-children	2, aged 8 and 4	3	0	2, aged 7 and 4	5, age range 4 to 13	2, one aged 4, one a baby	1, aged 3	0	0
Type of accommodation	Own house in Essex	Council maisonette in Essex	Lives in her mum's house in East London	Council flat in Essex	Council flat in North London	Privately rented property in Essex	Housing association house in Essex	Council flat in Essex	Council flat in Essex	Own house in Essex	Own house in Essex	Housing association house in East London	Rented house in Essex	Own flat in Essex	Own house in Essex

Figure 1.3 Profiles of the fifteen interviewees, arranged by length of time with Ann Summers

Name (cont'd.)	Vanessa	Cherry	Helen	Donna	Trish	Diane	Melanie	Sarah	Joy	Beth	Cathy	Laura	Dawn	Lucy	Justine
Self-description: class	'Oh I don't know. Mmm, don't know. Bit common I suppose really. Middle, I don't know. Whatever.'	'As in what? Rich, famous, what?' [Laughs.] [Merl: Yeah, well I've got some examples here like upper class, middle class, working class.] Say working class, definitely, 'cause my husband works and we find it a real struggle.'	'Um, I've never got any money. We've never – we've never got any money. [. . .] No, um, I – I try and look smart, but I haven't got extreme amounts of – I haven't got any money, until I get paid.'	'Oh, I don't know. As in what? [Merl: Middle class, upper class, working class . . .] Oh, I'm a working class person, yeah.'	'Common.'	'Middle class.'	'Normal. [Laughs.] [. . .] Normal, yeah!'	'Working class.'	'Oh God knows! [Sighs.] Well, I'm definitely not upper class. [Laughter.] Definitely not upper class! [. . .] I don't know. I don't really know what the – the, um – how they work out what class you are supposed to be in, or what class you are in.'	'I don't know, they don't have nothing for nutters do they? [. . .] Lower middle class, I suppose.'	'Middle.'	'Um. . . [laughs]. . . I don't know, 'cause I've never thought of myself as a class, in all honesty, so . . . [. . .] I'm just me.'	'Working class.'	'Oh, middle class.'	'Middle class.'
Self-description: ethnic/racial background	'Don't think I've got one, it wouldn't bother me, no.'	'English.'	'I'm English.'	'Oh, just plain English.'	'English and proud of it! Pure English through and through!'	'Well, I'm English.'	'Um, I don't know, 'cause my mum was English and my dad's Maltese, so . . . mixed up! Mix-up!'	'I'm English.'	'White English, I think. [. . .] I think. Well I – I'm adopted, so . . . [. . .] I know my – my natural mother's white English, well she's Scottish actually. Don't know what my father was, he could be anything. So. . .'	'I don't know. Well, race as in being white, or. . .? I don't really know. I'm just me, so – I'm me and whoever – I've got no – I'm not prejudiced against anyone. You are what you are.'	'White, is that right?'	'British, English I suppose. British.'	'I'm British.'	'White. English. Well, white English.'	'British white.'

Name (cont'd.)	Vanessa	Cherry	Helen	Donna	Trish	Diane	Melanie	Sarah	Joy	Beth	Cathy	Laura	Dawn	Lucy	Justine
Self-description: sexuality	'Normal. [Laughs.] If there is a normal!'	'Hetero-sexual.'	'I'm not shy. I'm not shy. I think – yeah, I think I'm very feminine. Yeah, that's about it really.'	'Um, just that I basically like men. [Laughter.] And men only! [Laughs.] And lots of them!'	'What words – what have I got to choose from? [Meri: Well, you – I mean, these are just examples, hetero-sexual...] Hetero-sexual.'	'[Meri: What words if any would you use to describe your sexuality?] No, I wouldn't. No.'	'Well I'm not a lesbian. [Laughter.] I'll say that. [Meri: Is that your last word?] Yeah. [Laughs.] Normal. Yeah, whatever normal is.'	'Um. ... normal [Laughs.] Regular.'	'Hetero-sexual.'	'Stark raving nympho-maniac! [Laughter.] That's what I get – that's what I get called! "Oi, leave me alone, you've had enough!"'	'I'd say normal. Er, just normal.'	'Er, I don't know, 'cause ... well, I'm not, um, gay or anything like that, I'm just straight, but ...'	'I'm straight.'	'Um, oh! [Laughter.] Oh hang on, what's the – hetero-sexual!'	'Hetero-sexual.'

Figure 1.3 Profiles of the fifteen interviewees, arranged by length of time with Ann Summers (*continued*)

ethnic diversity of London and urban Essex more generally. I did occasionally encounter black party organisers of African or African-Caribbean descent, and one of 'my' units recruited a black party organiser during my fieldwork. (She did not meet my interviewing criteria because she had not yet organised a party.) I never saw or heard of any Asian party organisers. Even more surprisingly, hostesses and guests at the parties I observed were only slightly more diverse in terms of class, age and ethnicity, and I never once encountered an openly lesbian or bisexual party-goer, although I did hear a few anecdotes about them from party organisers.

This homogeneity is at least partly explicable by the reliance on individuals' social networks both to recruit party organisers and to obtain party bookings: party organisers and party hostesses tend to know, invite and recruit women who are more or less like themselves. I did encounter some rare examples of overt racial discrimination, including one memorable incident when a unit organiser refused to recruit a woman of South Asian descent. (This incident is discussed in detail in Chapter 2.) But for the most part the 'whiteness' of the sales force was, so to speak, both unconscious and unselfconscious. For example, one interviewee, describing to me a previous, 'jungle'-themed catalogue launch, told how one unit had come in fancy dress as 'tribal people' wearing grass skirts and blacked-up faces; this was clearly regarded as unproblematic by all concerned, and indicates the extent to which it is taken for granted that party organisers are both willing and able to black up their white faces. Heterosexuality is similarly taken for granted: the very fact that party organisers told each other anecdotes about lesbian party guests shows that such guests are sufficiently unusual to be anecdote-worthy.

This unconsciousness of whiteness and heterosexuality is reflected in some interviewees' reticence in naming themselves as white or heterosexual. Only two of the fifteen interviewees unequivocally identified themselves as white. Most of the interviewees interpreted the question ('How would you describe your race or ethnic background?') purely in terms of nationality, which invariably meant some permutation of English or British (or in Melanie's case Maltese). Beth recognised the existence of 'white' as a racial category while simultaneously denying her own membership of it on the grounds that 'I'm just me', thus asserting a kind of abstract individualism over ethnic identity; Vanessa even denied having any kind of race or ethnicity at all. These silences around the women's own whiteness are significant but not surprising: 'Naming "whiteness" displaces it from the unmarked, unnamed status that is itself an effect of its dominance. Among the effects on white people both of race privilege and of the dominance of whiteness are their seeming normativity, their structured invisibility' (Frankenburg 1993: 6). Whiteness is routinely regarded in white culture as an *absence* of ethnicity or 'race' such that 'race' belongs only to the non-white; the 'unmarked' status of whiteness arises from and perpetuates white dominance and privilege. In a similar dynamic of dominance, privilege and normativity, heterosexuality is often invisible as such to hetero-sexuals themselves (Dyer 1997). Five of the interviewees named them-selves unequivocally as heterosexual or 'straight', although even in these cases, as Lucy's fumbling for the 'correct' term suggests, their hetero-sexuality may not be a very active part of their everyday sense of identity. Two others named themselves as heterosexual after some hesitation or prompting, while Beth, Donna and Helen described their sexuality in terms of their personal likes or attitudes. Others described themselves as 'normal'; and just as Vanessa claimed not to have an ethnicity, Diane declined to describe her sexuality at all. All of these 'normal' women were participants whom I came to know fairly well during my research, as was Diane, and there was never any question mark over their heterosexuality, either in my mind or in any of their peers' minds. The invisibility of heterosexuality in their responses represents the very pinnacle of heterosexual dominance, privilege and normativity.

As a white woman in my mid-thirties I fit the party organisers' demographic profile fairly well myself. However there were two import-ant respects in which I differed from my participants: class and sexuality. My university education and my job as an academic – of which all my research participants were of course aware as the context of the research as such – clearly position me as middle class. I do not have a 'posh' accent, and I grew up in a lower-middle-class home not unlike those of many party organisers; but many other, more subtle markers of class difference, such as fashion sense, TV viewing preferences and tastes in food and drink, became apparent as I participated in parties and meetings.[5] I was also aware of the sometimes huge gap between my own income and those of party organisers and party-goers. This was part-icularly brought home to me at one party where one of the guests announced to her friends that she had received a large pay rise at work. She was effusively congratulated on what her friends regarded as a

---

5. These differences, which include gait, posture, dress, taste and so on, are what Pierre Bourdieu calls 'habitus'. Bourdieu's account of class is discussed and drawn upon in Chapter 5, and the concept of 'habitus' is returned to in Chapter 6.

brilliant salary, but which to me seemed rather paltry. Several feminist commentators have noted that the relative earnings gap between women of different social classes is now wider than that between women and men of the same class (e.g. McDowell 1992): that party vividly illustrated my own relatively privileged position in such inequalities.

The situation in relation to my sexuality however was much less straightforward in terms of difference and privilege. I am bisexual. All of my research participants were heterosexual and indeed, as already suggested, heterosexuality was so taken for granted as 'normal' that it barely registered as a form of sexuality at all. Anticipating that this would be the case (it is, after all, the way heterosexuality is usually viewed by heterosexuals in British society at large), I made a conscious decision even before beginning my fieldwork that I would allow my research participants to assume that I was heterosexual too. If directly asked about my sexual orientation, I would not lie; but otherwise I would not make any move to 'come out' to participants. This was fundamentally a tactical decision about how I would deal with heterosexism and homophobia, the exercise of which in Ann Summers settings placed me in a position of disadvantage and even potentially of subordination in relation to my participants. It was also a practical decision in that the research would probably have been simply impossible if I had been out to my participants. There were times at parties in particular, especially during some of the more tactile or physical party games, when I felt sure that I would have been excluded, and perhaps verbally or even physically abused, if the party-goers had known that I was bisexual. Such moments were themselves of course extremely revealing of the ways in which heterosexual femininity is constructed at Ann Summers parties, and allowed me to observe facets of heterosexuality which would otherwise have remained hidden from me. Nevertheless, being less than completely open about my sexual identity (I never was directly asked, and so never 'came out' to anyone) was uncomfortable, particularly when party-goers and party organisers were generously welcoming me into their homes and their lives. All I could do was to try to proceed without harming or distressing any of the participants, and without putting myself at risk of undue harm or distress – in the hope that my position as a queer sociologist observing heterosexuality would yield some insights into the usually hidden power relations in which heterosexuality is embedded, and in the knowledge that the ultimate responsibility for the exercise of dominance and privilege in the research would be mine when I came to analyse the fieldwork.

'The No 1 Fun Company'

Given that they are all so similar in terms of age, class, ethnicity and sexual orientation, why are party organisers and unit organisers alike so convinced that they are 'liquorice allsorts'? The answer is that party organisers look for diversity not in sociological categories or demographic profiles but in ages, body sizes and personality types:

> The thing is, when you – you've been to the meetings, you've seen, like, there's a great big fat woman, there's really thin women, like, size eights, you know, wandering around, there's, like, really old people, there's, like, people that have barely – you know, only just turned eighteen, it's amazing. You've got really loud, lively, bubbly people like FX. I mean, FX's brilliant, you know, and some of them are just so loud and that, and then you've got people that are really quiet and really shy. So, you know, I – I just get amazed when I go to the – like, the – not so much our meetings, 'cause I know all our girls now, but when we go to the catalogue – catalogue launches, you know, you meet people that, like, are so different. (Lucy)

> [Merl: So do you think you need special kinds of skills to do this job?] No, not at all. I mean, as I say, I used to be really quiet, and um, you know, I was probably one of the last people you'd think would do it. But I don't think – I mean all – all shapes, sizes, ages, everyone could do it. Um, and you say – it's sales, but at the end of the day you have a catalogue and it sells itself to some degree. Um, so you don't even have to be that good at selling. (Sarah)

When Lucy says there are 'really old people' doing Ann Summers she probably means women like Diane who are in their forties. The oldest party organiser I encountered during my fieldwork was sixty, and I know her age precisely because other party organisers were constantly remarking upon how exceptionally old she was. Moreover although, as Lucy notes, some party organisers have just turned eighteen, in fact many unit organisers and even party organisers are reluctant to recruit eighteen-year-olds:

> Unfortunately the ones that are just eighteen are the nightmares [laughs.] [Merl: Are they?] 'Cause they live at home with their mum, and they've got no responsibility, and it's a bit of a laugh. I must admit I do tend to – I really enjoy signing people up that have actually got – like, they're living away from their mum and dad, they have got a child or two children, they've got responsibilities. (Dawn)

Ages, then, are not generally quite as diverse as party organisers like to think they are. However even though age is often cited as a form of diversity, ideas about different body sizes and, more especially, personality types are far more significant as a factor in the sales force's collective self-image as 'liquorice allsorts'. Being a different body size or shape, and having a different kind of personality, are key factors in what it means to be a different 'sort' of woman. Lucy's classification of women according to binary axes of body size – 'fat' vs. 'thin' – and personality type – 'loud' vs. 'shy' – is standard amongst party plan members, and being 'loud' or 'bubbly', 'shy' or 'quiet' is the most commonly cited form of diversity at Ann Summers events.

Personality, skill and emotional labour

As Sarah's words above indicate, the claim that Ann Summers party organisers are diverse goes hand-in-hand with the claim that anyone can do this kind of work, with no special skill involved. This claim, like that of diversity, is part of the everyday 'common sense' of doing Ann Summers, and was regarded as an obvious 'truth' by most interviewees. Only Vanessa was prepared to consider that some skill might be involved, and compared the interpersonal skills required for party organising with those required for her daytime job as a hairdresser; all the other interviewees were adamant that no skill was required in party organising. My own observations at parties and meetings however suggested that this was by no means the case. Although the paperwork involved is relatively straightforward (but also cumbersome and widely disliked), party organisers display considerable interpersonal skills during parties: they must be entertaining, witty, knowledgeable about products and especially about lingerie and bra sizes, patient, cheerful, good listeners, tactful, persuasive, alert, and above all able to control groups and group dynamics without appearing to be bossy or domineering.

This impressive range of skills is not regarded as such by party organisers themselves, who tend to regard them as matters of personality rather than of skill: being able to handle and entertain a group of strangers is described simply as 'adapting your personality', or even more simply as just 'being friendly' or 'being cheerful'. The following interview quotes are chosen from many:

> The minute you walk through the door, you're hear – listening to their conversations. 'Cause at the end of the day you've got to adapt your

personality to theirs. So to – to be in this job you've got to be an actress. You've got to take on whatever personality you want to take on. So when you walk through the room you're listening to them. If they're saying – if there's hardly any conversation going on you know it's going to be really hard work. You know that you've got to try and find games that are going to break the ice first of all, you know, it's – it's – it is, it is hard. But as long as you can adapt yourself your parties will go OK. (Dawn)

[. . .I]t's not the product always that sells. It's yourself and what you do at a party. Basically your personality is what sells it. And your games are your personality, really. It's whether – I mean I can walk out of this house and I can quite often say 'I really can't be bothered tonight', but once I'm in there I – I let Ann Summers take over what – I don't – don't even think about what I thought when I was in here [i.e. at home]. I could have a – the worst day on earth in here, but when I walk in that house that all goes out the window, I forget, and I – I'm their entertainer for the night, so you've got to be an entertainer [laughs], you've got to give them a good time. (Cathy)

[. . .I]f you go into someone's house that you don't know, you can be any-body you want to be. I mean, I do it. I walk in, um – I mean people that know me know that I'm a loudmouth cow and – [laughter] I get on with it and if I don't like something I will say so. Um, but if I go into some-body's house and they're all this really quiet person, and they're like 'Oh we're having a party, but it's going to be a really quiet party', then that's fair enough, and I will be a quiet person. But if I go into a house and they're all, like, 'Oh look, here she comes!' and all that, and they don't know me, then fair enough, I'll be a totally different person. I go 'Yeah, I'm here! [Claps hands.] Come on, let's all go!' and I don't care. Because they don't know me, the only person that'll see me again is whoever's booked a party and, um, who I'm going to deliver to. And in all honesty I can be that person over and over again for that lot, but I'll go to another house and I'll be [adopts a formal tone] 'Hello, I'm from Ann Summers' [laughs], you know, and it's all – all, like, um, you sit there all pristine and proper and tell them all about it, and another one I could go in and not care less, because they can't care less [laughs], so . . . It doesn't take anyone [i.e. any particular type of person to do Ann Summers], really. I mean, anyone could just turn around and do it. (Laura)

These and many other interview quotes, alongside my observations at parties and meetings, indicate that a large proportion of the work performed by Ann Summers party organisers and unit organisers is what sociologists following Hochschild (1983) have called emotional labour. Emotional labour is often performed by women working in the service industries and/or face-to-face with the public, but is rarely recognised *as* labour by them, precisely because it involves the kind of emotion work routinely performed by women in everyday private life in their interactions with family, especially children and male partners:

> Emotional labor [is] the management of feeling to create publicly observable facial or body display; emotional labor is sold for a wage and therefore has exchange value. [. . .T]he synonymous terms emotion work or emotion management [. . .] refer to these same acts done in a private context where they have use value. (Hochschild 1983: 7)

Smiling when one may not feel like it, being patient or sympathetic when others are being demanding or tiresome, making an effort to get along with people regardless of one's own mood: these are all forms of emotion work in which Ann Summers members are highly skilled, both at parties and meetings and at home with their families. Indeed the effective performance of this kind of emotional labour for others is arguably in some sense constitutive of heterosexual femininity. Beverley Skeggs (1997) has argued that 'caring' skills are regarded by young working-class heterosexual women not simply as skills but as essential aspects of femininity; the same is true of party organisers and their social skills, which they regard not as skills but as 'natural' kinds of feminine know-how. In particular, neither Skeggs's participants nor mine recognised that they had developed their emotion work skills in the context of sexual or domestic inequality – of caring physically and emotionally for children and other adults, especially adult men.

Emotion work involves a kind of change of consciousness which Hochschild calls 'deep acting', whereby one does not simply pretend to feel cheerful or patient or friendly, but actually induces oneself really to feel that way, without realising that one is doing so. As Cathy and several other interviewees put it, Ann Summers 'takes over' as soon as one arrives at a party; regardless of how she felt at home, when she gets to a party she does not just pretend to feel cheerful, she really does feel that way, even though, as Dawn and Laura reflect, a certain amount of acting or self-invention *is* involved. Although Hochschild draws anxious attention to the damage that may be caused by this commercial use of emotion, the testimonies of my interviewees suggest that there are also considerable benefits. Several interviewees spoke at length of the ways in which doing Ann Summers, particularly going to parties, helped them to deal with a range of personal problems, from bereavement to depression and even mild agoraphobia, as well as the more mundane issues of boredom and isolation faced by many women at home with small children. Indeed for most party organisers – with or without children at home – the prime motivation behind their participation in Ann Summers is not only to earn money, or even in many cases to earn money at all, but to enjoy the social side of Ann Summers parties and meetings, having fun and meeting people. The 1999 Party Organiser Training Manual describes Ann Summers as 'the **No 1 FUN** Company'. Many party organisers wholeheartedly agree, and this is another factor behind many participants' reluctance to see what they do as skilled work, or even as work at all:

And also, when you do go out, it's not like going out to work. [Merl: A lot of people have said that to me.] You get paid to have fun! You're going to have a social night out with the girls, you meet a whole new circle of friends. (Dawn)

[Merl: How do you think of [Ann Summers]?] As a night out. As a night out, to have a laugh and – to have a laugh [Merl: It's the fun of it], meet – to meet other people, you know. I mean sort of like I'll be walking down here and sort of like 'Hello!' 'cause they've known me from a party, and things like that. Which is what I like. [. . .] [Merl: So it's more the social side of things you like by the sounds of things.] Yeah. Yeah. Oh yeah, definitely. (Melanie)

[Merl: What's your favourite thing about doing it, about doing Ann Summers?] Getting out for the night and earning some cash! [Merl laughs.] Um, and if it is a friend's party, um, it's also getting to meet the friends, um, and if it is local then I can have, like, one drink at the end of the evening and have a little chat with them before I come home. [Merl: So it's like a social thing for you as well?] Yeah, social. Yeah. Yeah. Your bonus is earning a bit of cash as well. (Trish)

It is very common for party organisers to rate the success of a party not financially but socially. A 'good' party is not necessarily a lucrative party, but a party at which everyone has joined in and had fun; and being able to create 'fun' for other people is both fun for oneself and boosts one's confidence and self-esteem. This discourse of 'fun' is also import-ant in relation to party plan economics. Although party organisers with experience of other party plans often commented on the relative generosity of Ann Summers commission rates, and in principle it is possible for party organisers to be holding lucrative parties six or even seven nights a week, in practice many party organisers (including most of the new recruits) are probably holding just one or two parties a week and meeting or only slightly exceeding the £41.40 standard commission rate. The discourse of 'fun' mitigates the precariousness of commission-based sales work as well as the hard emotional labour involved in each party.

'Young mums'

As already noted, direct selling in general is attractive to women, and the Ann Summers party plan in particular is an entirely female business, although some men do work at the Ann Summers head office. The combination of fun, familiar types of emotion work and part-time evening hours exerts an especially strong pull on women with young children who are unable to work full-time and/or during the day, particularly when the emotional labour involved feels more like 'having fun' and 'getting a boost' than doing serious work. This at least partly explains the bunching of party organisers' ages in their twenties and thirties: many of these women are doing Ann Summers as their only form of paid work while caring for young children at home. The notion that 'young mums' are the core of the Ann Summers party plan is widely taken for granted, and such women are often deliberately targeted both as potential recruits and as a source of party bookings. This is neatly expressed by Sarah, who is herself a 'young mum':

> [Merl: So they tend to be mums then that make a good crowd [at parties]?] Yeah. Yeah, definitely mums. They're the people we target as well when we're canvassing [for bookings], if they've got a pushchair. [Merl: Oh really? You go for people with pushchairs?] Yeah. One, 'cause they can't run away fast enough [laughter], and um . . . But yeah, definitely. Because they are the people that tend to want to – want to have a bit of fun and a girls' night in as well as sort of a girls' night out. But they're not really at – having to go out to a pub and things like that, you know. And they're only out for two, three hours, so if they have got young kids it's easy for them anyway. (Sarah)

> Mums, young mums. [Merl: Mums. Yeah, mums are, like, the backbone of Ann Summers, I'm realising.] Yeah, yeah, very much so. Because also

what happens is they fit – because it's – it's mums wanting to get back into the workplace, um, but trying to fit it around the children, which, as I say, you don't get jobs – unless you work in a school, you don't get jobs that fit in around children. And this obviously does. So long as you've got someone that can look after the kids at home of a night. But you only need to go out once a week, you know, it's not – for what, three, four hours probably maximum by the time you've gone sort of from door to door. You know, so anyone really can do that in – as long as they've got someone willing to help them a little bit. If – you've got to have that. If you've got – I mean, if they've got a partner that's non-supporting, doesn't want them to go out, they'll be getting no end of trouble at home, sort of moaning at them that they're going out again and all that, and then they'll just pack it in. So there's – there's just no point. I mean [my unit organiser]'s just lost a girl because her husband don't want her doing it. (Sarah)

This view that 'you need a supportive partner' to do Ann Summers is universally held by party organisers and unit organisers with children, as is the view that doing Ann Summers should not disrupt one's 'home life', by which women mean one's responsibilities for childcare and domestic work. As Sarah points out, the many benefits of party organising for young mums are available only within the context of a traditional marriage or marriage-style partnership. Even the most optimistic commentators agree that, with some exceptions, the overwhelming majority of heterosexual partnerships still rest on a grossly unequal division of labour in the domestic sphere, with women bearing responsibility for most of the housework and childcare (Sullivan 2000). In the context of such domestic inequalities, going to Ann Summers parties is a kind of 'fun' available to guests for a few hours a night only, in a private home rather than the public, masculine space of the pub, on condition that women's primary responsibility for childcare is not disrupted. Becoming an Ann Summers party organiser not only allows one to continue that primary responsibility, but according to Sarah it also depends upon one's living with a husband or partner who will (as women often put it) 'baby sit' his own children for a few hours a week. The division of labour, especially of childcare, between husband and wife means that she can only do Ann Summers with his consent. In practice this consent is often being constantly re-negotiated, and is the site of many domestic power struggles. The following interview quotes are chosen from many:

[Merl: How does your partner feel about you doing Ann Summers?] Um, he wasn't too pleased at first. And then he learnt to live with it. And then a couple of weeks ago when I said 'Oh I –' I said, I said 'I'm thinking of giving it up', after he'd got down off climbing the ceiling, he went 'Oh, it's down to you'. But you know when you can tell that someone's, like, really pleased that you've stopped doing it, you know? [. . .] [Merl: What is it about it that he doesn't like?] I don't know. [Merl: Don't know? He won't say?] No, he just doesn't like me, you know – I mean, sort of like, I said to him 'I'll give it up and I'll, um, go and get a job, like, in Asda's or something like that', but he doesn't want me to do that either. [Merl: Right.] I don't think – he just don't want me to work. [Merl: He'd just prefer you to stay at home?] Yeah, I mean, sort of like now he's talking about, um, buying a burger van, you know, one of those catering vans, and me and my brother running that. Well that's fine to him, 'cause I'll be with my brother all day. You know, and if I get out of turn, he'll think my brother's there to sort me out. [Merl: Oh right, to keep an eye on you?] Yeah. (Melanie)

[Merl: But you never have anyone be really strange with you [about the fact that you do Ann Summers].] No. Only him. [Merl: Yeah, why is he strange about it?] Selfish! [Merl: Oh really?] I'm getting him out of that, don't worry! [Laughter.] [Merl: Yeah, you can't afford to be that with Ann Summers around, can you?] No. He don't mind me doing it, um, he has took a few, um, 'phone calls for me. Even though – 'cause normally he forgets people have 'phoned me, so it's – I'm trying to get him into the swing of writing people's name and numbers down. Um, but, like, he's passed on the messages and what have you. But, um, like FX, she's – her husband will take orders and things on the 'phone, no way would he do that. No way. He'll say 'Oh, I'll give you her mobile number' [laughter] if I'm not here, you know, or ''Phone back at so-and-so time'. Um, and he don't like me having my stuff out when we've got people here. [Merl: Oh really?] That's all got to be put away. So I have to do it [i.e. paperwork and orders, in the] evening when I come back from a party. (Trish)

[Merl: So do you think of it as a job?] I do. I do. He doesn't always. He doesn't always, because I'll say to him 'I've got to go and do this delivery', or 'Can you be in for this time 'cause I have to go and do this party', he'll stroll in and I'll have to run out the door. And I say to him 'Now if that was your job, you'd be gone. I can't do that 'cause I've [sic] got two kids sitting here'. And I'm sorry, but men, and women working like I do in the evenings or whatever, they seem to think it doesn't matter, and they're a bit selfish about it. And um, I've said that to him and he – he knows that's what he's like about it. But he prefers me to do it. He says to me, like, 'You enjoy it, you do it'. But when it comes to him stopping something for me to do it, he doesn't like it. (Laura)

These quotes demonstrate that the giving or withholding of male partners' consent for women to participate in Ann Summers places real material constraints on women's freedom. Trish's boyfriend forces her to complete her paperwork late at night (and his attitude to her customers on the telephone may lose her some sales too); Laura's boyfriend could literally prevent her from leaving the house simply by failing to arrive home; Melanie's boyfriend, who seems to be about to force her to work for him and under the everyday surveillance of her brother, is perhaps the most blatant example of men's material power over 'their' women.

This paradox – that direct selling organisations offer women self-esteem, financial reward and a sense of personal empowerment which is actually founded on a traditional and unequal sexual division of labour – is noted by Biggart, who writes:

DSOs [direct selling organizations] give women a sphere in which they can develop competence, a degree of economic independence, and the opportunity to interact in ways that do not do violence to their sense of themselves as women. But DSOs [. . .] do not challenge the prevailing sociopolitical arrangements of society. In fact, it is probably the compromise direct selling represents that has made it attractive to many women. They can be personally empowered – *feel* liberated and modern – without upsetting the traditional premises of their lives. [. . .] [E]conomic organizations that emulate the domestic sphere [e.g. by focusing on interpersonal relationships] can be used not only to empower women, [. . .] but also to maintain their submission. (Biggart 1989: 97)

Moreover, as Sarah's comments about unsupportive partners suggest, whether one upsets the 'traditional premises' of one's life at home with the children is not simply a matter of personal preference or willpower, but lies in the realm of personal and economic necessity. Men have the power to refuse to 'baby sit' their own children, and at the same time women lack the power to support themselves financially outside of a traditional heterosexual partnership. Few party organisers or even unit organisers would be able to support themselves and their children on their Ann Summers commission.

Ann Summers as post-feminist fun

Reflecting on this paradox in the gender politics of direct selling, Biggart concludes that 'Women's DSOs might be characterised as *pre-feminist*, celebrating womanly abilities and values but not challenging dominant social structures' (Biggart 1989: 97). This characterisation however does not seem quite right in the case of Ann Summers. The US-based direct selling organisations studied by Biggart, such as Amway, Tupperware and Mary Kay, make no claims to be challenging dominant social structures, and indeed in some cases openly espouse conservative ideologies of patriotism and Christianity. But while the structure of the Ann Summers party plan is clearly based on a traditional model of family and gender relations, it does at the same time claim to be reject-ing traditional views of women's place in society and in particular of women's sexuality. Jacqueline Gold's oft-stated personal philosophy is 'to encourage women to feel good about themselves and their sexuality' (e.g. Party Organiser Training Manual 1999).[6] In its celebration of women's heterosexual desire and heterosexual pleasure, Ann Summers appears to challenge the traditional but still widespread view of women as sexually passive. One of the arguments of this book is therefore that the Ann Summers party plan, unlike those studied by Biggart in the 1980s, is not pre-feminist but *post-feminist*.

Like pre-feminist organisations, Ann Summers fails to challenge women's socio-economic inequality while at the same time offering them pleasure and self-esteem. This is evident in many comments and interactions at parties and especially at meetings, where women's empowerment is spoken of and even experienced in terms of 'confidence' or 'inner strength':

> There are powerful – up until a few years ago we had no men working for us [at head office]. We were a predominantly female company. Which gives women inner strength basically from knowing that. You know, it makes you take control of – it's given women, mums and housewives, the opportunity to be a businesswoman. Which not a lot of places out there will do that. [. . .] [Merl: It sounds like you think Ann Summers is a good thing for women.] Oh definitely. (Dawn)

This sense of 'inner strength' is immensely important in party organ-isers' lives, and I certainly do not wish to denigrate or underestimate

6. This statement also appears on the homepage of Jacqueline Gold's personal website, www.jacquelinegold.com.

it. But nevertheless *feeling* empowered is not the same as *being* powerful. In effect this 'inner strength' is a kind of compensation for women's lack of real socio-political power. This was strongly brought home to me during a meeting of Dawn's unit, when she presented one of her 'girls' with a necklace to mark the latter's imminent promotion to unit organiser. Dawn had had the necklace engraved with the words 'Whatever you can conceive and believe, you can achieve.' The presentation was very emotional, and the party organiser receiving it became quite tearful: both the necklace and the engraving clearly meant a great deal, not just to the recipient and to Dawn, but also to the other unit members present. And yet of course it is simply not the case that this party organiser, or any of the other working-class or lower middle-class women present, could achieve whatever they wanted simply by believing it. In effect this discourse of 'inner strength' encourages women to feel empowered by refusing to see the many obstacles and inequalities which structure their everyday lives, including the inequalities which underlie their participation in Ann Summers itself. For example, although young mums in Ann Summers need the help of a supportive (and gainfully employed) husband, they are strongly discouraged from supporting each other by working together in pairs or teams. This discouragement comes indirectly from the structures of commission, prizes and competitions within the party plan, which are all based on the assumption that party organisers work as lone individuals; and directly from unit organisers and area managers who explicitly advise party organisers not to try to work together. Donna was one of the rare party organisers who worked in partnership with another woman in Ann Summers. I heard her being openly told by her unit organiser that they would inevitably fall out over money; I saw their unit organiser pointedly giving prizes to only one of them when they had won competitions as a pair; I heard Donna describe the complex and downright convoluted arrangements the two of them had to make to process their sales and calculate their respective shares of the commission. If Ann Summers gives 'inner strength', it does so on the condition that that 'inner strength' is not shared with your female friends.

Unlike pre-feminist organisations, Ann Summers also celebrates not only traditional 'womanly abilities' in emotional labour and domestic organisation, but new kinds of 'womanly values' which emphasise the primacy of pleasure and the centrality of an active (hetero)sexuality to women's selves and lives. It is these new 'womanly values' that give Ann Summers its post-feminist character. Esther Sonnet (1999), writing about the Black Lace series of erotic novels for women (which also regularly appear in the Ann Summers catalogues), has discussed post-feminist values, especially in relation to women's heterosexuality and pleasure. Sonnet suggests that post-feminist values combine an emphasis on individual empowerment (rather than collective power) with a sense of *entitlement* to pleasure; and further that this pleasure is regarded not as a right gained by social struggle or feminist argument, but simply as a consumer good. In the case of my research with Ann Summers this sense of entitlement was evident in the oft-repeated phrase 'it's the nineties'. Party organisers would often tell their guests not to feel embarrassed about buying vibrators because 'it's the nineties', a phrase which encapsulates both the sense of consumerism (you have a right to buy the product) and the sense that social change is not the goal of ongoing struggle but has already been achieved.

The Ann Summers version of post-feminism supplements these emphases on empowerment and entitlement with other values which, by themselves, are perhaps pre-feminist but which in combination take on a post-feminist edge. Chief amongst these is the idea that 'men are useless – but we love them anyway', which is often more or less explicitly stated and is even more often implicitly assumed at parties and meetings. 'Men are useless' in effect allows women to complain about domestic inequality, albeit in the exculpatory and attenuated form where men's failure to share domestic tasks, or to perform such tasks adequately, is represented as inability rather than refusal. (An occasional variation on this theme is the praising of those rare husbands who do share responsibility for household chores, who are held up as paragons of almost superhuman virtue.) In the context of Ann Summers parties such complaints often extend not just to domestic chores but also to sexual reciprocity: men can no more stimulate the clitoris than they can do the ironing. 'But we love them anyway' acknowledges men's shortcomings without challenging either the shortcomings themselves or, more importantly, the social structures within which they occur. 'Men are useless but we love them anyway' suggests that sexual inequality is an inevitable element in heterosexual relationships, but that heterosexual women can find comfort and even 'empowerment' in their own superior abilities. That those superior abilities are expressed in an unequal division of emotional and physical labour at home is merely the 'natural' order of romantic relationships.

Another important post-feminist value in Ann Summers settings is that of sexual openness. Being 'open' and 'honest' about one's (hetero)-sexual pleasures and desires is regarded as an end in itself. To some extent this may be seen as part of the 'confessional culture' circulating

in the media, especially in popular confessional day-time TV shows like
Oprah and *Trisha* (see e.g. White 1992, Squire 1994). It is summed up
by Beth:

> But yeah, I think it – I think it – it says that, you know, just because we're
> women we're not allowed to stand in a pub and say we – we don't like
> sex, or 'Ooh you shouldn't talk about that'. And I think it's bringing a
> lot more people out of their shells, definitely. And making people better
> for it. [Merl: So it sounds like you think it's quite a – it's a positive thing
> for women.] I think it is, I think it is. 'Cause I was quite shy myself until
> I did Ann Summers. And now I'm not embarrassed to say that I've used
> a vibrator or I've done this or I've done that. Whereas before it was 'I'm
> not going to talk about that' [Merl laughs.] But it has, it's brought me
> out. [. . .] [Merl: So it makes people feel more open and more relaxed about
> it.] Yeah, I think it does. Makes you a better person once you can be like
> that as well, I think. Because you're not living a lie. Most definitely. (Beth)

As Beth rather dramatically puts it, to be shy or embarrassed about sex
is to live a lie; to be open about sex makes a woman not just more
relaxed but actually 'a better person'. Women's sexual liberation consists
not in challenges to the unequal structures of heterosexuality but in
an individualised freedom from embarrassment. Again, as with the values
of empowerment and self-esteem, I do not mean to underestimate the
importance of this kind of self-confidence and sexual openness for
many women, for whom it can mean the difference between sexual
pleasure and sexual coercion; a great deal of literature on sex education
and HIV prevention has stressed the importance of being able to talk
openly about sex, especially for women and girls negotiating sexual
practices with male partners (e.g. Holland et al. 1998). But the post-
feminist version values sexual openness for its own sake, rather than
as a means to an end of sexual equality.

Indeed post-feminism tends to assume that the major battles for
sexual equality, in the sphere of sexuality and elsewhere, have already
been won, and that all that now stands between individual women and
'empowerment' is self-confidence and the exercise of a consumerist kind
of choice (cf. Whelehan 1994, Sonnet 1999). Between the pre-feminism
of the party plan structure in general and the post-feminism of Ann
Summers values in particular, *feminism* is smoothly elided. There is no
sense in Ann Summers settings and values that women continue to face
systematic or structural socio-economic inequalities in contemporary
Britain, much less of women as collective agents of social change.

Indeed there is barely any sense of 'women' at all. One of the more curious observations about Ann Summers settings – both parties and meetings as well as interviews – is that the words 'women' or 'woman' are hardly ever used. Party organisers and party-goers refer to themselves and each other as 'girls' (in an informal register) or 'ladies' (in a formal register), but never as 'women'. Similarly, general remarks about women – such as those made by Beth above, for example – are phrased using the words 'person' or 'people' rather than 'woman' or 'women', even in contexts where it is very clear that only one gender is being discussed. There is no such squeamishness about 'men', who are rarely referred to as 'boys' (and never as 'gentlemen'). It is as if the word 'women' itself is too politically loaded to be used.

Hidden depths

Thus party organising and, as the rest of this book argues, party-going both offer a kind of fun which has some rather murky hidden depths. Although at first glance Ann Summers parties may offer (in the words of one heterosexual feminist responding to my research) a 'safe space for women to talk about sex', on closer scrutiny it becomes apparent that neither parties nor meetings offer such safe space in any straight-forward sense. What they do offer is a *pleasurable* space – but pleasure and safety are not the same thing. Indeed this book argues that much of the pleasure in Ann Summers settings comes not from safety but from the successful passing of unspoken tests, and from gaining victory in unconscious power struggles.

Some of these hidden depths are hinted at in the existing academic literature on home shopping parties. Davis (1973) points out that Tupperware parties harbour hidden dangers for participants, because social interactions such as parties always run the risk that they may go wrong and end in disaster: 'party-giving is a delicate activity requiring considerable skills to maintain the right level of artifice: it is easy to make mistakes, to attract condemnation for pretentiousness, resent-ment at the too-palpable imposition. [. . .T]he skills required may not be widely diffused' (170). A more sustained discussion is provided by Gainer and Fischer (1991), who suggest that home shopping parties may be understood as arenas for two specific kinds of social 'ordeal' or test. Firstly, home shopping parties are an 'ordeal of civility, [. . .] a recurring test of who "passes" as a member of a certain cultural group'; and secondly they are also an 'ordeal of conviviality, [. . .] a symbolic demonstration of signs of fraternity (or, in this case, sorority)' (600).

By successfully 'passing' these ordeals, they argue, women at Tupperware and Discovery Toys parties demonstrate to themselves and other women their 'membership in the social category of "good wife and mother"' (600) while at the same time conducting a kind of female bonding. Success is a source of both pleasure and a sense of identity for participants, and Gainer and Fischer conclude that home shopping parties 'appear to have become a ritual female activity [. . .] used in the social construction of femininity itself' (602).

These ideas – of home shopping parties as risky, as ordeals to be 'passed', as forms of female bonding, and as arenas for the construction of group membership and feminine identity – are all developed in my argument in the chapters that follow. However there is one crucial element to which none of the existing home shopping literature devotes sufficiently critical attention, and which is foregrounded by Ann Summers parties in particular. That element is heterosexuality. Ann Summers parties are not just about the social construction of femininity in general, but the construction of white, working- or lower-middle class and above all *heterosexual* femininity. Where previous studies of home shopping parties have tended to take the heterosexuality of participants for granted as simple background information, this book seeks rather to interrogate it. Heterosexuality for women offers both privilege and dominance over the non-heterosexual, and inequality and subordination in relation to heterosexual men. The paradoxes and ambiguities of heterosexual femininity are the very stuff of Ann Summers.

About this book

The central argument of this book is that heterosexual female gatherings such as Ann Summers parties and meetings can be understood as examples of *female homosociality*. Female homosociality, far from being peculiar to Ann Summers, is an everyday phenomenon occurring in many different settings, including both workplaces and leisure settings. The aim of this book is to offer, as it were, an anatomy of female homosociality, which has a basic structure and a number of core characteristics, through the detailed consideration of Ann Summers settings. Further research in other settings will be required to establish the ways in which Ann Summers is the same as or different from other female homosocial arenas, although I do offer some pointers and suggestions on this question in the Conclusion.

Chapter 2 introduces the concept of female homosociality and sets out its basic structure. It does so through a systematic comparison with the structure of male homosociality as it has been conceptualised in previous feminist work, and through an analysis of my interviews and participant observation. Chapter 3 continues and extends this discussion of the structure of homosociality with an analysis of the forms of exchange that take place within it. These exchanges centre on represent-ations of men and masculinity. Chapter 4 analyses the ways in which female bodies and female (hetero)sexuality are constructed and repres-ented at Ann Summers parties. Chapter 5 discusses party organisers' and party-goers' tastes and preferences for lingerie and other items in the Ann Summers range, focusing on the role of class distinction in the construction of a markedly post-feminist version of heterosexual femininity.

A central theme throughout all of these chapters is that of identification and exclusion. Homosociality is fundamentally about identification between women, and about the exclusion of those who do not 'fit in': in other words, it is about affirming and legitimating the femininity of some women while rejecting that of others. The hierarchies, conflicts and power struggles which take place over the terms of such identific-ation form much of the substance of my analysis. Ann Summers may be the 'No. 1 Fun Company', but the fun and laughter can be aggressive as well as convivial. And the women are not always laughing: some-times, as we shall see in the next chapter, it can end in tears.

two

'The Ultimate Girls' Night In'

Join in the celebration and experience the **Ultimate Girls Night In** (Jacqueline Gold's introduction to the autumn & winter 1999 Ann Summers catalogue)

The world of Ann Summers parties is a women's world. Only women may attend parties; only women may become party organisers. It is also a profoundly heterosexual world, both literally (party organisers and party-goers are almost universally heterosexual) and culturally (the products, the parties and the party plan itself are all oriented around a heterosexual lifestyle). Ann Summers parties are presented as 'the Ultimate Girls' Night In' at which heterosexual women can buy products 'that will make him succumb to temptation' or 'make any man purrrr!' (autumn & winter 1999 catalogue descriptions of Tempt PVC top and Feline leopard-print chemise respectively).

In itself this is not particularly remarkable: there are many other settings similarly occupied by heterosexual women. These include paid work settings where heterosexual women work predominantly or entirely with other heterosexual women (such as might be the case for nurses, cleaners, secretaries or teachers) as well as leisure settings where heterosexual women socialise together. These leisure settings encompass specific environments, which may be as public as the local shopping mall or as private as each other's living rooms, as well as specific events such as the 'girls' night out'.

Although a great deal of work in both sociology and cultural studies has considered women's work and leisure in considerable depth, little of this has paid sufficient attention to the simple observation that heterosexual women get together. The exception to this neglect is a significant (though relatively small) body of sociological research on women's friendships in work and leisure settings, including work which

37

explores married women's friendships with each other.[1] Some authors argue that such friendships provide married or cohabiting heterosexual women with valuable emotional resources which may compensate for, or even enable resistance against, the domestic, emotional and material inequalities of their sexual relationships with men (e.g. Oliker 1989, Harrison 1998). Others are more ambivalent about the role of heterosexual women's friendships in relation to gender inequalities, suggesting that they exist in tension with those inequalities without necessarily challenging them (e.g. O'Connor 1992, Marks 1998).

Some of this literature on heterosexual women's friendships includes explicit discussion of the phenomenon of the 'girls' night in' which may appear to offer some starting points for understanding Ann Summers parties. Kaeren Harrison (1998), for example, considers her middle-class research participants' insistence on having their 'girls' nights' together, despite their husbands' opposition, to be an important form of resistance to domestic inequalities. However the 'girls' nights' discussed in such literature are usually private and fairly intimate gatherings of women who have mutual, pre-existing and often long-standing bonds of friendship. This is by no means the situation with Ann Summers: parties and (even more especially) meetings where all the participants already know each other are the exception rather than the rule. Moreover, even though parties in particular are saturated with talk about supposedly intimate sexual relationships and sexual practices, that talk itself is very far from the trusting, mutual self-disclosure which authors such as Jennifer Coates (1996) regard as a constitutive feature of women's friendships. Talk about men, sex and bodies in Ann Summers settings is more likely to be ritualised and masking than spontaneous and confiding, as I argue at length in Chapter 4. Indeed Coates begins her book by explicitly distinguishing her own friends' regular 'girls' nights' from the kinds of female interaction found at home shopping parties, describing the latter as 'polite but empty' (1996: 3). Ann Summers parties and meetings are in fact neither polite nor empty, but Coates is correct insofar as Ann Summers events cannot simply be treated as instances of women's friendships. The same of course can also be said of many other heterosexual women's gatherings in work and leisure settings for which notions of 'friendship' cannot provide an appropriate analytical frame.

Heterosexual men, of course, also spend a lot of time together, in a wide variety of work and leisure settings – from snooker halls to

---

1. Thanks to Kaeren Harrison for drawing the importance of this body of work to my attention.

corporate boardrooms – which are not necessarily characterised by ties of friendship. Rather more attention has been paid to these settings than has been the case for heterosexual women's gatherings, particularly by scholars concerned with the relative cultural and social positions of men and women. One of the most suggestive concepts developed by sociology and cultural studies to analyse these heterosexual male-dominated settings is that of *homosociality*. It is the contention of this book as a whole that the concept of female homosociality is not just useful but crucial to an understanding of the dynamics of Ann Summers parties and meetings – and, by extension, to many other kinds of heterosexual women's gatherings. This chapter draws on existing literature on male homosociality to develop a new model of female homosociality, and introduces some of the latter's key characteristics. The chapters that follow then develop and deepen the analysis of different facets of female homosociality in Ann Summers settings.

Conceptualising Homosociality

Male homosociality

The term 'homosociality' refers to social relationships between members of the same sex. It has usually been used specifically to describe to men's social relationships with other men, and has been applied not just to men's leisure pursuits (such as playing and/or watching football and other sports), but also to men's working relationships, and to all-male institutions such as the armed forces. Homosocial relationships are non-sexual; how, if at all, male homosociality is connected to male homosexuality is one of the key questions posed by scholars in the field.

Scholars who use the term 'homosociality' sometimes do so rather casually, without presenting any theoretical or conceptual definitions of it. However, among those who attempt an explicit conceptualisation of the term, there appear to be two alternative versions. One version predominates in sociology, the other in literary and cultural studies, and scholars who reference one version never (to my knowledge) refer to the other. In effect, there have been two entirely separate debates taking place over the same concept.

Sociological discussions of male homosociality have tended to take their cue from the work of Jean Lipman-Blumen (1976).[2] Lipman-Blumen defines homosociality as a preference for members of one's own

2. Lipman-Blumen in her turn is explicitly drawing on the interactionist work of John Gagnon and William Simon, especially Gagnon and Simon (1967).

sex – a social rather than a sexual preference. She places this within the context of the profound gender inequalities which characterise our society, which is both divided and stratified by gender: men and women are socially unequal and sharply divided. Moreover, social and political institutions which are exclusively or predominantly male, such as the armed forces, the government, the judiciary and the global business élite, have the lion's share of access to social, political and economic power. Male homosociality is for Lipman-Blumen both a cause and a symptom of male dominance: 'the different institutions of our society [. . .] all act in an integrated and reinforcing way to maintain a male homosocial world in which only men are included and allowed access to the various resources of a society' (24). Thus male power and male homosociality reinforce each other: 'men homosocial in outlook prefer other men's company and also work to maintain all-male institutions' so as to maintain their own power in wider society (Britton 1990: 425). However, according to Lipman-Blumen, homo*sociality* must always clearly distinguish itself from homo*sexuality*: thus homosocial institutions tend to be strongly homophobic, precisely because homosexuality is an ever-present threat where men form strong attachments to and/ or preferences for other men.

Moreover male homosociality according to Lipman-Blumen operates as an 'exchange system' in which men seek resources from each other, and women seek resources from men. In this system women themselves become 'resources' or commodities:

> The dominance order among men is based upon control of resources, including land, money, education, occupations, political connections, and family ties. Women, forced to seek resources from other men, in turn become resources which men can use to further their own eminence in the homosocial world of men. The acquisition of a beautiful woman is a resource that heightens the status claims of a man vis-à–vis other men and provides him with a sexual resource as well. (Lipman-Blumen 1976: 16 –17)

Lipman-Blumen argues that the commodification of women as 'sex objects' is not therefore something which has been forced onto women by men. It is rather a strategy actively (though not necessarily consciously) adopted by women themselves to entice men away from their homosocial bonds with other men.

Literary and cultural critics tend to take their cue not from Lipman-Blumen but from the work of Eve Kosofsky Sedgwick (1985). Drawing on feminist anthropology, particularly Rubin (1975), Sedgwick defines male homosociality as a form of male bonding with a characteristic triangular structure. In this triangle, men have intense but non-sexual bonds with other men, and women act as the conduits through which those bonds are expressed. Rubin's anthropological argument[3] shares with Lipman-Blumen's account the view that women are positioned as 'exchange objects' in transactions between men, as symbolised by the moment in the Christian wedding ceremony when the bride's father 'gives her away' to her new husband. For Sedgwick, the exchange of women in male homosociality need not be as literal as this (although it might be in some contexts). It can also be the positioning of women as intermediaries (her primary example is the classic 'love triangle', where two male rivals for the same woman are in fact more interested in their rivalry with each other than in their romance with her); as signifiers (where men exchange *talk* about women as sex objects, as in sexual boasting or sexist jokes (cf. Lyman 1987)); or as the conduits of male bonding in other ways. Like Lipman-Blumen, Sedgwick suggests that homosocial bonds are inherently homophobic, because homo-sexuality is an ever-present threat: there is a constant danger that 'being a man's man' (homosocially) will tip over into 'being interested in men' (homosexually) (Sedgwick 1985: 89).

Lipman-Blumen's insights about the relationship between male homosociality and men's relative social power, and about heterosexual women's active investment in their own status as 'exchange objects', are extremely valuable and important. But Sedgwick's argument, originally intended as a framework for reading a series of European literary texts, has a great deal to offer to sociological and cultural as well as literary analysis.

Firstly, Sedgwick's emphasis on structure makes for both a more powerful and a more nuanced analytical tool. Lipman-Blumen concept-ualises homosociality as a 'preference' which men acquire through socialisation during childhood and adolescence. This emphasis on attitudes and preferences means that her framework is only loosely tied to historical change – or, for that matter, to historical continuity. Have there always been men with homosocial preferences? Have these homosocial preferences always taken the same form? How do changing historical or social conditions affect the prevalence of male homo-sociality, or the forms it takes? Lipman-Blumen's framework neglects

3. Rubin is here explicitly drawing on structuralist anthropology, particularly the work of Claude Lévi-Strauss.

these questions; indeed her introduction (albeit tentative) of evidence from primate studies tends to rule out the issue of historical change altogether. Sedgwick's account, on the other hand, is explicitly situated in relation to historical change.[4] Sedgwick is very clear that homosociality takes different forms at different historical periods: the Ancient Greeks, for example, lived in a homosocial society where certain kinds of sexual contact between males were permissible (Sedgwick 1985: 4).

Secondly, Sedgwick's definition of homosociality as a structure rather than a preference has greater potential to accommodate not just the ways in which homosociality may have changed, but also the ways in which it stays the same: the ways in which the *structure* of homosociality may persist despite the dissenting *preferences* of the individual heterosexual men who may find themselves caught up in it (or indeed expelled from it). Sharon Bird's (1996) study of North American masculinities, for example, found that many individual heterosexual men disliked the sexist talk and aggressive competitiveness which were the staple of male homosocial gatherings, but that they never felt able to challenge the sexism and aggression during those gatherings themselves: all of their dislike was expressed in other, non-homosocial settings. However, this does not mean that the question of preference is irrelevant – far from it. Sedgwick herself argues that men's homosocial bonds are infused not just with 'entitlement' and 'rivalry' (1985: 1) but also with friendship and pleasure, love and desire; Lipman-Blumen's insight that many heterosexual men actively prefer the company of their own sex remains extremely important. If homosociality is a structure, it is also – at least in some contexts – a source of pleasure and comfort. Heterosexual men don't just go to snooker halls in passive obedience to the requirements of a social structure; on the other hand, their preference for snooker halls rather than home shopping parties is a matter not just of individual whim but of social structures of gender. Moreover men's preference for, and access to, some homosocial spaces rather than others is also of course structured by class and ethnicity. White working class men who visit snooker halls are probably unable to join a polo team or for that matter to attend a corporate board meeting; they are probably just as unlikely to visit their local African-Caribbean men's barber shop. In this sense it would perhaps be more accurate to characterise homosocial relationships as an *interface* between social structures and social

4. This is not to say that Sedgwick's own periodisation is always or necessarily successful; merely to point out that Sedgwick's argument, unlike Lipman-Blumen's, at least includes some attempt at historicisation as an essential part of the analysis.

preferences (or, in more sociological language, between structure and agency).

Thirdly, although both authors argue that homosociality tends to be accompanied by homophobia, Sedgwick offers a clearer account of the relationship between homophobia and homosociality in its current form. Lipman-Blumen notes that male homosocial institutions tend to be strongly homophobic but, as Britton (1990) points out, she does not offer any sustained explanation for it. Indeed if one takes seriously Lipman-Blumen's description of male homosociality then it becomes unclear why men should attempt to develop any kind of affective or domestic relationships with women at all, other than the bare minimum required for men to reproduce and thus to acquire the social status of paternity:

> Women are excluded from [male homosociality] because their lack of resources makes them less useful and interesting both to men and to other women. Men, recognizing the power their male peers have, find one another stimulating, exciting, productive, attractive, and important, since they can contribute to virtually all aspects of one another's lives. (Lipman-Blumen 1976: 30–31)

If they find each other so terribly alluring, why don't men in homosocial groups have sex with each other? Why is male homosexuality vehemently excluded from homosocial groups rather than being welcomed or even promoted? By implicitly assuming men's heterosexuality rather than critically interrogating it in this context, Lipman-Blumen misses a crucial feature of male homosociality, one which Sedgwick explicitly foregrounds. In Sedgwick's model, homophobia is not just a contingent feature of homosocial institutions, but an essential part of both male homosociality and men's power. This is precisely because homosociality and homosexuality are dangerously close to each other – not because heterosexual men are all 'really' or 'repressed' homosexuals by preference, but because of the *structure* of homosociality:

> To put it in twentieth-century American terms, the fact that what goes on at football games, in fraternities, at the Bohemian Grove, and at climactic moments in war novels can look, with only a slight shift of optic, quite startlingly 'homosexual', is not most importantly an expression of the psychic origins of these institutions in repressed or sublimated homosexual genitality. Instead it is the coming to visibility of the normally implicit terms of a coercive double bind. [. . .] For to be a man's

man is separated only by an invisible, carefully blurred, always-already-crossed line from being 'interested in men.' (Sedgwick 1985: 89)

Sedgwick conceptualises male homosociality as existing along a continuum (Figure 2.1). At one end of the continuum is male homosociality – men bonding with each other and acting to further each other's interests. At the other end of this continuum is male homosexuality – men loving men in an explicitly sexual sense. Although in some patriarchal societies and historical periods, such as Ancient Greece, 'the continuum between "men loving men" and "men promoting the interests of men" appears to have been quite seamless' (Sedgwick 1985: 4), in contemporary over-industrialised societies such as the UK and USA it is regarded as imperative that male homosociality be sharply distinguished from homosexuality. Homophobia in such societies is the active boundary marker between the homosocial and the homosexual, the roadblock erected to separate either end of the continuum. In other words, male homosocial events, environments and institutions are homophobic *because* they are homosocial: it is precisely because male bonding is in danger of tipping over into male sexual love that homosexuality must be so emphatically rejected. Sedgwick writes:

What European-style homophobia delineates is thus a space, and perhaps a mechanism, of domination [. . .]. So far as it is possible to do so without minimizing the specificity and gravity of European homosexual oppression and identity, it is analytically important to remember that the domination offered by this strategy is not only over a minority population, but over the bonds that structure all social form. [. . .] [H]omophobia [is] a mechanism for regulating the behavior of the many by the specific oppression of a few. (Sedgwick 1985: 87–8)

Homophobia in our society is not only about the rejection of homosexual individuals or homosexual behaviour; it is also about the regulation of heterosexual men. Precisely *which* heterosexual men are able to set the terms of this regulation is, for Sedgwick, one of the key sites of power struggle between classes (and, we might want to add, between ethnic and racial groupings too). The two-dimensional, linear model of the continuum in Figure 2.1 is therefore rather misleading because, despite its apparent simplicity, the homosocial continuum actually encompasses many different power relations. There is the power of men over women: the role of women in male homosociality is to act as the conduits of male homosocial relationships. There is the power

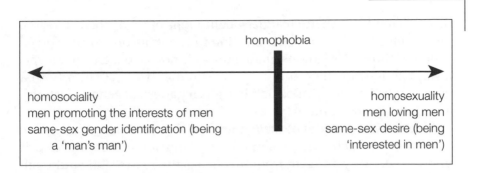

Figure 2.1 The male homosocial-homosexual continuum (extrapolated from Sedgwick 1985)

of heterosexual men over those men defined as homosexual, who are forcefully and sometimes violently excluded from male homosociality. And there is the power of heterosexual men over each other: the power of some men to manipulate the terms of inclusion in and exclusion from homosocial bonds, which in some cases takes the form of class or racist power, but may also take the form of more attenuated struggles over what counts as 'acceptable' or 'unacceptable' versions of masculinity (Connell 1995; Bird 1996; Hutchins and Mikosza 1998).

I suggest that these multi-dimensional power relations can be encapsulated in R. W. Connell's concept of *gender régime*. Connell defines a 'gender régime' as 'the state of play in gender relations in a given institution' (Connell 1987: 120), where 'institution' is understood fairly loosely to include both formal institutions such as schools and informal arenas such as the high street. He distinguishes gender régimes from the 'gender order', which is the state of play in gender relations at the level of a whole society.[5] The particular configurations of specific gender régimes (and indeed of specific gender orders) are historically specific and perpetually open to change. As such they are sites of conflict, resistance and violence – and also of compromise, complicity and negotiation. Thus the forms of masculinity which are hegemonic (to use Connell's term) in particular institutions at particular historical moments may be subtly or even radically different from those in others, and this need not be a problem for the dominance of men in the gender order as a whole. According to Connell (1995), the term 'hegemonic masculinity'

5. The problem of what constitutes a singular 'whole society' in a globalising world is not addressed by Connell.

does not imply any particular personality type or set of characteristics, but simply locates a particular position in the 'state of play' in a given gender régime: '"Hegemonic masculinity" is not a fixed character type, always and everywhere the same. It is, rather, the masculinity that occupies the hegemonic position in a given pattern of gender relations, a position always contestable' (76).

To take two examples of male homosocial institutions, the form of masculinity which is hegemonic in a professional football team is undoubtedly very different from that in a gentleman's club – although they are also likely to have some similarities, such as competitiveness or a reluctance to show 'soft' emotions in public. The configuration of ethnicity and gender is different in each case – one is far more likely to see black African-Caribbean faces in a football team than in a gentleman's club, although in Britain at least one is fairly unlikely to see any South Asian faces in either setting. The class nature of the respective forms of hegemonic masculinity is markedly different, almost by definition. Each of these dimensions – class, ethnicity, emotionality, rivalry – and many more besides are constantly open to challenge and revision, but for that very reason are also likely to be strongly defended within the respective institutions. This is why gender régimes are a 'state of play': they are neither monolithic nor fixed.

The concept of gender régime provides a context within which to place male homosocial institutions (in Connell's loose sense of 'institution'). Put simply, I suggest that male homosociality is a significant variety or subgroup of gender régimes which have certain structural features in common. These common structural features are: homophobia; an interest in the continuance of male dominance within both the institution itself and the gender order as a whole; and a 'state of play' in which a particular form of masculinity is hegemonic and acts as the focus of members' gender identifications, although *which* particular form of masculinity this is will vary between different institutions. (In contemporary Europe and North America it is unlikely to be quite the same as the nineteenth-century 'man's man' type of masculinity evident in Sedgwick's European literary sources.) Not all all-male institutions have this structure: gay male settings, for example, are clearly not homosocial in this sense – and these can be understood in terms of different gender régimes. Moreover not all homosocial gender régimes are the same, as the examples of football teams and gentleman's clubs demonstrate. Connell insists that the state of play in any gender régime can only be established by 'concrete study' of institutions in action (86).

Female homosociality

So can the concept of homosociality be applied to heterosexual women? Sedgwick does suggest that there is such a thing as 'female homo-sociality'. However she sees it as very different, in both structure and meaning, from male homosociality:

> [T]he diacritical opposition between the 'homosocial' and the 'homo-sexual' seems to be much less thorough and dichotomous for women, at least in our society, than for men. At this particular historical moment, an intelligible continuum of aims, emotions, and valuations links lesbianism with other forms of women's attention to women: the bond of mother and daughter, for instance, the bond of sister and sister, women's friendship, 'networking,' and the active struggles of feminism. [. . .] [I]t seems at this moment to make an obvious kind of sense to say that women in our society who love women, women who teach, study, nurture, suckle, write about, march for, vote for, give jobs to, or otherwise promote the interests of other women, are pursuing congruent and closely related activities. (Sedgwick 1985: 2–3)

As Stephen Maddison (2000) points out, for a number of lesbian commentators this passage makes no 'obvious kind of sense' at all.[6] Teresa de Lauretis (1994), for example, angrily condemns Sedgwick's model of female homosociality which, by blurring the distinction between lesbianism and heterosexual female bonding, effectively erases the distinctively *sexual* nature of lesbian love and desire. To put it bluntly, wanting to vote for another woman is *not* the same as wanting to fuck her (cf. Castle 1993). Moreover, Sedgwick's claim that the 'homosocial' and the 'homosexual' are less thoroughly and dichotomously separated for women than for men simply ignores the phenomenon of anti-lesbian homophobia (lesbophobia), particularly as it occurs among women themselves.[7] Many heterosexual women are very concerned indeed to distinguish themselves from lesbians.

De Lauretis situates these failures in Sedgwick's model as part of a wider trend in feminist thinking which simultaneously romanticises

6. But for an interesting exception to this lesbian hostility, see Vermeule (1991).

7. This aspect of Sedgwick's model is arguably part of a wider trend amongst scholars who pay more attention to homophobia directed against men than to that directed against women. Britton (1990) for example, whose explicit aim is to offer an explanation for homophobia, nevertheless excludes lesbophobia from her account, focusing instead on heterosexual men's and women's hostility to gay men.

non-sexual relationships between women and de-sexualises lesbian relationships. More specifically, she sees Sedgwick's account as just one of many misappropriations of the concept of 'lesbian continuum', a concept first elaborated in a celebrated essay by Adrienne Rich (1981) and to which Sedgwick herself refers in a footnote. Rich's lesbian continuum embraces 'forms of primary intensity between and among women, including the sharing of a rich inner life, the bonding against male tyranny, the giving and receiving of practical and political support' as well as explicitly sexual relationships between women (23-24). In de Lauretis's view, Sedgwick's (and others') mistake has been to take Rich's lyrical feminist vision too literally. In fact, de Lauretis suggests, the 'lesbian continuum' should not be read as 'a sociological hypothesis to be verified. [. . .I]t is less in the realm of what is than in the realm of what if, less a factual description than a passionate fiction. [. . .] The feminist political fantasy of a diasporic yet continuous community of women' (1994: 191). Sedgwick's picture of brave and loving homosocial bonds between women has simply mistaken a feminist fantasy for a female reality.

In response to the flaws in Sedgwick's model, Maddison (2000) offers an alternative account of female homosociality. Sedgwick's problem, he suggests, is that she fails to account for the ways in which hetero-sexual women often do not act to further the interests of other women – indeed, they all too often act to further the interests of men:

> The gap in Sedgwick's work lies in her failure to suggest that some hetero-sexual women may actually act in the interests of men, that is, act against the interests of other women (politically, sexually, culturally, emotionally, psychologically) and thus may functionally require homophobia against lesbianism to naturalise a radical *dis*continuity between women who act in the interests of women and women who desire women. (Maddison 2000: 82)

But this does not quite make sense either. Why do women who act in the service of men 'require' homophobia in this model? For the sake of brevity, let's call 'women who act in the interests of women' femin-ists, and 'women who desire women' lesbians. Why do non-feminist (or even anti-feminist) women – women who act in the interests of men – need to distinguish feminists from lesbians? On the contrary, the stereotype that all feminists are 'man-hating lesbians' is all too common among such women, and often acts as an effective mechanism to regulate any heterosexual women who show signs of wanting to further their own interests instead of those of men. If anything, then, non-feminist women 'require' the *continuity* of feminism with lesbianism, which allows non-feminists to reject them both all the more vigorously.

But in any case, I am not convinced that 'acting in the interests of men' always or necessarily excludes 'acting in the interests of women' quite as straightforwardly as Maddison implies. Heterosexual women's interests are often closely bound to those of men precisely because of the social, political, cultural and economic inequalities between women and men. As Lipman-Blumen puts it:

> By now, it is practically a psychological truism that individuals identify with other individuals whom they perceive to be the controllers of resources in any given situation. This is true of children vis-à-vis parents as well as of workers in an occupational setting. It is no less true of the relations between the sexes. (Lipman-Blumen 1976: 16)

Thus at the level of the heterosexual couple, women in unequal partnerships with men are likely to identify with those men's interests, and to do so on a very material basis. As we saw in the previous chapter, Ann Summers largely rests on the assumption that its party organisers will be living with male partners who will both provide the household's primary income – party organisers (as opposed to unit organisers or area managers) are not expected to earn a living wage from Ann Summers, especially not when they first join – and also provide other forms of support, from childcare during the evenings to emotional support and encouragement. Such forms of dependence have class as well as gender dimensions: a woman with young children who earns enough to be able to pay a childminder will not be dependent on her male partner in this way. There may also be ethnic dimensions, such that for example black women of African descent may draw on fictive kin relations and practices of 'othermothering' to share childcare responsibilities with other women (Collins 1991). But for the white working-class and lower middle-class women who made up the vast majority of party organisers encountered during my research, forms of dependence on men imply an interrelationship between men's interests and women's interests.

Many heterosexual women are also likely to identify with men's interests at a more general level too. As we saw above, Lipman-Blumen proposes that not only do men hold the lion's share of social, political, economic and cultural resources in what Connell would call our current 'gender order', but that heterosexual women can gain access to those resources by forging alliances with men – using their sexuality to do so. Beverley Skeggs's (1997) research with young working-class women similarly found that 'when they [the young women] traded their femininity and appearance on the marriage market [. . .] they were able to negotiate more power [than they could access by themselves] but only in interpersonal terms rather than gaining access to wider instit-utional power. The trading of femininity, however, also involves them as the object of the exchange' (9). This 'marriage market' dynamic between men who have resources and women who lack them effectively ties women's interests with those of men in a relationship of inequality and dependence. This does not mean of course that all men have resources which all women lack: the young women in Skeggs's study were forming partnerships with often unemployed working-class young men who actually had very little in material terms, and certainly had a great deal less than many middle-class women have in this sense. But within the gender régime of this working-class 'marriage market', the men's 'hard' form of masculinity was itself a source of social status which gave them power over the working-class women – and to which those women in turn sought to gain access by presenting themselves as desirable 'objects'.

With all of this in mind I wish to propose my own model of female homosociality. Figure 2.2 represents female homosociality in a way which may easily be compared with male homosociality in Figure 2.1. Thus female homosociality is a variety of gender régime with three distinctive structural features: women promoting the interests of women who promote the interests of men; gender identification, which in the case of Ann Summers is defined as being 'one of the girls'; and lesbophobia.

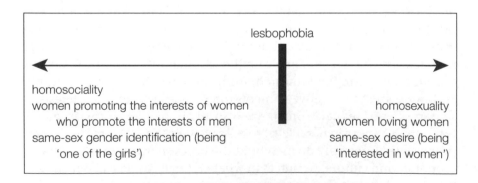

Figure 2.2 The female homosocial-homosexual continuum

Firstly, female homosociality promotes the interests of women who promote the interests of men – or, to put it slightly less tortuously, *female homosociality helps heterosexual women to further men's interests*. It is important to recognise that this means helping the women in question as well as helping the men. At the level of the heterosexual couple, my baby-sitting for my married friend means helping her, because she has a child-free evening for a change; helping him, because he has a child-free evening as usual; and also helping her to help him, because her evening off gives her time to recuperate, 'recharge her batteries', ready to return to her childcare responsibilities the following day without posing any fundamental challenge to basic inequality in their household. In fact this sense of a 'night off' from responsibilities for the care of both children and other adults (particularly adult men) precisely characterises many girls' nights out, including Ann Summers parties as we shall see below. At the level of the 'marriage market', helping women to look and feel sexy or attractive, whether through the purchase of Ann Summers products or simply through mutual affirmation, both helps women to maximise their 'marketability', and maintains the unequal status quo of male dominance and the existence of the 'market' itself.

Secondly, just as there is always a hegemonic or favoured form of masculinity within male homosociality – which, in the literary cases analysed by Sedgwick, are about being a 'man's man' – so there is a favoured form of femininity within female homosociality. Connell (1987) argues that women's unequal status in the gender order means that forms of femininity cannot acquire the same kinds of power or status as masculinity; he therefore insists that one cannot speak of 'hegemonic femininity' in the same way that one can speak of 'hegemonic masculinity'. However he argues that there *is* a particularly favoured kind of femininity, widely accepted and supported in the current gender order, which he calls 'emphasised femininity' and which is both acquiescent to and oriented around men's interests. He argues that 'this kind of femininity is performed, and performed especially to men' (188). But female homosocial gender régimes, although oriented around men's interests, do not involve the direct performance of femininity to men; femininity is performed or displayed in such settings to gain the approval and affirmation of other women. In the case of Ann Summers, the favoured form of femininity around which gender identification revolves is 'being one of the girls'. Female homosocial settings are by definition a forum for gender identification *between women*. Identification is a *process* rather than a state of being, and as such is constantly under negotiation and revision (Fuss 1995). 'Being one of the girls' is not just a passive state of being but an active construction in which heterosexual women mutually recognise and affirm their femininity as coherent, acceptable and appropriate. This provides women with the opportunity for emotional nurture and support: being 'one of the girls', being recognised and affirmed by others, can be a powerful and positive experience. But it also gives women the power to judge each other's femininity – to refuse each other recognition as appropriately gendered women. Female homosocial spaces, both within Ann Summers and under other homosocial gender régimes, are racked by power struggles over what constitutes 'proper' femininity, who decides what the criteria are, and who has the power to judge whom.

Thirdly, the favoured or 'proper' form of femininity in such settings, whatever its class, ethnic or other criteria, is of course always by definition some form of *heterosexual* femininity. In this sense the lesbophobia which marks the boundary between homosociality and lesbianism acts to police not just sexual desire but also, no less importantly, gender identification. Thus lesbophobia is intrinsically linked to 'being one of the girls' in Ann Summers settings. Moreover both lesbophobia and gender identification in female homosocial settings are themselves intrinsically connected to women's service of men's interests: 'being one of the (heterosexual) girls' in this context involves *identifying with men's interests* – both specifically, with the interests of husbands and boyfriends, and generally, with those of the gender order. For many of the women who become Ann Summers party organisers, as we have seen, this identification is entwined with the very material ties of financial and other kinds of dependence on individual men. Identification with men's interests may also have other threads, for Ann Summers women and for others, including class or ethnic solidarity, aspirations for (or fear of) social mobility, positions of authority or prestige within kin networks, and so on. In particular, as I argue at length in Chapter 3, the form of femininity involved in 'being one of the girls' under the gender régime of Ann Summers is one in which women 'fashion themselves as sex objects to attract men' (Lipman-Blumen 1976: 17) – in other words, the kind of femininity favoured within this female homosocial gender régime is precisely the kind which at least some *male* homosocial gender régimes treat as objects of exchange between men. Thus the continua in Figures 2.1 and 2.2 should not be regarded as parallel lines, but – in relation to some sets of institutions at least – as intimate and interlocking structures.

Ultimately all three characteristics of female homosociality – lesbo-phobia, gender identification, and identification with men's interests – seek to secure heterosexual women's privilege. As Eve Sedgwick writes, 'often in history, "patriarchy" is not a monolithic mechanism for subordinating "the female" to "the male"; it is a web of valences and significations that, while deeply tendentious, can historically through its articulations and divisions offer both material and ideological affordances to women as well as to men' (1985: 141). Such privileges and 'affordances' for heterosexual women obviously include privilege over lesbians and bisexual women, as well as access to men's status and resources in ways discussed above.

The model of female homosociality proposed here may appear rather negative, even pessimistic, to some readers, particularly feminists. My claim that female homosociality is about 'women helping each other to further the interests of men' may seem to some to imply that such women are passive in the face of their own oppression, or that they lack the intelligence, imagination or resources to assert themselves in a male-dominated world. In fact the reverse is true: the women I met at Ann Summers events, and indeed the events themselves, were active, vibrant, imaginative, resourceful, intelligent, assertive, emotionally nourishing, and side-splittingly funny. None of this necessarily means that they were feminist, in either intention or effect. As Valerie Walkerdine (1997) has argued, academic scholars have been too eager to look for signs of 'subversion' and 'resistance' in working people's everyday social and cultural lives, and have conversely simply ignored or dismissed the un-exotic cultural practices of 'ordinary working people, who have been coping and surviving [. . .], who are subjects formed in the complexities of everyday practices' (21). In the case of feminist scholars, as Rachel Moseley (2002) points out, this has meant a rush to find examples of women's 'cultural resistance' against patriarchy when in fact for many women everyday life is not about resisting power relations but coping with and surviving them. Female homosociality may not present a challenge to power relations within either the gender régime or the gender order; but it does help women to cope with those power relations. In this sense I would argue that female friendship groups, such as those discussed by Oliker (1989) and Harrison (1998) in which women compensate one another for and support one another through heterosexual inequalities, may be regarded as a variety or subgroup of female homosociality. Thus, as my baby-sitting example suggests above, when I describe female homosociality as 'helping women to further men's interests' I do so in two senses: helping to further men's interests as such, but also helping the women who do so to cope with, survive, recuperate from, reward and compensate themselves for the demands of everyday life.

The analysis of Ann Summers as an example of female homosociality is the central concern of this book. In later chapters I will consider in detail the objects of exchange or conduits of female relationships at Ann Summers parties (Chapter 3); the ways in which female homosociality produces particular versions of male and female bodies at Ann Summers parties (Chapter 4); the ways in which struggles over femininity are waged in Ann Summers settings through the dynamics of taste and consumption (Chapter 5). For the rest of this chapter I will explore in more detail how the homosociality of Ann Summers party organisers and guests enacts female homosociality's defining characteristics: helping women to serve the interests of men; gender identification; and the lesbophobia which polices and supports them.

Ann Summers and Female Homosociality

Although this chapter, and this book as a whole, obviously focus on Ann Summers parties, it is worth reminding ourselves at this point that Ann Summers parties constitute just one of a number of homosocial spaces in the lives of party organisers and guests. Many guests and party organisers also spoke of leisure pursuits which were either implicitly or explicitly homosocial: these included bingo nights, shopping trips, slimming clubs, nights out clubbing with the girls, trips to see the Chippendales or similar male strippers' acts, hen nights, and indeed other kinds of home shopping parties such as Tupperware.

Many of the party guests in paid employment also worked in homosocial settings, and in some cases workmates made up a significant proportion of the guests at a party. At a party organised by Sarah, for example, approximately half of the guests were the hostess' non-work friends and neighbours, and the other half were her fellow healthcare workers; at another party organised by Joy, *all* of the guests were current or former workmates of the hostess, with the exception of two women, one of whom was the hostess's mother. It was particularly evident at Joy's party that gatherings of the women outside the workplace offered them, among other benefits, the opportunity to 'let off steam' about their various male work colleagues and bosses: a great deal of conversation at this party revolved around the difficult personality, mood swings and suspected cocaine habit of one man in particular. It was clear that the women were unable to challenge or confront this man at work; talking about him amongst themselves was a way of coping with him.

However, the female homosocial space of Ann Summers is temporally limited and heavily circumscribed, at both parties and meetings. Not only does a great deal of conversation at parties and meetings revolve around husbands, boyfriends and children, but those men and children themselves are often ready and waiting to bring the female homo-sociality to an end – literally, in the cases of the many husbands and boyfriends who arrive at parties and meetings to take the women home again at the end of the evening. The closing stages of both parties and meetings are often heralded by the ringing of mobile 'phones around the room, as husbands and/or baby-sitters call to find out how much longer the women are going to be away from home; and women themselves, especially party guests, sometimes call their husbands or boyfriends during parties, whether to check on the children left in their care or just simply to maintain contact.

Ann Summers party nights are often also homosocial nights for the male partners of party-goers, particularly of hostesses. Party organisers strictly enforce the 'no men' rule at parties, and men whose partners are hosting an Ann Summers party almost always leave the house altogether rather than sit in another room during the duration of the party, often going to male homosocial spaces such as the pub or snooker hall. This has two consequences to men's advantage. Firstly, because the 'no men' rule means that the men's return automatically means the end of the party, men have the power to bring the female homo-social event to an end whenever they choose simply by deciding to come home, a power which women cannot exert over male homosocial events: for example, at a party organised by Sarah, the hostess's husband had pre-arranged that he would come home at 10.00 p.m., thus strictly demarcating the party time available to his wife and her friends. Secondly, if the hostess and her partner have young children, by leaving the house to go to a male homosocial space or event the man leaves his partner with responsibility for the care of the children, who are usually in bed and/or in another room during the party. Guests at Ann Summers parties will often help their hostess in such cases by taking care of and/or entertaining the children for her, so that she can still have some kind of 'time off' during the party, and it is not uncommon for babies or small children to be present during at least some of their mother's Ann Summers party. Needless to say, it is never the case that fathers take their children to male homosocial events or spaces: men's spaces are strictly for adults only.

Helping women to serve the interests of men

Despite these limits and conditions, however, it is undoubtedly the case that Ann Summers parties represent a highly pleasurable 'night off' from women's everyday responsibilities. In the case of women in paid employment, this can mean time off from dealing with male colleagues and bosses; for women with partners and/or children, it means at least some form or degree of time off from domestic responsibilities for the care of children and especially of adults, notably adult men[8] – even if children are still in the house, the men at least have gone for a few hours. As Dawn once remarked during a unit meeting, when you go to an Ann Summers party 'you're there to have fun, you've left the kids and the husband at home for the evening'. The pleasures of female homosociality as 'time off' are consciously touted by party organisers in their attempts to get party bookings:

> [Merl: So they tend to be mums then that make a good crowd?] Yeah. Yeah, definitely mums. They're the people we target as well when we're canvassing [for party bookings], if they've got a pushchair. [. . .] Because they are the people that tend to want to – want to have a bit of fun and a girls' night in as well as sort of a girls' night out. (Sarah)

This 'time off' is a pleasure not just for guests but also for party organisers themselves:

> Oh, it was fun. I mean that's why I – mostly why I do it. I mean, I do like the money [laughter], I do like the money, but, no, the – the games and all the laughs and everything, it's just, um – it gets me out, and with having the two – the two kids I do need it. (Laura)

> [I]f I wasn't going out to someone's house [i.e. to do a party] I'd most probably just be sitting in front of the telly or sorting the kids out, putting them to bed and doing a bit of housework. So, you know, whatever [money] you make it's a bonus. And you've had a – a couple of hours out. So that's the way I look at it. (Trish)

8. It should be noted though that men are not the only adults for whose care party guests or organisers are responsible. Diane, for example, shares (with her sister) responsibility for the care of her elderly mother; she also helps her own adult daughter by baby-sitting her grandchildren. Indeed on some days, including the day I conducted her interview, Diane does both at the same time.

Indeed, for Ann Summers party organisers, some of the promotions, prizes and other 'perks' offered by the company as motivational tools are themselves opportunities for homosocial leisure, such as the promotional offer of a weekend away at a Pontins holiday resort:

> Oh I booked up – we're going to Pontins as well, me and the girls! [Merl laughs.] [. . . A]ll the girls that are friends of mine that have had parties for me and done me the favour type of thing, I've said to them, like, 'Come with me, we'll have a girls' – get rid of them lot, the kids and what have you, it's a good excuse, I'll say 'No, no, you can't come, it's for Ann Summers, it's women only' [Merl laughs], they don't know, see. [Laughter.] [Merl: Oh poor things.] You wouldn't be saying that if you saw them all, believe me! [Merl laughs.] They have me running round riots for the rest of the year! (Trish)

As Trish's remark that she is 'running round riots for the rest of the year' attests, taking 'time off' in a female homosocial setting, no matter how pleasurable, does not really represent a challenge either to unequal childcare responsibilities or to other domestic inequalities faced by heterosexual women. Indeed, elsewhere in her interview Trish says that she joined Ann Summers because she wanted 'basically the money, and time out. I mean, I'm in here every day. [. . .] So if I've got a couple of parties booked then [. . .] he's got to stay in and look after the kids, and it gives me a night out. And also earns a bit of money.' In other words, doing Ann Summers is her alibi for *making* her partner stay home and take responsibility for childcare for a couple of nights a week; otherwise, childcare is her job. Thus Ann Summers parties could be said to help women who serve men's interests by allowing them the time off they need to be able to return refreshed to their domestic and/or paid work responsibilities to and for adult men.

If the 'time out' that Trish refers to is in men's interests as well as women's, the same can also be said of the 'money' she mentions as her other motivation for doing Ann Summers. In fact husbands and boyfriends may benefit from the money even more directly than they do from the 'time out' (as well as from some of the prizes offered in the bigger competitions, which include holidays 'for two' and even gifts specifically for men such as a day at the motor races). Twelve of the fifteen interviewees live with husbands or boyfriends; ten of these, when asked about the money they make from Ann Summers, said that they spend it in ways which are arguably of benefit to their male partners at least as much as to themselves. Perhaps the most naked expression of this occurred not in a formal interview, but during participant observation at a unit meeting. When each of the unit members was asked to stand up in turn and state her personal goals, one party organiser announced that her goal was 'to pay off my boyfriend's overdraft, and to be able to feed the kids without grovelling to my mother.' None of the interviewees spoke of handing over their money to their partners so directly. However, some of the married or cohabiting interviewees did say that they spent at least some of their money on gifts for their partners:

> That's just my pocket money. It's just, like, to save me asking my husband for money, basically. If it's his birthday, whatever, and I want to buy him something, or, you know, if I want to buy myself something. (Cathy)

> When I very first started it I started to do it for my other half's birthday. And I know sort of like I could go – say to him 'I'm going to the bank to get some money out', but I wanted to do it for myself. So by the time his birthday come round I'd saved up sort of like about a hundred and thirty quid, and I went out and bought him his birthday present. [. . .] Like the other week, last weekend actually, we went down to [Essex] and I said 'Oh what do you want for Christmas?' 'Oh, I don't know', and he – he was going out, and he said 'Oh I think I'll go and get a pair of trousers'. So we was queuing up and I went, 'Oh', I said, 'I'll get them for you for Christmas'. (Melanie)

More often, however, party organisers spend their money in ways which benefit their partners more indirectly, by taking over responsibility for family purchases which have hitherto been the responsibility of the men:

> If I want something, I haven't got to take it out of the housekeeping or the bank balance. It's – it's there if I need it. (Diane)

> Sometimes if I really want something I can save it up. But it's – it's just, um, floater money really. If I want to go down to Asda's and get something, or if I want a pair of shoes, I know I've got money. I don't have to keep asking my husband 'Have you got a tenner?' (Beth)

> I'd say after Christmas, um, maybe for a change I'd like to say to my family 'Come on, I'll – I'll take you on holiday, I'll pay for the holiday'. Yeah, maybe something like that. (Vanessa)

Then in August it's my little girl's birthday. So I just went absolutely mad. And my parties were going well then. And, um, I mean, I – she had a bouncy castle, she had how many friends was it? Twenty? Twenty-four friends? At FX's birthday party. About twenty-four friends round for her birthday party. MacDonalds for everybody. Like, it cost me about – oh, plus her birthday present, it must have cost me about two hundred and fifty pound. And I got so much pleasure out of saying to him at the end of the day 'I need fifty pound off you for the bouncy castle'. And he said to me 'What about everything –' 'No, it's all paid for.' I'd paid for everything else, all as he had to pay for was the bouncy castle. [. . .] [I]t's more the independence than anything else. I mean, [my partner] wouldn't qualm if I went down the bank and got a hundred pound out to buy him something, but it's just, like, the self-satisfaction to think I can do it for myself. (Melanie)

Sometimes the party organisers' spending takes the form of specific purchases for the family home: Diane, for example, spent some of her money on new carpets for the house, and Donna bought a new sofa. In other cases the women's Ann Summers money just becomes a more or less undifferentiated part of the family budget: in Cherry's words, 'sometimes I think it's probably going to be, you know, you pay your electric bill [. . .] It's a case of – depends on how much you make and when you make it as to what you use it on.'

However, although it is undoubtedly the case that husbands and boyfriends benefit materially from party organisers' earnings, it is important not to forget that, as argued above, men's interests and women's interests are by no means mutually exclusive. Indeed, the very fact that they are able to take financial responsibility for some or all of the family's outgoings is itself a source of great pleasure and satisfaction for many party organisers, as the quote from Melanie demonstrates. This is particularly the case when it comes to spending money on their children (or, in Diane's case, grandchildren):

Yeah, I suppose you can call it treat money, 'cause that's what it does. I – I put that straight in the bank, and we are saving up to go on holiday next year so that will be it, and also, as I say, if there's anything in the home that I need, or if anything – you know, the children, if I want to treat them, I can do it, I haven't got to think 'Oh, you know, I can't do it this week', I can, I can just go and treat them if I want to. So – 'cause I do – I – I mean, I do spoil my grandchildren, and I think I might – I can do that even more now. Because I'm earning the money. (Diane)

Well it just gets spent – I mean, it always gets spent on everybody else and not me anyway, but — [laughs] 'cause that's just the way I am [Merl laughs], you know, I – I can't help it, you know. My husband always has a go at me, he'll give me a sort of hundred pound, like, 'Go and treat yourself', and I'll come back with trainers and that for the kids, you know! [Laughter.] And he'll 'Oh God, not again', you know. I can't help it, you know, I – I walk round shops and I think 'Oh I'm not paying that . . . Oh they look nice!' But it gives me the freedom to go out and think 'Right, I can get that'. I haven't got to ask my husband 'Oh can I have some money to get that?' You know, just – just give me that extra little bit of freedom, you know, like, I've been able to buy a Playstation game and bought their coats and bought some shoes for myself and all that, rather than having to ask him for money. 'Cause I always used to be very independent and very career-minded when I was in the bank, and then obviously got pregnant and married and all that, and it – it all went. And I missed not having my own money. Even though it's not a lot, [laughs] it's mine, I can do what I want with it. (Sarah)

I mean, I done a very good party, um, last year. Er, that was for just under a thousand pound in one party, that was. And that was a very good party, I like that. And I did get commission – good commission off that. Um, and me being me and the kids come first [laughs], I went out and I bought my son some lovely things. [Laughter.] And um, I did actually buy myself a new – a new top. I got a new top out of it. [Laughs.] [Merl: But you spent more on the kids?] But I spent more on him than I did, yeah. I did. And I don't know – that gives me satisfaction though. To get my kids something, it gives me satisfaction . And I think – yeah, I decorated their bedroom with it as well. So I like that. [Merl: Oh that's good.] So I was happy to [do] that, because if it – if it's putting it into something that I can see, then I like it. 'Cause it doesn't have to be on – on me, I don't have to go out and lavish myself with new clothes and all the rest of it, but if I can do it once in a while I'm happy. But if I can make, like, my kids happy, and make the place look nice, then I'll do it. (Laura)

Although Laura and Sarah both think that this tendency to spend their money on the children rather than on themselves is a personal foible ('that's just the way I am', 'me being me'), in fact this is a widely noted feature of heterosexual women's relationship with money, especially the spare money or 'treat money' left over when bills and other essentials are paid: men spend such money on themselves, women spend it on their family (Pahl 1989). The problem is not that women make a financial contribution to the home, but that this is not matched either by an equal contribution by their partners to childcare and domestic responsibilities, or by an equal use of 'treat money'. Nevertheless, despite the material inequality which this kind of spending both represents and exemplifies, the *meaning* of that spending for the women concerned is overwhelmingly positive: it represents self-worth, independence and personal achievement; indeed, spending their money on the family is often experienced by the women as a way of spending the money on themselves, for their own enjoyment. Diane calls her Ann Summers money her 'treat money' *because* she spends it on carpets, family holidays and gifts for the grandchildren.

Party organisers do also, of course, spend their Ann Summers money directly on themselves. This usually means treating themselves to clothes (Melanie in particular spoke at length of her insatiable shopping trips for shoes and handbags, although even here it turned out that some of these shoes were actually for her daughters), but there were other kinds of personal expenditure. Beth sometimes spent her money on taking (female) friends out to breakfast; Lucy (who does not have children) divides her money between motorbike maintenance, vets' bills, and paying off her credit card debts. There are also of course ongoing expenditures related to Ann Summers itself – buying stationery and other necessities, and buying new or extra stock to carry in one's kit. As we saw in the previous chapter, party organisers occupy an ambiguous position as both customers and retailers in relation to Ann Summers Ltd, and this ambiguity means that buying for one's kit can also be buying for oneself. Most party organisers routinely order kit items in their own size, so that they can keep any item for themselves if and when it is removed from the Ann Summers catalogue – or, indeed, wear it themselves in the meantime. Many party organisers were already Ann Summers customers and/or party-goers before they were recruited, and the line between 'clothes for my kit' and 'clothes for me' can become blurred. Helen, for example, boosts her kit by including some Ann Summers items she already owned before she joined; Donna, conversely, boosts her own Ann Summers collection by ordering kit items in her own size. Even here, though, there is some question mark over whether this source of enjoyment for women is also ultimately of benefit to men:

> Although you say you treat yourself, if anything I think the real winners out of – out of the Ann Summers really is the men [Merl laughs], because you – you find, see, they're the ones that get the real enjoyment. We get

to feel sexy wearing it, yes. But they get to get the enjoyment of us feeling sexy. So you know, I do think that the men still win more than the women in this – in this business. (Cherry)

Ann Summers guests' and party organisers' definitions of 'the real winners' in heterosexual encounters raise complex questions about heterosexuality and pleasure, which are explored in more detail in Chapters 3 and 4. Even putting these questions aside, however, it is clear that the female homosocial world of Ann Summers fits the description of 'helping women to serve the interests of men' in a number of ways, specifically in the cases of women living with male partners. The 'time off' offered by Ann Summers parties to guests and organisers alike benefits the women themselves in helping them to cope with their domestic and other responsibilities; it also benefits their husbands and boyfriends in that it accommodates rather than challenges domestic inequalities, especially childcare responsibilities. The money exchanged between women at parties and earned by Ann Summers party organisers is of benefit to the organisers, not necessarily because they spend the money on themselves, but often (in the case of married or cohabiting women) because it represents a degree of independence and offers feelings of pleasure and satisfaction; but in material terms it is more likely to be used to benefit partners and children than to treat the women themselves. Thus in the case of married/cohabiting women in general, and mothers in particular, Ann Summers time and money clearly serve the interests of those women, but they also ultimately serve the interests both of specific men (the women's husbands and boy-friends), and of the gender order which shapes the unequal material conditions of women's paid and unpaid work.

Being one of the girls

The forms of femininity in circulation at Ann Summers parties are historically and culturally specific to turn-of-the-century Britain. (Indeed, given the precise geographical location of my participant observation, some aspects of them may be specific to south-eastern England. For example, party organisers and unit organisers would sometimes make jokes about being 'Essex girls' at area meetings, using the stereotype of the brash, sexually active 'good-time girl' and investing it with positive value: 'Essex girls' know how to enjoy themselves, unlike say the (by implication) staid girls from Kent or other counties who might be present at the meeting.[9]) The forms of femininity at Ann

Summers parties are not exactly anti-feminist, but can more accurately be described as *post*-feminist, within the terms set out in Chapter 1. The 'girls' at Ann Summers parties take it for granted that women have an equal right to sexual pleasure with men, and that women are free to make sexual and other choices. However they do not question or challenge the prevailing divisions of paid or unpaid labour, nor do they question the 'naturalness' of either heterosexuality or gender. The ways in which this apparent contradiction is tacitly negotiated at Ann Summers events forms one of the threads running throughout this book.

Being 'one of the girls' at Ann Summers events is a source of great pleasure for party organisers and partygoers alike. In this sense Ann Summers parties may be typical 'girls' nights out', organised around culturally coded 'feminine' preoccupations with clothes, food – especially chocolate – shopping and relationships. The feminine gender identifications involved in these pursuits are of course thoroughly circular: chocolate and shopping make you 'one of the girls' while at the same time women's investments in them make chocolate and shopping 'feminine'. The simple fact of being recognised and affirmed as 'one of the girls' through such pursuits is itself an important source of comfort and pleasure for women: 'getting rid of the men for the night' (as Trish put it during her interview) opens up a space for women to experience themselves and each other as something other than girlfriends, wives or employees in a gender-stratified society. But I also suggested above that gender identification at Ann Summers events is a site of power struggle between women.

As we saw in Chapter 1, Ann Summers party organisers (or at least those I observed during this research) are surprisingly homogeneous in terms of class and 'race'. This homogeneity is a source of gender identification in itself: being 'one of the girls' at the Ann Summers events I observed usually meant being a *white* girl. The most ethnically diverse of the parties I observed was organised by Dawn in North London: although white women still formed the majority, five of the fifteen party-goers (including the hostess) were of Mediterranean or 'Middle Eastern' descent, and another two were of South Asian or African descent. This party started late because the guests were late in

9. Jokes about 'Essex girls' are a common form of sexist joke which was particularly popular in the 1980s and 1990s. Sample joke: 'How do you know when an Essex girl has had an orgasm? She drops her bag of chips.'

arriving and settling down, and it also resulted in slightly below-average sales figures. Dawn was very disappointed and unhappy with this party (although she maintained her fun-loving and patient persona throughout the party itself), and did not solicit further party bookings from it. Discussing the party with me on the way home, Dawn put the relatively low sales down to the ethnic composition of the partygoers: she told me that 'you have to think of their background', that guests like these never bought much because of their religion (although there had been no talk of religion during the party, and none of the party-goers had been wearing any clothing or jewellery indicative of any particular faith). She also explained the late arrivals in terms of ethnicity: while waiting for guest to arrive at the beginning of the party, Dawn told me that 'mixed' parties always started late because the guests 'have no concept of time', and said that one of her regular hostesses, who was Turkish, always put a 7.00 p.m. start-time on her invitations because she knew then that the guests would actually arrive at 8.30 p.m. Dawn explicitly contrasted this with white party-goers who she said would always arrive and start the party on time. This did not seem to me to be direct racism on Dawn's part: the tale of the Turkish hostess did seem to back her claims about different perceptions of time-keeping and, as Dawn herself pointed out, one of the Mediterranean guests at this party did also say that she would never be able to have an Ann Summers party of her own because none of her friends or relations would buy anything. I also heard a great deal of anecdotal evidence from other party organisers that parties for non-white women were rare; as one party organiser once put it, 'Ann Summers isn't really black people's sort of thing'. Whatever the true figures on ethnic composition of parties might be (and no-one actually records any such figures), it is clear that party organisers' own perception is that Ann Summers girls are usually white girls. Most importantly in this context, this perception is about gender identification rather than, say, the logistics of parties: no-one ever suggests making changes to the party format to accommodate late arrivals, for example; ethnicity is an issue in terms of whether non-white women can behave (and buy) like 'one of the girls' with the white women at parties.

This becomes clearer on the extremely rare occasions when the tables are turned on white women at Ann Summers parties. Helen organised one party in East London at which she was the only white woman present, and she plainly found it difficult to negotiate, even though the hostess was one of her oldest friends:

Well anyway, all her friends – I've met a couple of her friends, but I don't know if you've sort of, like, come across, like, Rude Girls. They were like, um, all these girls from North London, about ten of them, and I'm thinking 'Oh my God!' Do you know what I mean? [Laughter.] But – but – and the – I can't remember, what game did I play first? I mean they arrived, they had the, um – the catalogues, and [the hostess]'s mum was, like, bringing food in , and it was like 'Oh I want some more of that', they didn't have any manners really at all. I'm thinking 'Oh God [laughs], this is going to be hard'. [. . .] But it was all right towards the end, well not towards the end, towards about the second game, but it was really hard. [. . .] I just said [to the hostess's mum], um, 'I'm enjoying myself now', like this was in – like, in the middle of the party, I said, 'but it was very hard at the beginning'. I said, like, 'FX [the hostess]'s really polite, and they were, like' – it felt like, oh I'm white and they don't like me. So – but they – they got over – I got over that, and they got over it I think, so it was all right in the end. But it – I thought 'Oh my God, this is going to be hard'. [Laughs.] [Merl: So you were the only white person in the room?] Yeah. Yeah. [Merl: That's really interesting, 'cause all the parties I've been to – well not quite all, nearly all the parties I've been to have been pretty white. I haven't really been to one where there's been a lot of black people there.] No, I think they don't tend – but let me count in the book, see how many people were there. (Helen)

Helen interrupts herself before finishing her final thought, but seems to be about to say that black women don't tend to have and/or go to Ann Summers parties much. Helen's words also make clear that what was 'hard' for her at this party was the lack of gender identification she felt with the partygoers when they first arrived. They were black 'Rude Girls' from North London; she is a white girl from East London; they inhabit a different (sub)cultural milieu, and a different kind of femininity, from her own. And because, on this rare occasion, the black women were in the majority and had the collective power to accept or reject the white woman, Helen was acutely aware of *their* power not to recognise *her* as 'one of the girls' – and acutely aware of the precise point in the party ('towards the second game') when they finally granted her that recognition. The moment of recognition was also of course the moment when the party became enjoyable for everybody: 'being one of the girls' grants access to homosocial pleasures.

Ethnic homogeneity is not just a source of gender identification in Ann Summers settings, but is also in some respects a result of such identification, specifically between party organisers and potential recruits. As explained in Chapter 1, most recruitment takes place through personal networks – through friends or acquaintances or their parties – and party organisers therefore tend to recruit women who are similar to themselves in age, class, and ethnicity. This is less straightforwardly the case, however, of recruitment through newspaper advertisements. The most direct and shocking expression of racism I encountered during this research occurred one morning when Cathy received a telephone call in response to such an advertisement while I was at her house. As the conversation progressed it became clear that the caller did not actually know what Ann Summers was, and Cathy explained that 'it's sexy underwear and vibrators, do you understand?'. The caller said she still did not understand, so Cathy repeated 'it's sexy underwear and sex toys basically, do you understand now?' The caller evidently said yes, and Cathy then began to explain a little about the work involved in party organising, emphasising that the hardest part of the job was getting party bookings and that the caller would have to persuade all her friends and family to have parties for her. Then Cathy abruptly changed tack and told the caller, 'I don't think this is your kind of thing, I think you'd be better off with something like Pippa Dee' and ended the call. (Pippa Dee is a party plan organisation selling clothing.) Once she had put the phone down Cathy told me that the caller had been 'a fucking paki' and that she would never take on 'Indians' because they were no good; that 'pakis' were never any good because their husbands never liked them doing Ann Summers and 'when they get the vibrators home they realise what it is' and did not want to do it.

In refusing to allow this Asian woman to join Ann Summers, Cathy is implicitly defining 'Asian femininity' as impermissible and excluding it from the homosocial circles of Ann Summers. Indeed the fact that Cathy homogenises the diversity of South Asian women/femininities as 'pakis' is precisely part of the racist effect of her explanation. Her thoroughly racist explanations why 'pakis' are never any good defines 'Asian' women's femininity as inappropriate for Ann Summers both because such women are supposedly sexually innocent and/or prudish (with the post-feminist implication that, conversely, Ann Summers women are sexually liberated), and because they are supposedly controlled by their husbands (with the post-feminist implication that, conversely, Ann Summers women are free of such control – thus defining their own heterosexual relationships as wholly egalitarian). 'Pakis' can never be 'one of the girls'. Moreover, as this example demonstrates, gender identification in this female homosocial context has a material base and material effects: it is not just about cultural definitions and struggles over meaning, but also about material power. Cathy's definition of the 'Asian' applicant as unacceptable is not just about the ascription of racist definitions, but is also of course about refusing the woman a job.

Power struggles take place not only with those excluded from the homosocial group, but also amongst those who are included. One highly charged example is the often fraught relations of gender identification between mothers and daughters. Mother-daughter couples are very common at Ann Summers parties (two thirds of the parties I observed included at least one mother-daughter couple). Among party organisers themselves it is not uncommon for mothers to recruit their daughters into the party plan and vice versa: I encountered one woman who was the Ann Summers 'baby' of her real-life daughter. It is also very common for party organisers to get their first party bookings from their mothers:

> I used to make my mum hold them. [Merl: Loads of people go to parties with their mums though, I've been really struck by how many mums there are at parties, it's really interesting.] Yeah. Yeah, yeah, no that is – there is quite a few. Some of them get really embarrassed and – but I think, I don't know, nowadays seems to be a bit – you know. But I remember when my mum came to my party and she – like, and her friend bought vibrators, and I was like 'Oh no! [Laughter.] Oh no!' [Laughter.] I couldn't believe it. Like, her and her friend were sitting there giggling away and, like – oh. I thought 'No, I won't go there!' [Laughter.] [Merl: Just let her get on with it!] Yeah! [Laughter.] (Lucy)

Attending an Ann Summers party provides mothers and daughters with a relatively safe space in which they can recognise one another as sexual adults. Having to obey the rules of certain party games ensures that mothers and daughters cannot avoid revealing at least some aspects of their sexual selves to each other; as Lucy attests, this recognition may be embarrassing, but the party context frames even the embarrassment as 'funny':

> I mean, my mum said she never would [attend an Ann Summers party], and she come to a party I done a few weeks back, and I've never seen that side of my mother before ! [Laughter.] [Merl: Really?] Yes. She was – oh, she was mad! [Laughter.] She was, um, more into it than some of the girls that I thought would be! [Laughter.] [Merl: Oh God, how funny.] I know. I mean, I went to an Ann Summers party with her before I even

done it, and, oh, I think I was actually pregnant with my son, so like four years ago. [Laughs.] And I went to an Ann Summers party with her, and I was so embarrassed, I sat there and I thought [Merl laughs] 'I can't talk to my mum about these things', and they done a game where you had to answer these questions, and if you got, like, 'Have you had sex in a car? Have you done this?' and move along a space, and I thought 'Shall I just sit here for the whole thing?' [Laughs.] But in the end I sort of like – I – I just thought 'Sod it', like, and I said to my mum – she said 'Well had you done all that?' and I said to her 'Well no, but I moved didn't I?' [Laughs.] I thought 'Well I'm not telling her anything!' [Merl laughs.] But now – now she's come to one of mine, and she just really opened up [Merl: Wow], so . . . And I'm like 'That's my mum!' [Laughs.] [Merl: So have you spoken to her since?] Yeah, yeah, yeah. [Merl: And did she say anything about it?] No, she just said she had a really good time. (Laura)

Playing Ann Summers party games enabled – indeed, according to the rules of games like that Laura describes here, effectively obliged – Laura and her mother to acknowledge each other as adult heterosexuals. And because they are specifically adult heterosexual *women*, this was also a moment of gender identification: 'That's my mum!' sums up Laura's surprised and delighted recognition of her mother as 'one of the girls' like herself. It may even be the case that attending Ann Summers parties together constitutes a kind of rite of passage for some heterosexual mother-daughter couples, enabling them to acknowledge each other's sexual and gender identifications and to enjoy the feeling of being 'all girls together'. Not all mother-daughter couples negotiate this recognition so smoothly, however. Laura herself told me during her interview of a party she had organised at which the hostess' mother had not just refused to participate as 'one of the girls' herself, but had prevented her daughter from doing so too:

Um, I've actually had a mother sit at a party with her twenty-one-year-old daughter and check everything as it came out. [. . .] Um, then I sort of bring out the little novelty bits, and the first thing I bought out was a condom, and it was like the novelty condom, the, er, little dragon and the elephant? [Merl: Oh yeah, I know.] I bought those out, and she took them very quickly off me [laughs] and said 'What are these?' I said 'They're, um, novelty condoms'. 'Oh, OK', and they sort of went round, and I thought 'Well, hang on!' And then I bought out, um, the cards, the playing cards, and she gave them straight back to me. [Merl: The playing cards!] The playing cards, she gave them straight back to me, um, and she said to me, um 'How – what else is in there?' and I said 'Well, what I call toys'. And she said to me, um, 'What are they like?' So I thought 'Oh!' [Laughs.] So I opened my bag, I said 'There, look, I'll just get them out', and she went 'Oh hang on, hang on', and all her friends are going 'Well, we want to look anyway!' Well, sort of like they was passed around, when it got to her daughter she went 'Pass it on!' and she would not let her look at them. And I – I felt, well I – I felt upset for the girl, because obviously she'd booked it, her friends and her were all up for a laugh, and – but most of her friends had to go by ten. And I'd travelled all the way over – I think it was [Hertfordshire]. So it's – I mean, the orders were OK, they was over two hundred pounds in the end, but the thing was her mum was just such a downer, it made her feel upset and embarrassed so much in front of her friends. (Laura)

(The playing cards Laura and I refer to here feature full-frontal male nude photgraphs on the back of each card.) This anecdote illustrates just how profoundly 'being one of the girls' is not just about individual preferences or intentions, but also about relationships with and power over others. The hostess at this party was effectively *prevented* from 'being one of the girls' by the behaviour of her mother and despite her own obvious desires to join in and make gender identifications with her friends. It also hints at the importance of Ann Summers products such as condoms and sex toys as hooks upon which gender identifications are fastened: I explore this in depth in Chapter 3. Such naked displays of one woman's power over the gender identification of another are relatively rare: conflicts and negotiations between mothers and daughters are usually lower key, although no less effective for all that. A party organised by Lucy in East London which I observed was made very awkward for one guest when the latter's teenaged daughter deliberately and successfully set out to embarrass her by 'showing off' in front of the other guests, especially by displaying items of lingerie or sex toys and announcing that they should 'take them home to daddy'. In this case the daughter was deliberately displaying more sexual knowledge (about both her mother and her own sexuality) than her mother was prepared to recognise. In fact there was aggression on both sides: the daughter was taking revenge on her mother because her mother, refusing to acknowledge the daughter as a sexually adult woman, was tacitly refusing to allow her to become 'one of the girls' at the party. At another party organised by Cathy in Essex, the hostess took advantage of a 'truth or dare'-type forfeit during a party game to ask her daughter whether she had ever had sex in her (i.e. the hostess's) bed. The ostensibly light-hearted context of the party both enabled the hostess to ask this question – which in a non-party context would probably be received as rather hostile, and might even form the prelude to a row – and obliged the daughter to answer. In this case the mother was demarcating the limits of her gender identification with her daughter: she was prepared to recognise her daughter as a sexual adult – the daughter after all was not only grown up but also had a baby of her own – but her willingness to be 'one of the girls' with her would only extend so far.

Even once one has gained recognition as 'one of the girls', gender identification is not all plain sailing, and one's status is always precarious. There are internal power struggles amongst 'the girls' in which recognition can be tested, made conditional upon a range of factors, or withdrawn altogether; and the question of who has the power to grant recognition to whom is itself fraught with tensions, rivalries and resentments. These battles and negotiations often occur at the micro-level of jokes, comments and conversations. Two of the most visible tactics used in these micro-struggles in Ann Summers settings are *bitching* and *teasing*.

Bitching is endemic to Ann Summers. It took me some time to be able to recognise this for what it was: as for many feminist researchers, my primary instinct was to challenge the stereotype of women as 'bitchy', and I did not want to accept that many women were devoting considerable energy to being plain nasty about each other (cf. Jones 1990, Coates 1996). My research participants of course were not so squeamish, and party organisers often bitched about the bitchiness of other party organisers. Indeed Trish regarded bitching as an occupational hazard not just of Ann Summers, but of female homosocial settings in general: 'I don't like bitchiness and all that, you know? And if you get all that [in a job] then I normally leave. I can't be bothered. That's why I prefer normally working with men than women.' Bitching is openly hostile behaviour which attempts to eject individuals from the female homosocial group: by bitching about somebody one is attempting to undermine or withdraw their recognition and status as 'one of the girls'. This is at its most hostile of course when the person in question is deliberately allowed to *know* that she is being bitched about by others. This happened to Cathy towards the end of my period of participant observation. She told me how a group of other unit organisers at an Ann Summers social event had sat at a table next to hers and bitched audibly amongst themselves about Cathy's physical appearance (they said she was 'anorexic' because she was too thin) and social conduct (they said she was an 'alcoholic' because she was drinking pints instead of shorts). Both comments were direct assaults on her femininity which left her in tears; although Cathy had been unhappy with Ann Summers for some time, this experience precipitated her decision finally to leave Ann Summers and join another party plan organisation. The bitchy comments therefore successfully excluded her from 'being one of the girls', not just in the context of that specific social occasion, but from the homosocial group of Ann Summers altogether. (Her more immediate response to the experience though was of course to bitch about the bitches to me during a telephone conversation.)

Although bitching most often enacts disapproval and exclusion, it can also be about competitiveness and envy, particularly over access to men's resources in the ways outlined above. Indeed competitiveness among women over their attractiveness to men and/or their access to men's resources is one of the most striking dynamics of female homosociality, and one of the ways in which it is most clearly oriented around men's interests and status. At an area-wide training event for party organisers, one unit organiser performed a 'kit demonstration' during which party organisers were called upon to play the role of 'guests'. One of those called to the front of the room to be a 'guest' was Joy, whom the unit organiser dressed up in the Kizzy lingerie set with fishnet stockings (all worn over Joy's clothes) and red plastic flashing devil's horns. Joy's long dark hair, hourglass figure and self-confident style, all dressed up in this sexy outfit, were greeted with a cry of 'Bitch!' from one of the party organisers in the audience. The comment was treated as a joke and everyone laughed, including Joy herself. In fact Joy did not only laugh at this comment; she was also excited by it. She commented repeatedly to her friends that she could hardly wait to tell her boyfriend about it, and indeed did so with great relish during a mobile 'phone conversation with him while driving home afterwards. The cry of 'Bitch!' was an envious and even rivalrous comment upon Joy's heterosexual attractiveness; Joy tacitly recognised it as such and relayed it to her boyfriend as if it were a trophy; it made Joy feel good because she was attractive, and her telling it to her boyfriend implied that she expected it to make him feel good for having an attractive girlfriend; every stage in this relay, from the original envious cry to the happy boyfriend, implicitly knows that what is being valued here is *Joy's ability to get and/or keep a man* – and, by extension, her ability to access both her own privilege as heterosexual and her partner's privilege as a heterosexual man.

The fact that everyone laughed at this cry of 'Bitch!' perhaps places it on the borderline between bitching and teasing. Teasing is less openly hostile than bitching. Indeed that is what gives it its power: teasing is supposed to be a joke, and if you fail to laugh and play along while you are being teased you expose yourself to censure and even exclusion from the group – 'what's the matter with you, can't you take a joke?' In this sense teasing is a test of group membership (cf. Goffman 1990); in the context of Ann Summers events, teasing functions more precisely both to reassert the boundaries of gender identification and to test errant individuals' membership of the homosocial group – in other words, to check to make sure that specific individuals are still 'one of the girls'. As such, teasing is triggered when a particular individual inadvertently says or does something 'inappropriate' which casts her gender identification as 'one of the girls' in doubt.

A clear example of this function of teasing as a form of discipline occurred at a party organised by Cathy in Essex. The hostess at this party, when asked during a hostess game what her favourite sexual fantasy was, replied 'lesbian sex'. This resulted in some teasing through-out the rest of the party by her guests as well as by Cathy herself. Thus, for example, one of the guests (who was also the hostess's workmate) made jokes such as 'I'm not staying the night here any more' and 'No wonder you bought me a Twix today'; the latter remark sparked more teasing from another guest, who asked 'Sure it wasn't a Kit Kat? Was it a chunky Kit Kat or a four-finger one?' No-one expressed any offence at these jokes, and eventually the hostess laughed and dismissed them with the words 'I *did* say it was only a fantasy!' In this case, the teasing successfully disciplined the hostess. Gender identification at Ann Summers events is always heterosexual identification: being 'one of the girls' means being straight. When the hostess's confession of lesbian fantasies threatened her inclusion in this gender identification, the teasing brought her back into line; by playing along with the teasing, she tacitly complied with its underlying lesbophobia, and in doing so reassured herself and everyone else that she really was still 'one of the girls'.

Lesbophobia

In the model of female homosociality proposed above, homophobia against lesbians (lesbophobia) marks the boundary between female homosociality and lesbianism. Ann Summers may be unusual[10] among female homosocial spaces in that the parties deliberately play with the tension between homosociality and lesbianism. It is worth noting in this connexion that hostesses almost invariably have all the lights on throughout Ann Summers parties – there is none of the subtle lighting or dark corners which one would expect at an 'ordinary', non-Ann Summers party. (On the rare occasions when hostesses do not put all the lights on, party organisers usually ask them to do so, ostensibly so that everyone can see the kit demonstration properly.) This use of lighting distinguishes the Ann Summers party from other kinds of heterosexual party at which men are present and at which heterosexual flirting, kissing and so on may be not just permissible but expected. In other words, lighting is used to attempt to de-eroticise the gathering of women. Nevertheless, flirting with the danger of crossing the boundary between homosociality and lesbianism is the source of a great deal of laughter, whether anxious or cathartic, especially during party games.

The flirting with danger can in some cases begin as soon as party guests walk through the door. One of the most popular games with party organisers is the name tag game. Each party guest (including the hostess, and sometimes though not always the party organiser herself) is given a name tag to wear for the duration of the party. Guests must call one another by their name-tag names instead of their real names; those who use their friends' real names during the party usually incur some kind of penalty, such as to perform a 'forfeit' (e.g. having to go outside and 'shag' a lamp-post for thirty seconds). For party organisers this has the immediate advantage of not having to remember the names of all their party guests, because they can address them by their name-tag names instead; it is also a very effective icebreaker at the beginning of parties, and guests take great and noisy delight in pointing out each other's infractions. Name-tag names routinely invoke heterosexual practices and/or female body parts (e.g. 'Rear-Entry Rebecca', 'Bucket-Crotch Belinda', 'G-Spot Gina'); some of them also invoke lesbianism or lesbian sex, as in 'Lesbian Lily'. Indeed, 'Clit-Licking Chloe' was one of the most commonly used name-tag names at parties, and was often greeted with shrieks of laughter. However, lesbian name-tag names are always very strictly in the minority – there are never more than two such names used at any party. The flirtation with danger in this game is always carefully restricted and contained.

10. Or then again, it may not be: until more research has been conducted on a range of female homosocial settings, I cannot be sure of this, or of what it means for female homosociality in general as well as for Ann Summers parties in particular.

Other games also explicitly flirt with connotations of lesbianism. Question-and-answer games, such as the points game or hostess games in which party guests and/or the hostess answer questions about their own or each other's sex lives, routinely assume that those sex lives have been exclusively heterosexual and that the women's actual or potential sexual partners could only ever be men. (I only encountered one party organiser, Joy, who deliberately altered these questions so as not to assume that the 'partners' were always men because, as she remarked to another party organiser during a unit meeting, 'you never know, I've had parties with lesbians there and I'm not asking them that'.) Nevertheless the hostess games in particular usually also include isolated questions about lesbian experiences. In one of the 'getting to know your hostess' games, for example, the hostess is asked to write down her answers to a series of innocuous questions, and then to read them out in response to a set of different, sexually explicit questions: the hostess thus finds herself giving outrageous answers to outrageous questions. The most common version of this game I observed is set up so that the hostess's answers explicitly flirt with lesbianism. Thus during the second, sexually explicit set of questions the hostess is asked whether she has ever had sex with a woman, and finds herself answering yes; she is asked who it was, and finds herself naming her best friend (who is also often at the party as a guest); and is asked 'who taught her', which turns also turns out to have been her best friend. This part of the game often produces great hilarity: at a party organised by Cathy, for example, it provoked gales of raucous laughter, with the hostess's best friend shouting out 'I taught you well!' Another hostess game, in which party guests have to guess the answers to questions about the hostess's sex life, includes the question 'Has she [the hostess] every kissed another woman sexually?' Given that the rest of the game is predicated on the hostess's exclusive heterosexuality, the answer to this question must always be 'no', and the guests always say so. In fact not only do the guests say 'no', they do so with more energy and emphasis than when answering any of the other questions in the game. Cries of 'None of that thank you!' or 'If we thought she had [done that] we wouldn't all be sitting here!' are common in response to this question.

Both of these hostess games, as well as the name-tag game, invoke the possibility (or threat) of lesbianism; but they do so only in order to repudiate it, as the responses to the question about kissing make clear. Interestingly, all of these games are usually played at or near the beginning of the party – indeed the name-tag game often 'frames' the party, so that the handing out of name tags signals the beginning of the party as such and the ending of the game is also the ending of the party games altogether. These games therefore set the terms for the rest of the party in part by making a tacit statement of the terms of gender identification which the party will enforce. No-one is in any doubt after these games that 'being one of the girls' for the duration of the party means being heterosexual, and everyone has signalled their consent to these terms by playing along with and laughing at the game.

Other party games provide opportunities for a kind of flirting with lesbianism, in which party guests engage in horseplay or play-acting with each other. For example, in one version of the vibrator relay game, teams of party guests form a line and then pass a three-foot tall inflatable penis along the line between their knees (an alternative version uses vibrators in place of the inflatable). This game is often accompanied by horseplay between guests, with one guest rubbing the inflatable suggestively between the legs of the next before passing it on. In this case, though, the sex act being invoked is actually a heterosexual rather than a lesbian one. This leaves the heterosexuality of the participants' gender identification intact: whether they are pretending to be heterosexual men having sex with a woman (actively pushing the inflatable), or heterosexual women having sex with a man (receiving the inflatable), they are still envisaging only one, hetero-sexual, version of feminine gender. In other words, this flirting with lesbianism is actually an assertion of heterosexual gender identification. It is significant that although I saw this kind of play-acting with the inflatable many times, it never took place during the version of the game which used vibrators instead of the inflatable. The inflatable cannot be read as anything other than a joke in this context, but vibr-ators are perhaps too 'real' to be safely played with in this way: I explore this question of 'realistic' vibrators in more detail in Chapter 3.

There were some contexts in which the lesbianism had different meanings and effects. One of the Ann Summers unit organisers, Dawn, is an example of this. During the period of my research Dawn separated from her husband, who moved out of the family home. After her husband had left Dawn often joked during meetings that she was 'turning gay'. This was very emphatically *not* because she sexually desired other women, but because, as she put it during her interview, 'I'm so anti-men at the moment. I really am! I kicked my other half out two months ago.' In other words, 'gay' for Dawn just meant not liking men; it had nothing to do with liking women – and so was not present as a threat during homosocial interactions at meetings. How-ever, as a single woman (indeed, the only interviewee who had no male partner at the time of the interview), supporting herself and her child on her income from Ann Summers,[11] Dawn arguably occupied an awkward position on the female homosocial/homosexual continuum: not only did her paid and unpaid labour no longer serve the interests of a male partner, but at this point she was emphatically not interested in even *having* a male partner. This of course did not make her a lesbian, but it did perhaps slightly recast her gender identification: no longer a woman-in-a-marriage, she now regarded herself as (in her words) 'a single girlie'. Her joke about 'turning gay' was perhaps a semi-conscious recognition of this alteration in what her feminine gender meant, either to herself or to other women and men. It is worth noting that Dawn only made this joke with people she knew; I never heard her make it at a party. The 'threat' of lesbianism has to be more carefully managed at parties than at meetings, precisely because parties flirt with lesbianism in the ways suggested above. It is also worth noting that party organisers would often respond to this joke by *teasing* Dawn and thus bringing her back into line as 'one of the girls' after all.

Lesbianism, then, is widely invoked, both implicitly and explicitly, during the interactions that take place at Ann Summers parties, and acts both to assert women's gender identifications and to position women in relation to heterosexual men. It is perhaps inevitable that this 'flirting with danger' sometimes goes wrong – that the line between homosociality and lesbianism is inadvertently crossed in a way which cannot simply be dismissed with laughter. In such cases more overt lesbophobia is invoked – sometimes aggressively so – to reassert the boundary between being 'one of the girls' and being a dyke. I encountered two major examples of this 'female homosociality gone wrong', and of the lesbophobia it produces, during participant observation at parties: once at a party organised by Helen, and a second time at a party organised by Sarah.

The party I observed with Helen was in fact her first ever party booking, held at her own home with her mother (with whom Helen lived) as the hostess. The moment when the female homosociality at this party 'went wrong' came while some of the guests (including Helen's mother and me) were playing the Walnut Whip game. During this game, teams are formed with two people per team. The first team member lies down on the floor on her back. The party organiser then

11. This may not have been Dawn's only source of income; I do not know whether she was receiving any form of maintenance or other financial contribution from her husband after their separation.

removes the top from a Walnut Whip and places it between the knees or thighs of the first team member – one Walnut Whip per team. The second team member then has to lick the cream out of the Walnut Whip without using her hands. In some versions of this game the second team member stands at the shoulders of the first, so that they are in what Helen called 'the sixty-nine position', but on this occasion some of the players objected violently to this position and so Helen told them to kneel between their team-mates' feet instead.

Helen introduced this game – the last of the evening – by saying that she didn't know how we were going to take it but we should remember that it was only for fun. She then asked for four volunteers (i.e. to make up two teams), but one of these was wearing a miniskirt and Helen, saying that this game couldn't be played while wearing a skirt, asked me (who was wearing trousers) to take her place. Thus I found myself lying on the floor while Helen's mother knelt between my knees. Helen's mother's counterpart on the other team was literally unable to lower her head to the Walnut Whip; Helen's mother did play the game as instructed, but was clearly not happy about it. After this game was over there was general consensus that it 'went too far' and should not have been played. At this point it appeared that the party had 'gone wrong', and Helen was at great pains to put it right again for the rest of the evening. She tried to reassure her guests by saying 'don't think of it as a lesbian thing'; later in the party, when she offered to model some of the lingerie for us, she still felt the need explicitly to reject any lesbian meanings to the party, and took great pains to say that her offer to model for us was without sexual intent: 'I'm not a lesbian or anything.'

There are two interesting observations to be made about this 'lesbian' moment at Helen's party. Firstly, although this was the first time I actually saw this game played, both Beth and Melanie mentioned this game as one of their particular favourites during interviews, and party-goers who played this game at two other parties I observed did so without any of the anxiety the game so clearly provoked among Helen's guests. Secondly, while trying to 'put right' the party after playing this game, Helen told us that there was another version using cartons of orange juice: one guest said that that would be ok if there were straws in the cartons, and another suggested that the game could be played using bananas instead of Walnut Whips. It was the Walnut Whips themselves which were too 'near the knuckle' (as Helen's mother put it). Playing the game with straws (a variation which I also observed at another party and which was indeed anxiety-free on that occasion) or with bananas would turn it into a bit of relatively harmless heterosexual play-acting: like the 'pretend heterosexual sex' with the inflatable willy, miming fellatio with a banana would still leave the heterosexuality of the players' gender intact, because one of them would just be pretending to be a heterosexual man. The problem, for these guests, was that there is no 'pretend man' in the Walnut Whip game to make it safe. It was therefore too lesbian to be funny.

The second example of 'female homosociality gone wrong', which occurred at a party organised by Sarah, was more openly lesbophobic; it was also an example of what can happen when party-goers refuse to play along while being teased. The incident arose from the hostess game in which the hostess writes down her answers to one set of questions and then reads them out in response to another set, so that some of her answers imply lesbian sex. This prompted one of the guests to comment laughingly to the hostess, 'Oh well, you've always said all women had lesbian tendencies!' There immediately followed a rather heated discussion, with some guests agreeing that all women did have lesbian tendencies and others disagreeing. One guest was particularly vehement, and said with some violence that 'Any woman who touches me is dead – *dead*!' Some of the others, including the hostess, began to tease her; the hostess said 'What do you do if you meet a friend you haven't seen for a long time? You give her a kiss, don't you?'; to which the guest replied, 'Yes but I don't snog her, I don't touch her up.' Another guest, agreeing that all women have lesbian tendencies, said that these were 'tendencies' present in both men and women and added that 'they aren't sexual, these tendencies.' Nevertheless, the lesbophobic guest, refusing to play along with the teasing, continued to express her hostility to this view, and to lesbianism in general. When Sarah initiated some party games shortly after this conversation, this guest refused to participate in even the most apparently innocuous of games, such as a game of passing an orange to one's team-mates from under one's chin; nor did she order anything at the end of the evening.

By refusing to play along with the teasing, this guest refused to submit to the others' attempts to discipline her: she was refusing to be 'one of the girls'. This self-exclusion from the gender identification at the party was both an expression of, and a response to, considerable aggression, both on her part and on the part of other party-goers, some of which was disguised (in the form of teasing) and some of which was overt (in the form of lesbophobia). The other party-goers disregarded her views and her bad mood and enjoyed the homosociality of the rest of the party – but they did not challenge her lesbophobia. In fact, although this one guest's lesbophobia was extreme and potentially disruptive, it was no less important to the other guests than to her that women not have *sexual* tendencies towards other women – even those who thought that women had lesbian tendencies somehow managed also to think that those tendencies were not sexual.

Sarah and I reflected on this incident during her interview:

> [Merl: I did think it was really weird the way that woman at that party that didn't want to –] Oh, the lesbian one! [Laughs.] Yeah, I've never – no – I've never seen anyone like that – I mean – [Merl: I was going to ask you if that was common or if you've seen anyone do that before.] I can never think anyone like that. I mean, most of the time they all mess about sort of kissing and cuddling each other and, like, getting on top of each other, you know, that – they go over the top with it. But I mean she was – she was terrible, she was, weren't she? Absolutely – wouldn't even play the orange-under-the-chin game 'cause she didn't want to come into close contact with another woman. Now that to me makes me think that she's got tendencies that way and doesn't want anyone else to know. [Laughs.] (Sarah)

Two things emerge from Sarah's comments here. Firstly, her description of the 'kissing and cuddling' which usually goes on at parties is further evidence that female homosociality at Ann Summers parties flirts, both implicitly and explicitly, with lesbian meanings. Secondly, she states that the eruption of lesbophobia at a party is very rare – indeed, she says she had never seen it before: Ann Summers parties may flirt with the boundary between homosociality and lesbianism, but the boundary marker itself is not usually as visible as it was at that particular party. By aggressively stating her lesbophobia, this guest forced all of the other guests explicitly to align themselves on the 'correct' side of the boundary. But thirdly, Sarah's comments displace the danger of lesbianism at this party by attributing it not to the party in general but to this individual woman in particular. According to Sarah, the threat of lesbianism was indeed present – not in the homosociality which is the very stuff of Ann Summers parties, but in the woman who insisted on making the threat visible. This neatly preserves the heterosexual credentials of female homosociality in general and Ann Summers parties in particular.

Thus the female homosociality of Ann Summers parties involves a complex interplay of flirtation, rejection and negotiation of lesbianism. There is also another layer of lesbian meanings with which the party guests and organisers have to negotiate, a layer of what one might call 'second-degree lesbian meanings', in which the negotiation is not so much with lesbianism itself, but with men's fantasies about lesbianism – or, more specifically, with the ways in which men's fantasies about Ann Summers parties collapse female homosociality with lesbianism, while positioning both as 'available' for a heterosexual male gaze and male desire. Many party organisers suggested that men tended to think of Ann Summers as 'sleazy', where 'sleazy' meant a mixture of lesbian sex – positioned as a spectacle or fantasy for male consumption – and heterosexual availability:

> [S]ometimes the men are a bit . . . [Merl: Oh, a bit funny?] Yeah, a bit funny. They seem to think that it's like – well, I know it's sex-orientated, but, like, that type of thing, and I don't know what they think we get up to! [Merl laughs.] (Trish)

> Every man wants to go to one [an Ann Summers party], don't they? They want to be a fly on the wall at one. [Merl: Have you had people actually say that to you?] Yeah, 'Let's come'. Loads of people. [Laughter.] 'Let's come'. I say 'No, you're not allowed, it's illegal'. [Laughter.] I say 'You can look through the catalogue, but you're not allowed to come to the parties'. I – [Merl: What is it about it – what do you think they want to go for [. . .]?] They want to see the underwear. And I – I suppose they think that we model it. I reckon they do. Yeah. [Merl: So you think they're imagining all these things going on?] Yeah. I do, I really do think so. (Helen)

> Um, I think you get it more – most – mostly from the male population. Because they look at it as a sleazy job. You know, it's, er, 'Oh, all women getting together', you know, 'oh, what are they going to be up to, using the vibrators and –' Um, you know, they tend – I think men tend to look on it that you're easy meat. (Diane)

In the male imagination, Ann Summers parties are about women parading around in their underwear and using vibrators on each other – which is itself about being actual or potential sex objects for hetero-sexual men, 'easy meat' as Diane puts it. Except, of course, that this is party organisers' perception of men's imaginations, which may or may not be an accurate assessment of what men really think about Ann Summers parties. Not having interviewed any men, I have no reliable data on what men think; these quotes are about what women *think* men are imagining (as my question to Helen makes clear). This may encapsulate a number of themes in the female homosociality of Ann Summers parties. It is partly of course another displacement of lesbianism, in that it situates lesbianism as a fantasy for men rather than as an option for women; this is also a mechanism for furthering the interests of men, insofar as it forecloses the possibility of a lesbian sexuality which is independent of men's desires. It is certainly an expression of gender identification, which in this case encompasses an assertion both of heterosexual femininity – we are not playing lesbian games at parties – and sexual propriety – we are not 'easy meat': I return to this question of sexual propriety in Chapter 5. It also alludes to a male gaze which is so much a condition of femininity – or at any rate, of the version of femininity which is 'acceptable' within the homosocial arena of Ann Summers parties – that it is present even at women-only gatherings. The presence of this male gaze, the pleasures of a particular kind of female gaze, and the different bodies those gazes fix, all form the basis of my discussion in the following chapters.

Summary and Conclusion

A gender régime is the 'state of play' in the gender relations in a particular institution. Some gender régimes are homosocial. Male homosocial gender régimes have certain structural features in common. The same is true of female homosocial gender régimes, of which Ann Summers is just one example. In the case of female homosociality, the common structural features are: *lesbophobia*, which separates homosociality from lesbianism; the furtherance of the interests of women who further the interests of men, that is to say, a kind of *compliance* with men's status and privilege rather than a challenge to them; and *gender identification*. In the case of Ann Summers, the specific form of femininity around which this gender identification revolves is 'being one of the girls'. Other female homosocial gender régimes in other institutions will doubtless involve identification with other forms of femininity. What it means to be 'one of the girls' in the context of Ann Summers forms the substance of the rest of this book.

Objects of Desire

One of the important characteristics of male homosociality as described by both Eve Sedgwick and Jean Lipman-Blumen is the positioning of women as objects of exchange in, or conduits for, relationships between men. This circulation of women is itself a crucial factor in the masculine gender identifications which take place in male homosocial settings, because it maintains the distinction between gender identification and same-sex desire. As we saw in the previous chapter, gender identification and same-sex desire in homosocial settings are always in danger of collapsing into each other, not because the individual men involved are 'really' or even 'unconsciously' homosexual but because of the structure of homosociality itself. The exchange of women (or of representations of women) in male homosociality is what makes this crucial separation between identification *with* other men and desire *for* other men. It does so by refracting desire through women: women become the ostensible objects of masculine desire, leaving the relations of male-male identification intact. Mutual desire *between men* thus becomes mutual desire *for women*. The exchange of women as objects of desire allows desire between men to circulate in a disguised form through an intermediary; it also acts as a vehicle for male bonding in the form of gender identification. For example, when a group of men on a building site collectively wolf-whistle a passing woman, they do so not just to express their collective desire for her but also for the mutual display and affirmation of their masculinity for each other. If the exchange of women *makes* the separation between gender identification and same-sex desire, homophobia aims to *maintain* it: the repudiation of homosexuality in homosocial settings is not just about the preservation of heterosexuality as such, but is also about the policing of gender identifications. Real men aren't poofs (Maddison 2000).

This raises two crucial questions about female homosociality. Firstly, how does women's position as conduits of male relationships impact upon their homosocial relationships with each other? And secondly, are men similarly positioned as objects of exchange in, or conduits for, bonds between women? This chapter considers these two questions in relation to Ann Summers parties and meetings. In doing so it fleshes out some of the structures and dynamics of female homosociality outlined in the previous chapter, and in particular it explores the ways in which expressions of desire for men act as vehicles for gender identification between heterosexual women. The first half of this chapter considers the ways in which men are talked about and represented by women in Ann Summers settings; the second half focuses on talk about and representations of the phallus.

Ann Summers Parties for Men?

Commenting on Sedgwick's model of male homosociality, Terry Castle suggests that homosocial bonds between women have the potential to disrupt the structure of male homosocial bonding:

> To theorize about female-female desire, I would like to suggest, is precisely to envision the taking apart of this supposedly intractable patriarchal structure. Female bonding, at least hypothetically, destabilises the 'canonical' triangular arrangement of male desire, is an affront to it, and ultimately – in the radical form of lesbian bonding – displaces it entirely. (Castle 1993: 72)

Castle goes on to use this 'hypothetically radical' conception of female bonding to produce a persuasively lesbian reading of Sylvia Townsend Warner's novel *Summer Will Show* (1936), in which two female characters establish a powerful relationship with each other through the exchange of a man who is the husband of one woman and the lover of the other. I wish to suggest however that this 'hypothetical' potential of female bonding in practice is only rarely achieved in real life settings – and certainly not at Ann Summers parties. I discussed in the previous chapter a party organised by Cathy at which the hostess had declared her favourite sexual fantasy to be lesbian sex. Later at that same party, one of the guests kissed her best friend's hand and announced to the room that she was her 'lover' and that she loved her more than she loved her husband; but no-one really thought that these two women were sexual lovers or expected them to leave their husbands for each other, any more than they imagined that the hostess might attempt to turn her lesbian fantasies into a reality. It is much more difficult to destabilise patriarchal structures in social settings than it is in textual readings; living subjects do not behave like texts (Rubin 1994). Understanding how the boundary between gender identification and same-sex desire, which appears so 'precarious' in Sedgwick's literary theory, can in fact be so durable in social settings is one of the main tasks of this book.

However, although female homosocial bonding may not often fulfil its hypothetical feminist potential, Castle's positioning of men as conduits of homosocial relationships between women is suggestive. It is certainly true that interactions between women at Ann Summers parties revolve largely around men and/or sex with men. This may take the form of talk about specific men, in settings where most or all of the party-goers already know each other and spend time talking about their boyfriends and husbands, or about men and (hetero)sex more generally. Do female homosocial settings involve the exchange of men analogous to the exchange of women in male homosociality? Some party organisers suggest that this might be the case:

> But yeah, I think it – I think it – it says that, you know, just because we're women we're not allowed to stand in a pub and say we – we don't like sex, or 'Ooh you shouldn't talk about that'. And I think it's bringing a lot more people out of their shells, definitely. And making people better for it. [Merl: So it sounds like you think it's quite a – it's a positive thing for women.] I think it is, I think it is. 'Cause I was quite shy myself until I did Ann Summers. And now I'm not embarrassed to say that I've used a vibrator or I've done this or I've done that. Whereas before it was 'I'm not going to talk about that' [Merl laughs.] But it has, it's brought me out. And – and a lot of my family, I mean, a lot of the girls in my family now, we'll – we'll sit here, when the blokes'll go snooker, we'll sit here and we'll have a chat and we're like – I suppose we're like a load of blokes down the pub really. [Merl laughs.] We'll sit here having a chat and 'Oh he done this and he done that', whereas before it was like, oh, you'd never mention that in front of your family. [Merl: So it makes people feel more open and more relaxed about it.] Yeah, I think it does. Makes you a better person once you can be like that as well, I think. Because you're not living a lie. Most definitely. (Beth)

Beth here explicitly compares female homosocial settings to 'a load of blokes down the pub', suggesting that women in such settings talk about sex *in the same way* that men do. As discussed in Chapter 1, she also regards this as a challenge to traditional conceptions of femininity in which women are 'not allowed' to talk so openly about liking sex; talking about sex with other women would thus appear to be an implicit endorsement of post-feminist values. Moreover, for Beth this female homosocial space has been opened up by Ann Summers itself, which by helping women to be open about sex has made a positive contribution to women's lives. The unstated premise of all this is of course that the sex women are talking about, being open about, and 'not living a lie' about is specifically *sex with men*.

But the kind of sex talk between women described by Beth is by no means the same as male homosocial talk about women and sex. In male homosocial talk, by definition, relationships between the men are structurally more significant and powerful than relationships with women, and the male speakers position themselves as superior to, rather than equal with, the women being discussed, whether those are particular women or just women in general. Male homosociality, as discussed in the previous chapter, is after all about maintaining heterosexual men's positions of power and privilege over (some or all) women. For this reason female homosociality cannot operate in ways which are simply analogous to or parallel with male homosociality. In particular, it is impossible to talk about 'female bonding' in the sense in which one discusses 'male bonding'. Men bond together in homosocial groupings to protect and promote their interests *as* a group; women in homosocial groupings, by definition, have no such interests except through their connections to, or identifications with, men – with whom their relationships are therefore far more structurally significant than their relationships with other women. To return to the terminology of Connell (1987) discussed in Chapter 2, 'female bonding' is as impossible as 'hegemonic femininity', and for the same reason: women's subordination.

This crucial distinction between male and female forms of homosociality becomes clear in interviews with Justine and Helen, when the conversation turns towards what might happen if heterosexual men were able to attend their own versions of Ann Summers parties:

[My dad]'s actually quite jealous that there isn't a male equivalent to Ann Summers. [Merl: Oh really?] Because he sees obviously that, you know, it's easy, easy money, and he thinks, 'God, you know, why can't the guys go out and do that?' [Merl: Yeah, yeah. Do you think that a lot of guys feel like that about Ann Summers, a bit jealous?] Mmm, yeah, yeah, my boyfriend does! [Laughs.] [Merl: Really?] Yeah, 'cause he was thinking of getting a second job, and he said 'Well even if I work – work in a bar a couple of nights a week I'll probably end up with twenty quid', he said 'you could do that in, like, the first five minutes at a party'. But yeah, there isn't an equivalent unfortunately. But then I don't know whether it would have the same effect anyway. [Merl: Why not?] Because I don't think men would be into that. I think they'd rather be down the pub having a drink. Um, I think they'd really good – they'd be really good ordering stuff, because whereas the women would say 'Oh', you know, 'I haven't got a top to match that', they'd be like 'Oh yeah, get the maid's outfit', you know, it doesn't matter what – what it matches [Merl laughs], order this, order that. But when it came to, you know, sitting indoors and playing games and – I don't think it would be the same. [Merl: Yeah. So they wouldn't do, like, the sitting – the – the at home, girls' night in bit wouldn't work for them.] No, they wouldn't do it. No, I don't think so. I think they would have to have a woman there as well [laughs] who'd be modelling. [. . .] [Merl: Yeah. I mean, thinking about the guys – men not doing the games or anything – [. . .] Um, it is really interesting. The thing that – the one thing – I mean it sounds really obvious. The thing that people do the whole time at Ann Summers parties is they're just laughing. And I can't imagine men sitting and just laughing about sex the way that women do. It seems quite –] No. Mmm, I think 'cause women are more open and they talk about things. Whereas I think a conversation with two guys, is like, 'Oh yeah, oh I screwed her last night' and that's the end of it. Whereas women are more like 'Oh yeah, we made love and he touched me there and they touched – done this and I done that and –', you know, go into more detail, whereas, yeah, I don't think you'd get the same conversation from men! [Laughter.] [. . .] And I don't think men would feel comfortable if a man was showing them a vibrator. [Laughs.] [Merl: Really?] They'd probably think there was something a bit odd there. [Laughter.] (Justine)

I know men aren't allowed to be at the parties, but I think there'd be a lot of sales if you did a men one. [Merl: Do you think – what, a men-only one?] Mmm, but you'd have to have, like, um, people with you to sort of like protect you. Not that I'd do it anyway, but I think there'd be a lot of sales going on. [Merl: Do you think it'd be the same as the women's parties that you've been to?] No. No. They wouldn't do the games. [Merl: They wouldn't do the games?] Don't think so. [Merl: So what do you think they would do then?] [Laughter.] They'd just want to order the stuff. [Laughs.] So – [Merl: So just sit there seriously and order the stuff?] Like, yeah. Yeah, I think they would. [Merl: That's really interesting.] Or you'd have to sort of like – I don't know, I'd never – I've thought about, like, oh I reckon there'd be a lot of sales if you did do a man's one. They wouldn't play the stupid games though. [Merl: Why not, do you think?] I don't – I don't think they would. Do you? I just can't imagine it, 'cause, er – I don't know. [Merl: I don't know. I can't imagine it either.] [. . .] No, I don't think they'd be up for it at all. They'd think it was totally silly, I think. [Merl: They wouldn't just get in the spirit of it, you don't think?] Yeah, mmm. I don't think they would. Mmm. But it'd be interesting – everyone – every man wants to go to one, don't they? They want to be a fly on the wall at one. [. . .] [Merl: What is it about it – what do you think they want to go for? 'Cause you – the – you know, if they won't play the games then why do they want to go?] They want to see the underwear. And I – I suppose they think that we model it. I reckon they do. [. . .] I reckon that – if there was one – one on – a fly on the wall, man, I think he'd be thinking 'Sad'. [Laughter.] I really really do, I do. But if they could see us laughing our heads off, then I don't know. It's weird, I just don't know. [. . .] You'd have to – you'd have to have, um, say another bloke or two blokes or at least some girls with you to sort of like – 'cause it could get out of hand, couldn't it? [Merl: Do you think?] I think it could, yeah. [Merl: In what way?] Um, um, them getting the wrong idea sort of thing. They'd think you was flirting with them I suppose, yeah. I reckon so. You'd have to have protection there. [Merl: Yeah, I can see that, yeah. It could be a bit dodgy.] Or . . . Mmm. But even though it's not anything sort of like flirty or disgusting with women, they'd think of it different I think. [Merl: Yeah. You think they'd read things into it.] Yeah, mmm. Definitely. And if you was on your own anything could happen, I suppose. [Laughter.] (Helen)

Justine's and Helen's musings on parties for heterosexual men reveal an implicit understanding of some crucial differences between male and female homosociality. Both Helen and Justine imagine that the sales figures would be high but that men as party-goers would not participate in the 'silly' games and laughter which characterise Ann Summers parties. Justine explicitly links this to the ways in which male homo-social talk about (hetero)sex *objectifies* women: men's objectifying talk about 'screwing' women leaves little room for lively conversation about sex, unlike women's talk which she claims represents both sexual partners as active subjects. Moreover the high sales figures would also be a result of men's interest in women as sexual objects (as suggested by Justine's allusion to the maid's outfit) rather than a reflection of what their wives and girlfriends might want to wear for themselves (e.g. items which 'go with' the clothes they already have). Secondly, both Helen and Justine also suggest that parties for men would have to have women present, whether to model the underwear or to demonstrate the vibrators: it is perfectly acceptable for women to model or demonstrate the items for other women, but this would not be the case of men modelling or demonstrating for other men. This reveals two aspects of male homosociality. It demonstrates Helen's and Justine's awareness of the homophobic boundary between male homosociality and homo-sexuality – as Justine puts it, 'there'd be something a bit funny there'. It also demonstrates the centrality to male homosociality of women's positioning as objects of exchange: both interviewees regard the presence of women as models to be not just desirable but *necessary* to these imaginary male parties – there would *'have to be* a woman there' (my emphasis). Indeed, Justine's insistence that a woman would have to be present to demonstrate the vibrators makes clear that this hypothetical woman would not only be acting as the conduit for the male bonding but would actually be situated at the boundary between gender identification and same-sex desire: it is her presence as such which would allow the men to ward off the threat of homosexuality in their interactions with each other. And lastly, as Helen makes clear, any woman who *was* there would inevitably find herself positioned as a sexual object for the male homosocial group, regardless of her own intentions or desires. She would need 'protection' because the male group would be seeking to exercise its collective sexual power over her as well as using her as an object of intra-group rivalries and identif-ications; male bonding would take place both around her and against her.

The position of women at actual or hypothetical male homosocial gatherings is very different from that of men at female homosocial gatherings, because women are routinely positioned as objects in a way that men are not. The women who participate in female homosociality, whether at Ann Summers parties or elsewhere, are themselves always already positioned as objects or conduits of exchange between men at the level of both gender régime and gender order. Talk between Beth and her female relatives about their menfolk in the living room is not the same as the talk between her husband and the other men at the pub or snooker hall, both because women are subordinated to men within their familial-domestic gender régime, and because female homosocial groups are subordinated to male homosocial groups within the gender order as a whole.

In the previous chapter I suggested that female homosociality serves the interests of women who serve the interests of men. The central argument in this chapter is that whereas men in homosocial settings position women (or talk about/representations of women) as conduits of male relationships, the conduits for relationships between women in homosocial settings such as Ann Summers events are men (and representations of men) *as exchangers of women*. The gender identifications which take place in Ann Summers settings construct and affirm a version of femininity which is complicit with men's exchange of women: to be 'one of the girls' is precisely to be an object of men's desire. In other words, female homosocial looking at or talk of men in Ann Summers settings is about negotiating with one's own position as a conduit of men's power relations with other men: not about destabilising, affronting or displacing it, but embracing it as an essential component of heterosexual femininity, acknowledging it in ways which are not just livable but also pleasurable.

She Likes Men

> Merl: What words, if any, would you use to describe your sexuality?
> Donna: Um, just that I basically like men.
> [Laughter.]
> Merl: She likes men.
> Donna: And men only! [Laughs.]
> Merl: OK, she likes men!
> Donna: And lots of them!
> [Laughter.]

Heterosexual women like men: what could be more obvious? I suggested in the previous chapter that homosocial relationships are about individuals' preferences and pleasures as well as about social structures. Although Donna's somewhat defensive tone during this exchange is marked by the structures of heterosexuality and lesbophobia, we must not lose sight of the simple fact that she really does *like* men. In this section I wish to trace some of the ways in which women's positioning as conduits or objects of exchange between men is itself a source of satisfaction, excitement and pleasure for the women themselves.

Feeling sexy

> Do you know what I think? I think, um, even if it was a normal – say if there wasn't an Ann Summers party, if girls went out for a girls' night out, and they did a bit of flirting, and they was totally faithful to their blokes and husbands, the husband's going to have a good time when they

get home. And it – especially if they go to an Ann Summers, they're all in the mood when they get home, I think. [Merl: So you think it helps?] Yeah, definitely. It's a girls' night out, so it's just – it's not disgusting, it's just funny. And I suppose men talk about things, and we talk about things as well. And it's just nothing disgusting, it's just a laugh. 'Cause it isn't crude, is it? [Merl: No, not at all.] You've been to loads of them. But it's just a laugh. And I reckon they're in, like, right – and the husband's thinking 'Yeah, she's gone to an Ann Summers party', you know. So everyone's happy. (Helen)

If female homosociality helps women to serve the interests of men, then Helen's words here certainly seem to suggest that men benefit from women's participation on 'girls' nights out' because the women will be willing to have sex with them when they get home (cf. Harrison 1998). But in the midst of this interpretation one must not lose sight of the otherwise rather obvious fact that heterosexual encounters, from 'innocent' flirting to full-on sex, are fun for women too, and that heterosexual women are not just sexual objects *for* men but also sexual subjects who actively *desire* men.

This dilemma between being an object and being a subject is resolved by heterosexual women at Ann Summers events in a paradoxical manner: women experience and express their heterosexual desires, but they do so from their position as sexual objects. Moreover they do so in a way which neither challenges their positioning as objects nor lessens their heterosexual enthusiasm for men. This is achieved by the construction at such events of men as desirable because they are powerful, strong or authoritative (or, if one is really lucky, all three). Men are desirable heterosexual objects insofar as they are recognisable as powerful heterosexual subjects: what is desirable about them is, precisely, their masculinity.

By this I do not of course mean to suggest that power, strength and authority are the only available versions of masculinity; a great deal of sociological and cultural work has been conducted to demonstrate that masculinity may take many different forms, and that these different forms are in turn desirable to different women and men in different ways (Connell 1995). However, it remains the case that versions of masculinity which emphasise power, strength and authority are the most highly valued and widely circulated in contemporary British culture. These forms of masculinity are currently hegemonic – in other words, they are still regarded as embodying what masculinity is supposed to be like, and even those men and women who actively resist them still have to do so by defining themselves *against* them. Nor am I suggesting that *all* heterosexual women *only* desire men who are powerful, strong or authoritative. On the contrary, many heterosexual women have written of their desire for and/or fantasies about men in positions of weakness, softness or vulnerability (Segal 1994). But we are dealing here with a group dynamic between women rather than with individuals: the exchange of masculine men at Ann Summers events is not about individuals' desires but about a homosocial structure of gender identification. One's status as 'one of the girls' is in part defined and secured by desiring the 'right kind' of men (i.e. authoritative, powerful, strong masculine men) where that desire is not individual but collective. Just as male homosocial exchange of women is about the mutual affirmation of men's masculinity, so 'the girls' cement their relationships with each other and secure the non-sexual nature of those relationships, by exchanging talk about and representations of masculine men.

In doing so they mutually construct, affirm and fantasise their own status as desirable objects for such men. For example, women at Ann Summers parties often talk about wanting to 'feel sexy'; indeed, this is usually the impulse behind their purchases of Ann Summers products:

> [. . .W]hy do people go to Ann Summers parties? Why do people buy, like, sexy underwear? Because they want to feel sexy. [. . .] Even – I know I don't wear the Ann Summers stuff, but yeah, like – the dresses, yeah, I do wear, the actual dresses, but – Because I know [my husband] thinks they're sexy. (Cathy)

'Feeling sexy' is simultaneously about desiring and being desirable, about being a subject and being an object. On the one hand Cathy feels sexy wearing things which she knows her husband thinks are sexy; her 'sexiness' in this sense consists in being the object of his desire. On the other hand, women's status as objects of desire is itself a source of sexual power over men, frequently formulated in Ann Summers settings as the power to 'turn him on' or 'get him going'; indeed one of the chief attractions of much of the Ann Summers range is the hope (of the party-goers) or promise (by the party organiser) that certain items will confer this power on the purchaser. This paradoxical construction of the 'sexy' woman as both subject and object lies at the heart of feminine gender identifications at Ann Summers events.

The paradox was vividly revealed during the launch event for the spring and summer 2000 Ann Summers catalogue, which took place in early December 1999. As described in Chapter 1, catalogue launches are the highpoints of party organisers' calendar, and this event was no exception. As usual it was a fancy dress event, and a great deal of time and money had been lavished on the preparation of costumes. It soon became apparent during the run-up to the launch itself that the 'problem' of reaching the venue while wearing fancy dress was an important part of the fun and pleasure of the day. There was a lot of laughing and joking at unit meetings about taking one's children to school while wearing one's fancy dress costume, or getting pulled over by the police for driving down the motorway dressed up as an alien. The anticipation was heightened by the fact that some party organisers' costumes were deliberately designed to be 'sexy' or revealing; and as this launch event had a science fiction/outer space theme, many of these incorporated items from Ann Summers' own range of 'silver' lingerie, especially the silver Goddess bra (Figure 3.1). When the big day finally arrived I travelled to the venue with members of Cathy's unit – two carloads of us in fancy dress. All of the party organisers in our car had a strong sense of themselves during this journey as a *spectacle*, and took great pleasure in smiling and waving at male drivers and pedestrians on the way, many of whom amusedly smiled and waved back. The gaze to which the women presented themselves was an adult male one: drivers of vans and lorries were particularly waved at, and the only pedestrian who was waved at was a man standing outside a police station with a video camera. Nobody waved at or remarked upon any of the female drivers or pedestrians or the children we passed along the way. In other words, being the object of a male gaze was a source of pleasure and fun, and this gaze was actively solicited. Both the pleasure and the solicitation were *collective*, that is to say, homosocial: I doubt that any of these women would have been smiling and waving at men if they had been on their own.

Moreover, there was a distinctive class dimension to the gaze being solicited, in that the most enthusiastic waving and smiling was directed at men driving vans and lorries rather than, say, expensive private cars. Part of the attraction of these men may simply have been a collective class fantasy about the working-class 'bit of rough' who is always ready, willing and able for (hetero)sex. Given the demographics of Ann Summers party organisers discussed in Chapter 1, it may also be that men who drive vans and lorries, whether as employees or as self-employed tradesmen, were perceived as being recognisably closer to the women's own class positions than Mercedes drivers. As such they would also inhabit the same or similar gender régimes to those of the women's

Figure 3.1 Goddess bra, from the Ann Summers catalogue autumn/winter 1999

own husbands, boyfriends and fathers, including male homosocial gender régimes as well as familial-domestic ones. As such the van- and lorry-drivers are perhaps recognisably types of men in relation to whom the party organisers are used to being positioned as objects of exchange, as well as actual or potential partners.

The gazes of heterosexual men are also actively solicited during some party games and forfeits, specifically those which involve going out into the street. Games and forfeits played in the street inevitably run the risk of being seen by male or female passers-by, but in some cases players deliberately accost men or even knock on neighbours' doors in search of a man. For example, Cathy sometimes makes party-goers pay their forfeit by knocking on neighbours' doors and giving a condom to the first man who answers. Similarly, the supermodel game involves going outside to find a male passer-by and inviting him to judge which team has made the best 'sexy' outfit out of dustbin liners and sellotape: during her interview Trish told me that 'everyone liked the – the black bags and the sellotape, they all loved that one. Especially when you get them to go out in the street and get a man to – to witness that'. Many party organisers make a point of playing games which solicit the attention of men:

> [. . .T]he second party I done, when there was only four people there, um, one of the forfeits was 'interview a bloke with a vibrator', and this girl, she went outside, and he was sitting on the wall, and she was talking to him like that, and he was talking into it as well, and I – she was out there for about five minutes. It was really funny. [Laughs.] We had to knock at someone's house to do that, Friday night. (Helen)

> Mind you, I like the new model one, with the – the bags. [Merl: Oh, that's a good one.] Yeah, I like that one. [Merl: Yeah, I like that one.] That's gone down really – I've played it every single party that I've done and it's gone really well. So I like the black bags one, like, the model game. And I have them outside in the street parading. [. . .] [Merl: I've noticed that people laugh their heads off when they're outside.] Yeah, because you're doing it outside, you've got a chance of all the neighbours seeing you [laughter], cars driving up and down, they might know someone. But it's a good talking point, it's – it's a laugh, it's something they've not [done] before. (Dawn)

At a hen night organised by Beth, being visible to passers-by (and subsequently to video spectators) was a feature of the whole party:

> Well I actually did, um, a hen night in July, and it was actually in a garden. But it was like – it was weird, because the garden was at the front of the house. It was a tiny, tiny little back garden, but a huge front garden. And all they had was trellis work, so everybody could see what was going on, so the whole party was outside, which was fun. But I thought 'Right, well I might as well make – like, take advantage of this', so every – [inaudible]

every game I played, and I actually video-ed it, well the girl video-ed it and she gave me a copy of it. [. . .] I would say that's the most fun party I've ever done. And they tried on every single item of clothing, literally. It wasn't just over their clothes, they had like a changing room. [Laughter.] And they was all coming down, and they was walking up and down the street in it, and posing, it was hilarious [Merl: Sounds fantastic], it was really funny. It was really funny. Yeah, I think that's probably the best party I've done. (Beth)

Being visible then, especially to men, is a site of gender identification for women at Ann Summers parties, and this gender identification is *pleasurable*: being looked at is both feminine and fun. It is not of course an unequivocal pleasure. For Dawn, the element of risk involved in going outside is part of the appeal: 'I think it is like a – an element of danger. It's like – a bit of taboo in it, it's not – it's not been done before, it's not to be seen, you outside playing games.' But many party organisers choose not to take their guests outside because they and/or the guests themselves find such self-display too uncomfortable:

I don't find [games played outside] appropriate. I don't find them appropriate at all. [Merl: Goes too far.] Definitely. What you do in them four walls – I mean, they say it's all confidential and everything else, which [is] fair enough. What you do in them four walls people will join in with. But once you go out of there and you've got to think someone lives there, and they've got to, like – it depends what type of neighbours they've got and things like that, you don't know what they're like and everything else. And like, I just don't think it's appropriate to do the outside games really. I don't – I don't enjoy doing them. (Melanie)

Um, before I started doing Ann Summers I wasn't too keen on the ones that you had to go outside for. [Merl: Why was that?] 'Cause you never know who you're going to meet walking down the street. [Merl laughs.] You don't know whether it's going to be someone nice, or whether it's going to be someone that's going to get offended by what you're doing. I mean, if you're outside and – I mean, some of the – the forfeits that can get played at parties, they're like handcuffed to a lamp-post outside, they've got to go outside with a vibrator and talk to the first man you see. Um, it can be extremely embarrassing. I tend to try not to do things that are going to be too embarrassing for people. (Joy)

Moreover, as Helen's comment that 'anything could happen' to a woman alone with a roomful of men suggests, being a sexual object can be not just uncomfortable but also dangerous. Party organisers do occasionally talk amongst themselves about the hazards of travelling home from parties late at night (especially by public transport), or of going to unfamiliar places (especially some of the more notorious council estates in Essex). However according to my observations these hazards are discussed surprisingly rarely by party organisers and even more rarely by party-goers. Ann Summers is really not about navigating the dangers of being a sexual object; it is about celebrating its pleasures.

Men in uniform – 'hello boys!'

If desirable masculinity at Ann Summers events is powerful, strong and authoritative, the apex of desirability is a man in uniform. The Ann Summers Christmas catalogue for 1999 even included a calendar of 'Dreammen in Uniform' ('Let these gorgeous uniformed hunks take you day-by-day through the millennium') (Figure 3.2). The uniforms in question are usually those signifying membership of male homosocial institutions, thus locating the men who wear them as exchangers of women. They must also of course signify power, strength or authority – the uniforms of postal workers, waiters or shop assistants will not do. Favourite men in uniform are firemen (best of all), policemen, members of the armed forces, or (peripherally) doctors.[1]

Driving me home from a party organisers' training session one night, Joy jokingly called out 'hello boys!' as we passed a fire station. She mused on why it was that women (not just some women in Joy's account, but women in general) find firemen so alluring – probably, she decided, because they are 'knights in shining armour' who would come and save your life if necessary. There were also many envious jokes and comments at a party organised by Sarah when one of the guests revealed that her current boyfriend was a fireman. 'Lusting over firemen' appears to be a homosocial activity which is not just confined to single-sex environments. Joy receives all of her Ann Summers deliveries at her workplace, and this provided an opportunity for homosocial interaction with another woman in her office:

1. Although I collected many instances of talk about men in uniform, I am not able to find any clear data on *why* some of these hegemonically masculine uniforms, particularly firemen's uniforms, confer greater desirability than others. Perhaps firemen are more desirable because they are imagined as more heroic and less authoritarian than policemen ('more knob, less rules' as one of my friends put it to me), as less violent than members of the armed forces, and as more physical and less intellectual or 'nerdy' than doctors.

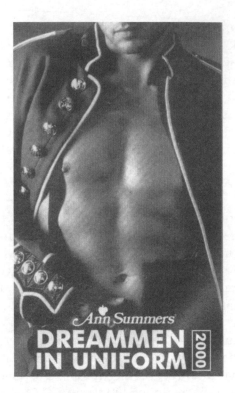

Figure 3.2 Dreammen in Uniform calendar 2000, from the Ann Summers catalogue Christmas supplement 1999

> Um, it had the dreamman calendar in it, Men in Uniform. [Merl laughs.] And me and one of the girls at work [were] lusting over the firemen in it. I said to the boss 'Do you mind if we have one of these up in the office?' and he didn't comment, so I think I might get one. (Joy)

By acting as conduits or objects of exchange between heterosexual women in Joy's workplace, sexualised images of men can be used to carve out a homosocial space in a mixed-sex environment. But since the images of men are sexualised precisely because they place men in positions of strength and authority, this homosocial space affords pleasure and fun to the women without unduly threatening their boss or other men.

While firemen are unequivocally regarded as providers of (actual or potential) pleasure, talk about policemen is both more common and more complex at Ann Summers events. The blue Light Up vibrator (Figure 3.3) prompts many jokes about policemen and police cars at parties and meetings; it is a standard joke used by party organisers that Light Up is handy for beating traffic jams because it can be used to imitate a flashing blue police light. Even more common than this are comments about 'getting arrested' during Ann Summers parties, particularly while playing games outside. These comments are often only half-joking, particularly for party organisers themselves, among whom being arrested for holding Ann Summers parties appears to be a fairly common kind of disaster fantasy:

> I mean, the very first party that we did was for my mum [laughs]. [. . .] And then a guy knocked in uniform, and we thought it was the police [Merl laughs], you know, we're going 'Oh my God!', you know, that's all we saw. It was Salvation Army! [Laughter.] [. . .] [Merl: Salvation Army, that's a classic! [laughs].] Yeah, they were collecting, but 'cause he was in uniform and he had a hat and that's all we could see. We was expecting something to go wrong that night [Merl laughs] and when he came to the door, 'cause we was standing by the window, just through the nets, we thought 'Oh my God, the police are arrived, oh no!' (Justine)

When party-goers playing a game in the street at a party organised by Cathy heard distant sirens and shouted out 'It's the Old Bill!', Cathy felt the need to reassure them that they were not going to be arrested and that on previous occasions when the police had found her playing

Figure 3.3 (L-R) Discovery, Flower Power, Reelfeel, Dynamite and Light Up Vibrators, from the Ann Summers catalogue autumn/winter 1999

party games in the street the policemen had only laughed. One party-goer replied that the obvious thing to do in that situation would be to tell the policeman to 'get out of the car and show us your helmet'. This little exchange perfectly captures the ambivalence surrounding police-men at Ann Summers events. On the one hand, as 'men in uniform', policemen are automatically positioned as objects of desire; on the other hand, as the representatives of Law and Order, they are also half-expected to be about to close down the fun and outrageousness of Ann Summers parties. This reveals an underlying sense that the kind of fun on offer to women at Ann Summers parties is itself somehow illicit and even borders on the illegal (a sense often reinforced by party organisers' claims that it would actually be 'illegal' for men to attend Ann Summers parties). It also reveals the extent to which the masculinity of the man in uniform also embodies real, concrete social power. Moreover this sense of 'illicitness' appears to be a component of feminine gender identification itself in such homosocial exchanges. 'The girls' are out-rageous, 'the girls' know how to have a good time – in short, the girls just want to have fun – but the idea that they behave so badly at Ann Summers parties as to risk arrest implicitly rests on the presumption that they all behave 'properly' the rest of the time and their almost-criminal outrageousness is only temporary. When the party is over they will all go home to their ordinary (that is to say, sexually unequal) domestic lives.

Uniforms are also of course a staple of male strip shows aimed at heterosexual women. The strip shows featured in the Ann Summers catalogue launch are no exception. Uniforms worn by the male perf-ormers during the December 1999 catalogue launch included doctors' white coats and stethoscopes, and Joy told me during her interview that the previous catalogue launch had featured soldiers' uniforms. The grand finale of the December 1999 launch which I observed had the two male strippers appearing not in formal uniforms as such but in the power-dressing City 'uniform' of sharp suits and ties; these suits were given an extra frisson of power by allusions (through both the compère's introduction and the theme music used) to the Hollywood film *Men in Black* (1997), in which mysteriously authoritative, gun-toting men in suits turn out to be working for a powerful secret organisation. Party organisers' reactions to the strip show are also revealing of the eroticised relationship between desirability and authority embodied in these 'men in uniform' and its relation to gender identification. The shows themselves generate extraordinary (and extraordinarily noisy) excite-ment, and the female spectators express this excitement in ritualised forms of group behaviour such as exaggerated screaming and, towards the end of the show which I observed, chanting in unison of 'Off! Off! Off!' in an (unsuccessful) attempt to get the men to remove their thong underwear. Such behaviour is about mutual identification within the audience at least as much as it is about desire for the men themselves (cf. Dressel and Petersen 1982, Mackinnon 1997, Smith 2002). Indeed, a number of party organisers commented after the event that the strippers this time had been disappointing and even unattractive, even though their participation in the screaming and chanting had been highly enthusiastic at the time. This highlights the extent to which all that screaming and chanting was not really for the men on stage but for the other women in the audience: the impressive display of collect-ive behaviour relayed all of the potentially homoerotic pleasures of looking at and being with each other ('sexy' silver outfits and all) through the men on stage; it also enacted the deliriously pleasurable gender identification between the women, by actively placing them all in the same structural position in relation to those men.

On the other hand, though, there were also many signs of both competitiveness and anxiety during the performance, particularly when strippers picked individuals from the audience to come up onto the stage with them. From my vantage point in the audience I could clearly see some women signalling a nervous and even slightly fearful refusal as they saw the strippers coming towards them through the crowd. Joy's shy friend (referred to here as FX) was one of those picked out at the previous catalogue launch, and seems not to have enjoyed the experience:

Um, you paid five pound to have your – you got a polaroid photograph [of yourself with one of the strippers], and you got a raffle ticket. And if at the end when they actually – they – they come on to do a strip, and they – they were pulling two names out to go up on stage to help them! And I'm sitting there thinking 'Please let it be me, please let it be me' [laughter], [someone else]'s thinking 'Please don't let it be FX, please don't let it be FX'. First one is no-one we knew, second one FX. I've screamed, FX's gone white, I mean she's pale at the best of times but the colour has just drained, and she's like – you can see she's, like, terrified. And I've – I've – luckily I had my camera, and I've took nearly a whole film of her on stage with this stripper. [Laughter.] [. . .] Um, they've come on stage in, like, green, er, soldiers' uniforms, and they've got the girls to stand behind them and rip their T-shirts off, or – I can't remember what it was, they had to rip other bits off, and then they've bent down, grabbed hold of their trousers and done that [gesture] and the trousers have come off, 'cause they're only on with velcro. Um, then they took – they've got a posing pouch on, and they've got the girls to lay on the floor and they're on top of them, and then they've turned round, whipped the posing pouch off and the hat's covering it, and then they've got on top of the girls again! And they're wiggling about, and I'm clicking away with the camera. [Merl: And poor FX's lying there.] FX's on the floor, like, 'What do I do?' [Merl laughs.] [Another unit organiser] said afterwards 'I'm so –' she was so glad it weren't me. [Laughter.] I'd have had fun! (Joy)

Some of FX's fear and discomfort may of course simply have been about appearing on stage in front of a large audience, but it seems clear that this was not the whole story, especially since the whole point of the catalogue launch for many party organisers is to wear a special sash and appear on stage as the recipient of prizes and honours during the earlier sections of the event. The male strippers during this performance not only represented hegemonically masculine power through their clothing, but also expressed that power through their behaviour with the women on stage: rather than the women actively undressing or dancing with the men, the men 'make' the 'girls' undress them and lie down underneath them. The sexual passivity of women could hardly be more clearly represented than in the spectacle of poor FX, supine on the stage, helplessly wondering 'what do I do?' This spectacle of masculine power is at least as pleasurable for the female onlookers as it is uncomfortable for the female participants, as Joy's excited photographing testifies. Moreover the discomfort of the female participants opens up another dimension of female homosociality – that is, women's competitiveness with and power over each other. Part of Joy's great pleasure in this situation is precisely that FX is so uncomfortable. This is not open hostility to FX on Joy's part – as Joy makes clear elsewhere during her interview, she regards FX as a very dear and close friend. To recall the terms of discussion in the previous chapter, this is not bitching, but is something more like teasing. Joy's aggressive delight in FX's predicament implicitly tests FX's gender identification – is she in fact *too* pale, shy and terrified to get through this ordeal and retain her status as 'one of the girls'? It is also intensely competitive: Joy wanted to go up there on stage with the men rather than FX, and what's more if she had done so she would have done a better job of 'being one of the girls' than FX did – she would have 'had fun', not just lain there.

Events such as male strip shows, and products such as the 'Dreammen in Uniform' calendar, thus position *men* as objects of *women's* gazes, turning the tables on the normative positioning of women as objects of male gazes. They do so however without diminishing the pleasure heterosexual women also take in being objects of men's desire, and indeed without compromising the power of hegemonic masculinity (cf. Mackinnon 1997, Smith 2002). Nevertheless Ann Summers parties themselves also offer women the opportunity not just to admire these representations of masculine authority, but also to mock them, as we shall see in the next section.

'All That's Missing is the Man!'

Stag nights and hen nights are among the most powerful examples of male and female homosociality in everyday life. These single-sex celebrations, traditionally held on the night before a wedding, herald the end of a single lifestyle and mark a 'rite of passage' into married life. They are often raucous affairs involving heavy drinking, serious heterosexual flirting (including or even especially by the bride or groom), dirty jokes and outrageous behaviour. Hen nights are also a source of bookings for Ann Summers party organisers, and in fact many complain that they dislike doing parties for hen nights precisely because they tend to be rowdy – and to produce poor sales, because the guests treat them as pure entertainment rather than as shopping opportunities.

The two passages below describe a stag night and hen night respectively. The account of the stag night was collected during participant observation at a Christmas party thrown by Cathy for the members of her unit. Party organisers' boyfriends and husbands were invited to this party, as were some of Cathy's friends and acquaintances from outside of Ann Summers; the story of the stag night was told by one of the party organisers' husbands. The account of the hen night comes from Cathy's interview.

> A funny story told by one party organiser's husband revolved around stag nights and strippers. He told how he was the last among his group of friends to get married, and had always been the one to arrange the strippers for the others' stag nights. On his own stag night his friends had duly arranged for a very attractive stripper to turn up, and he had been pleased. Then, later during the evening when he was very drunk, a second stripper had arrived – a very fat one with breasts 'down to her kneecaps', who (unlike the first stripper, who had only gone down to her G-string) had stripped completely naked. Throughout this anecdote he referred to the second stripper as 'it'. This was related as a particularly

funny story and provoked a lot of laughter among both men and women present. (Participant observation at Cathy's Christmas party)

[Merl: So what's the difference then between a hen night and a normal Ann Summers party? How would you do it different?] I'll dress the bride up, put a veil on her, um, dress it up with condoms, stress willies, swinging willies coming down [laughter], everything you can think of. And um, basically all party streamers coming off of her. The one – that particular one I actually had a bridal gown, like, it was a long sort of jacket. I know it's just a jacket but it was a bride's one which we – I done all that up as well. Had a wig on her, that was just – you know, we put the wig on her so she looked totally different to normal. You know, we – I play the similar sort of games, but basically it's the giggle of getting the bride dressed up and everything, they take photos and, you know, it is slightly different. (Cathy)

The story of the stag party is a perfect example of strip shows as a male homosocial event (Erikson and Tewksbury 2000). Neither stripper is considered as a subject – indeed the second stripper, referred to as 'it', is barely considered as a person. They are both simply objects of a homosocial male gaze – an approving, desiring gaze at the first stripper, a disgusted, mocking gaze at the second. They are clearly positioned as conduits of the more important relationships between the men themselves, particularly of the relationship between the groom and the men whose stag nights he had arranged in the past.

In Cathy's account of a 'typical' hen night, the question of what constitutes the object of exchange between the women is less straightforward. There are two important features to note in Cathy's account. Firstly, the bride, rather than being presented with an object for her gaze (as the groom is presented with a female stripper), is herself gazed at by her party guests, who dress her up, alter her appearance, and take photographs of her. This reflects both women's pleasure in men's gazes (in this case from actual or potential passers-by), as discussed in the previous section; and also women's pleasure in looking at each other, which will be discussed in detail in Chapter 4. More importantly for this section, the second feature emerging from Cathy's account is that the bride is literally laden with phallic symbols – the condoms and 'willies' attached to her veil and clothing. In fact it is 'willies' and their various representations, in the form of sweets, party games, dressing-up costumes, novelties, and above all vibrators, which are the core focus, not to say obsession, at Ann Summers parties in general, not just hen nights in particular – much more so even than men in uniform. Consider, for example, the centrality of willies to popular Ann Summers party games such as:

- Pin the willy on the man. Players are blindfolded (as in the children's game 'pin the tail on the donkey'), and then have to pin a paper cut-out willy onto the life-size image of a naked man whose genital area has been left blank. The player who pins the willy closest to the genital area is the winner. Importantly the willy has to be not just in the right place but also 'the right way round', i.e. erect.
- The Kit Kat game. Players are given a plate containing a finger of Kit Kat and two Maltesers, arranged to represent a willy and balls. They have to eat all of the chocolate from the plate without using their hands.
- Meat and two veg. Players draw the outline of a man onto a piece of paper, leaving the genital area bare. They then have to place the piece of paper on top of their heads and draw the willy in what they think is the right place. This is often immediately followed by another game in which the players hold the piece of paper in both hands behind their backs and tear out a willy shape. The torn out shapes are always of erect willies, although the party organiser never explicitly instructs players to do this.
- Candle in the bottle. This can be played in pairs, or in teams as a kind of relay race. One player stands or kneels with an empty bottle between her knees or thighs. The second player holds a candle between her own knees or thighs, and the object of the game is to insert the candle into the bottle without either player using her hands.
- Willy in the cup. This is played in teams as a kind of relay race. Each player has to put on a pair of pants which have a Dashboard Pecker inside a stocking or popsock dangling from between the legs.[2] She then has to run to a cup, dangle the willy into the cup without using her hands, run back to her team, remove the pants and pass them on to the next player.

To this list one must add many other willies, such as the jelly willy stress busters and their miniature counterparts, often given as prizes (Figure 3.4); willy-shaped novelties and sweets also given as prizes, such as pink

2. Some party organisers, specifically those who have been with Ann Summers for a relatively long time, in fact use a discontinued line of men's underwear for this game rather than the pants and popsocks.

willy-shaped lollipops, a willy-shaped lipstick, a 'dick lighter' (cigarette lighter shaped like a willy), 'pecker earrings', willy-shaped keyrings, toothbrushes with willy-shaped handles, pink willy-shaped soap bars, the Dashboard Pecker (an ornament for one's car dashboard), the Water Willy Bath Plug (a bathplug to which a floating plastic willy is attached by a chain); other novelties in the Ann Summers catalogue, such as the willy pasta shapes, willy-shaped drinking straws, willy-shaped candles, willy-shaped pencil-top erasers, an ice tray which produces willy-shaped ice cubes; the use of vibrators during games and party forfeits, as in the popular forfeit in which the guest must place a condom over a vibrator using only her mouth; various embellishments made to otherwise non-phallic games by individual party organisers, such as home-made willy-shaped packaging used by one party organiser during pass-the-parcel; and, of course, the demonstration and purchase of willy-shaped vibrators themselves. To call Ann Summers a phallocentric culture would be something of an understatement.

In what follows I shall explore in detail the meanings of this obsession with 'willies' at Ann Summers events. I shall also be arguing that this is not only or necessarily about reflecting or confirming men's possession of social power, strength or authority, but is often also about acknowledging and even mocking their shortcomings. In making this argument I will be drawing on a crucial distinction between the penis and the phallus.

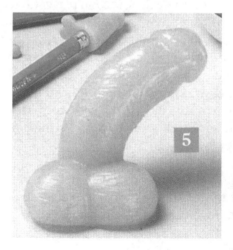

Figure 3.4 Jelly Willy Stress Buster, from the Ann Summers catalogue autumn/winter 1999

The penis and the phallus

The distinction between the penis and the phallus comes from psycho-analytic theory,[3] and has been widely used by scholars in other discip-lines, particularly cultural, media and literary studies. To put it simply, according to this distinction the *penis* is a fleshy physical organ, whereas the *phallus* is a signifier (Lacan 1989). (The term 'signifier' comes from linguistic theory. Those unfamiliar with this terminology may prefer to substitute the term 'symbol' or 'sign' in the discussion which follows. These terms lose the conceptual nuances of 'signifier', but they convey the gist.) The phallus signifies (among other things) patriarchal power, male privilege, and the difference between masculinity and femininity.[4] Indeed it signifies precisely the mixture of hegemonic masculinity, social authority and sexual power regarded as desirable at Ann Summers events, as the following image of the policeman's 'truncheon' suggests:

> Monday's one was a good one, 'cause the woman that I know, she lives on my mum's estate, and we live – like, she lives right near a police station. So I got her out with the Light Up blue and white vibrator [Merl laughs], you know the one? And I've told her she's got to keep turning the switch so it flashes on and off, shouting out 'Police! Police! I need help! I need a big truncheon!' [Laughter.] Which is quite funny, 'cause she is up for a laugh, and everybody knows her round there, and I made her run through the flats. [Laughter.] (Trish)

But the penis (organ) is not the phallus (signifier). Indeed, not only do men have humble penises rather than mighty phalluses, but as a signifier the phallus represents a level of power and masculinity which no man (or woman) could ever really attain. However, it is an important feature of our culture that the penis is routinely mistaken for the phallus in everyday life. In fact there is a certain ambiguity about the status and meaning of the phallus in everyday culture: the phallus is not the penis, but at the same time there is some kind of relationship between the two, insofar as the phallus is connected to men, masculinity and male bodies far more directly than it is to women, femininity or female bodies.

3. It specifically comes from the psychoanalytic theory of Jacques Lacan, whose work has been highly controversial, particularly among feminists. See e.g. Mitchell and Rose (1982) and Grosz (1990).

4. In Lacanian psychoanalytic theory the phallus is in fact the 'primary signifier' without which culture, language and human subjectivity are impossible.

A neat and useful illustration of the distinction between the penis and the phallus is given by Carol Smart in an anecdote about her experience of teaching Freud to her students:

> When I come to Freud I inevitably give my students the (in)famous quotation so critically cited by [Kate] Millett:
> (Little girls) notice the penis of a brother or playmate, strikingly visible and of large proportions, at once recognise it as the superior counterpart of their own small and inconspicuous organ, and from that time forward fall a victim to envy for the penis. (Freud, quoted in Millett 1972: 181)
> At this point they usually fall about laughing, or at least the women do. I have usually chided them that their laughter is inappropriate because [. . .] I explain that what the little girl finds awesome is the power and privilege which accompanies masculinity and which are symbolised in the phallus/penis. At this point they stop laughing. (Smart 1996: 162)

The women in Smart's class laugh at the idea that little girls should wish that they had a dangly genital organ (the penis); Smart replies that what little girls wish they had is not the male organ but male power (as represented by the phallus). But as Smart goes on to reflect, the women in her class are not so wrong to laugh after all: 'I now wonder what I have done to successive cohorts of students in suppressing this mirth about the supposedly awesome penis' (162). Freud's theory of 'penis envy' assumes that the penis and the phallus *are* the same thing, that envy for men's power *is the same as* envy for men's genitals. The women students are laughing because they already know that, on the contrary, penises are not as impressive as all that. Despite their unfamiliarity with psychoanalytic theory, they immediately recognise that penises are not phalluses, and the difference between the mighty phallus and the humble penis makes the latter look rather ridiculous.

Reading this anecdote, I was certainly reminded of my own attempts to teach the theory of 'penis envy', which have similarly been greeted with hoots of laughter from my women students. But I was also reminded of Ann Summers parties, where 'willies' are the stock-in-trade of jokes, games, prizes and products – and are also greeted with laughter. I wish to suggest that much of the laughter occasioned by these objects stems from party-goers' and party organisers' intuitive perception of the difference between phalluses and penises. Men's willies can never measure up to phallic signifiers. For example, as embodiments of hegemonic masculinity and sexual power, male strippers can themselves be regarded as living phallic signifiers, as Susan Bordo suggests: 'What is eroticised in the male stripper routines is not the strip, nor the exposure of nakedness, but the teasing display of phallic power, concentrated in the hard, pumped-up armour of muscles and the covered frontal bulge, straining against its confinements' (Bordo cit. Mackinnon 1997: 229).[5] But this illusion of phallic power can only be preserved as long as the strippers' penises are hidden:

> Well, he – they – they led [the women] off the stage afterwards, and the one that FX was with walked right off and out of the building – out of the – the auditorium. He's then come running back through doing a streak, completely starkers. Um, it – it – it still gets mentioned now. Um, he must have been intimidated by us. [Merl: Oh poor thing.] Yes, it was absolutely hilarious. And I'm so upset I didn't have film left in my camera [laughter], 'cause I would have taken a shot! 'Cause – 'cause I've said to people how small it was and they don't believe me! [Merl: Oh that poor man!] It was. But it must have been the intimidation of us lot screaming at him. [Merl: I'm sure it was!] [Laughter.] (Joy)

As a living phallic signifier, this man was the object of excited female adulation; but as soon as his poor little willy was visible his pretensions to phallic power were revealed as not just illusory but 'absolutely hilarious'.

At the same time, however, there is also a certain refusal at Ann Summers parties to distinguish the phallus from the penis. The term 'willies', for example, is used interchangeably to refer to penises, vibrators and three-foot-high pink inflatables alike; and a high premium is placed upon vibrators which are 'realistic', where 'realistic' means looking (and sometimes feeling) like a penis. Faced with such vibrators, party-goers often laugh out loud and exclaim 'all that's missing is the man!' This exclamation encapsulates the ambiguous relationship between the penis and the phallus; it also suggests that women find the un-phallic penis not just ridiculous but also disappointing. Is the

5. Smith (2002) has challenged this kind of 'phallic' reading of male strippers as too limited in its understanding of strippers' performance of masculinity. She cites performances by the Chippendales – undoubtedly the best known troupe of male strippers – in which the men perform versions of masculinity which long for and/or seek to please women in a way which she regards as decidedly un-phallic. However, the male strippers' performances at Ann Summers events, according to both my own observations and the accounts of my participants, never enacted such 'longing' or 'pleasing' versions of masculinity: they were unremittingly phallic.

man 'missing' because he *ought* to be attached to a phallus? If so, the women's laughter may be taken as participating in the fantasy that real-life men both can and should hold the impossible phallic status of hegemonic masculinity. Or is he 'missing' precisely because he cannot be attached to a phallus, only to a penis? In this case the laughter may be taken as mocking and aggressive, expressing both the recognition that real men cannot hold such status, and the disappointment that the phallic promise of firemen, male strippers and ordinary husbands alike always turns out to have been empty after all.

In the previous chapter I suggested that Ann Summers parties provoke anxious and/or cathartic laughter by flirting with boundary between homosociality and lesbianism. In what remains of this chapter I want to suggest that parties also provoke knowing, delighted and/or aggressive laughter by playing with the distinction between the penis and the phallus. Insofar as this laughter mocks men's pretensions to phallic power, it has the potential to challenge men's social and cultural privileges in gender régimes and the gender order. But, as I shall argue in what follows, it never quite fulfils that potential. It is never allowed to present a real challenge to men's power or to hegemonic masculinity: the disappointment and mocking aggression do not become political anger or political action. Laughing at willies at Ann Summers events enacts a gender identification – it makes you 'one of the girls' – which recognises the fraudulence of men's claims to power without taking that fraudulence seriously, as if to say 'we know they don't really have the phallus but we'll let them carry on pretending' – a potent version of the post-feminist sentiment that 'men are useless but we love them anyway' discussed in Chapter 1. In other words, laughter at willies enacts a gender identification with a distinctively *post-feminist* version of femininity.

Pass my penis

One of the most popular games played at the parties I observed was vibrator relay, sometimes also known as 'pass my penis'. This game is sometimes played with vibrators (either switched on or switched off, according to the party organiser's preference), but is far more often played with a three-foot high inflatable willy (complete with balls). The version with the inflatable is usually played out of doors, and can be played either as a race between teams, or with everyone together in the same team playing just for fun. Players stand in a line, and the inflatable is passed down the line from one player to the next. The catch is that the inflatable must be passed between the knees, without using one's hands. Sometimes the inflatable is then passed back up the line again, with players having to pass it to each other from behind rather than from in front, a method which many party organisers call 'doggy style'. This game always provokes gales of laughter, and is a staple of the party games repertoire. Unit organisers teach it to their party organisers by getting them to play it themselves during meetings.

I wish to highlight a number of points about this game, and about the inflatable itself. The latter is sold under the name Party Pete. Party organisers sometimes use this name amongst themselves and in their interviews with me, but never do so at parties. At parties it is referred to as a willy; or, in the different names given to the game, as a vibrator ('vibrator relay') or a penis ('pass my penis'). It is perfectly obvious to all concerned of course that in fact it is not a penis; but with its pink flesh-tone plastic and neat pair of balls, it is clearly a *representation* of a penis. It is also an image of the phallus, impossibly large and always erect (because always inflated – party organisers always inflate their Party Pete before starting the party, indeed usually before setting off for the hostess's address). Interestingly, it is also often coveted by party-goers. It is quite common for guests to ask party organisers whether they can buy one (Party Pete is not an Ann Summers product and does not appear in the catalogues), and two Party Petes were even stolen during a large party organised by Dawn at a student union bar. Dawn and the party organiser who was assisting at that party were both baffled that it was the Party Petes that were stolen rather than any of the vibrators – because, they reflected, unlike vibrators, you can't actually *use* a Party Pete for anything other than Ann Summers party games. The point, perhaps, is that what is attractive about Party Pete is not its use value but its symbolic value – not what it does (which is not much, taken out of its party context), but what it signifies. What it signifies, I would suggest, is precisely the ambiguous relationship between the phallus and the penis, which it both does and does not resemble; and this is also perhaps what makes it an inherently funny object at which women laugh as soon as it appears.

Because this game is almost always played outside, it is one of the games most open to the gaze of neighbours and passers-by, including men. A common response to the sight of this game on the part of men is to shout comments at the women. (Significantly, the men who shout comments are always with other men, never on their own: shouting comments at women playing Ann Summers party games thus appears to be a male homosocial pastime, positioning the women as objects of a homosocial male gaze.) The shouted comments are invariably about Party Pete rather than about the game as such or the women themselves. For example, when Cathy played this game on the streets of an Essex council estate, two men watching from an upstairs window heckled us along the lines of 'come here darling I've got a bigger one than that' throughout the entire game. If this was intended as a joke on their part, its tone suggested that it was not a particularly good-natured one. On this occasion everyone simply ignored the comments: perhaps the men's claims to be the proud possessors of over-three-foot-long phalluses did not warrant a reply.

On other occasions when men heckle during this game the players and/or party organisers answer back. For example, when Dawn taught this game to her party organisers by taking them outside to play it during a unit meeting, there was some heckling by a group of young men who shouted comments such as 'stick it up yer bum!' and 'do you want to see a real one?' Dawn quickly responded to the latter with 'not unless it's as big as this one!' Dawn's heckle not only highlighted the inadequacy of a real penis compared with a three-foot permanently erect phallus, but also expressed some of the unconscious disappointment with and aggression against men discussed above. The women found Dawn's reply funny; the men ignored it and carried on heckling. These men's attempt to silence us was ultimately successful this time in that everyone rushed to finish the game and go back indoors, exclaiming 'hurry up, they're coming towards us!' (in fact they were doing nothing of the sort). (It should also be noted here that Dawn did not reply to the cries of 'stick it up yer bum', a point to which I return in Chapter 4.)

On still other occasions, women playing this game in the street do not merely respond to male heckling, but actively and aggressively heckle men. When Dawn played this game at a party in North London, one of the hostess's male neighbours had the misfortune to be crossing the road to his house just as Dawn was leading us out through the front door with Party Pete. The man said nothing, but kept looking back at us in amazement as he opened his front door and went inside; 'He's scared, look, he's locking the door, he knows he can't match it!' said Dawn. At another party organised by Cathy, women shouted comments at the men who could be seen watching us from their windows, but the men themselves were silent.

Thus men respond to the sight of Party Pete in silent amazement (when on their own) or with defensive comments about their own penises (when in groups). Women, on the other hand, respond with mocking and even aggressive laughter, deflating the men's claims to

have a 'real' or 'bigger' phallus. In some cases this means deflating the
actual claims of men watching; but even when the game is not heckled
by men, I would suggest, the laughter provoked by this game deflates
everyday assumptions that there is an inherent relationship between
being a man (having a penis) and being powerful (having a phallus) –
that men's privilege and entitlement are 'natural'. Sharing this 'secret'
knowledge about men enacts gender identification between the women
– 'we' all know the truth about men. But the identification takes place
on post-feminist grounds: the 'truth' we all know is that men are not
naturally powerful – a 'truth' which does not actually tackle the problem
of men's very real *social and political* power.

   If men are intimidated by Party Pete (which, borrowing Freud's words,
one might describe as 'strikingly visible and of large proportions'), they
are also sometimes intimidated by the jelly willy stress buster, to which
party organisers and guests often refer simply as 'jelly willies'. Jelly
willies in many ways the opposite of Party Pete: where Party Pete is
large, smooth and always rigid, jelly willies are small – extremely small,
in the case of the miniature jelly willies often given as prizes – and (as
the name suggests) soft and sticky. While Party Pete is always greeted
with delighted laughter, jelly willies are met with more ambivalence.
Some guests like them, particularly because the miniature willies will
stick when thrown at mirrors, windows or gloss-painted doors; but other
guests find the soft, sticky quality unpleasant. Both the liking and the
dislike are usually expressed by laughter.

   The purpose of jelly willies is to be abused. As the name 'stress buster'
implies, they can be pulled and stretched with considerable force:
significantly, the catalogue invites customers to 'get to grips with your
aggression!' Much of the joking around jelly willies at parties revolves
around the discomfort and even intimidation of men; indeed this is
often regarded as its main attraction. At a party organised by Diane,
the hostess helped to persuade one of her guests to choose a jelly willy
as her prize by telling her that she had once taken a jelly willy to work
with her and put it on her desk; this had made her (male) boss so
uncomfortable that he had asked her to put it away. She laughed and
mimed her boss's squirming as she told this story; and her guest chose
the jelly willy. At a party organised by Joy (at which most of the party-
goers were workmates), the jelly willy was offered as one of the raffle
prizes, and provoked a lot of laughing comment as it was passed round
before the raffle was called. Several guests commented that it would be
a good thing to take to work, particularly as one man in particular was
always telling them that he had a small willy. Joy said it was also good

for winding up your partner as you could pull it around, and she demonstrated by stretching it, saying you couldn't do this with a real one. When one of the guests said 'Oh yes you can!' Joy replied laughing, 'Yes, but he doesn't cry when you pull this one!' The jelly willy was highly sought after in the subsequent raffle. It seems that the jelly willy is appealing to women, and discomfiting to men, not just because it is a tool of extraordinary symbolic violence against men at home and in the workplace, but also because it is the precise opposite of Party Pete. Rather than being too phallic, the jelly willy is too *un*-phallic, a visible and tactile reminder of the relative softness and smallness of the penis compared with the phallus. It also provides an opportunity for female homosocial interaction in the workplace which seems to be rather more threatening to hegemonic masculinity than the images of hard, muscular, 'pumped-up' phallic men in the Dreamman calendar.

However, although it may be permissible to 'wind up' one's male partner by abusing a jelly willy, or even to wind up one's male neighbours by brandishing Party Pete at them, there are limits on how far this winding up of men is permitted to go. As discussed above, Party Pete is an object with symbolic value rather than use value, and the same is true of the jelly willy. Despite its marketing as a 'stress buster', I never heard any party organiser or party guest seriously suggest that it be used for stress management – its only 'uses' are to be thrown at the door and/or to be displayed to men. This symbolic value may indeed make some men uncomfortable, particularly in the context of workplace gender régimes organised around a hierarchical work relationship (male boss, female employee) and a construction of the workplace as a rational space governed by minds rather than bodies. However, in the more intimate context of heterosexual relationships, it appears that the symbolic value of jelly willies is the focus of light-hearted play rather than serious threat. The situation is rather different, however, when it comes to phallic and/or penis-shaped vibrators. Since these have a use value as well as a symbolic value, they offer a greater potential threat to men's masculinity in intimate relationships.

Feel it, believe it!

The Ann Summers catalogue for autumn and winter 1999 lists twenty-six vibrators, of which only six are non-phallic in design (the Bath Massage Ball, the Climax Creator, the Little Beaver, the Vibromatic Ring, Eva's Love Egg, and the Heart Throbber). Of the remaining twenty, eight are moulded to resemble a penis, with penile heads, moulded veins, and in some cases even foreskin. These include one pink sparkly vibrator (Promise), one purple vibrator (Purple Pulser), one self-illuminating blue vibrator (Light Up), and one black vibrator (Black Prince). The others are 'flesh-tone' in colour – that is to say, they resemble not just penises in general (if indeed it makes any sense to speak of 'penises in general'), but specifically the penises of white men. I never heard Black Prince described as 'realistic' by party organisers or party-goers; nor is it described as 'realistic' in the catalogue (unlike Warrior, Foreskin and Reelfeel). Although the demand for large black vibrators and dildoes on the part of white consumers has often been noted (Findlay 1992), this racialised longing for a 'big black phallus' does not seem to play a part in the homosocial culture of Ann Summers. As we saw in the previous chapter, the gender identifications at Ann Summers events are usually specifically *white* gender identifications, and this may be part of the explanation for the absence of expressed desire for black phalluses: to want a black phallus might disrupt the gender identification with white femininity. This does not of course preclude the possibility that Black Prince was simultaneously undesirable to the homosocial group and yet highly desirable to some women as individuals. On the one hand, Black Prince appears to be largely ignored by the homosocial group – the only time Black Prince was ever directly discussed during any of my interviews or observations was when Joy mentioned it as one of the items she dislikes; but on the other hand, she did also tell me in the same breath that she once sold as many as three at one party.

The very fact that these 'white' vibrators are referred to as 'realistic', both at parties and in the catalogue, recalls the instability of the distinction between the penis and the phallus. (Moreover, the only time I ever heard a party-goer talking about vibrators and expressing a desire for a 'black one', her friend retorted 'you get a black one all the time!' because her male partner was black – again conflating penis with phallus.) Many white men are, of course, in positions of relative social power in relation to men of other ethnic groups in the UK; given the demographics discussed in Chapter 1, party-goers' and party organisers' past and present (and even potential future) sexual partners are themselves more likely to be white men. Thus the fact that 'realistic' vibrators are those resembling white penises plays on the ambiguity between the penis, in this case the genital organs of actual white sexual partners, and the phallus, here signifying the relative power of white men.

By far the most popular of the 'realistic' vibrators during the period of my research was the Reelfeel (Figure 3.3), described by some party organisers to their guests as 'the most realistic vibrator on the market'.

Several party organisers mentioned that this was one of their best selling items; even Cathy, who rarely demonstrated vibrators at her parties for fear of embarrassing the guests, found that Reelfeel was 'selling like hot cakes' during October and November 1999. Donna, who had joined Ann Summers with a friend (referred to here as FX) so that they could organise their parties together, regarded Reelfeel as a particular favourite:

> And the Reelfeel vibrator is a very very good seller. We sell on average about four or five a month. We sell an awful – as soon as you take it out of the kit, and – if you say to the girls 'I've got one, it's very good, it's excellent', they buy it. [Laughter.] 'Cause it is just – it is very – it's a very nice – it's got a very nice feel 'cause it's actually made of latex. And it sells so well, it really does sell really well. That one's been very very common. [Laughs.] [Merl: That's funny, 'cause at the parties I've been to where that's come out of the kit bag, all – everyone in the room's gone 'Eurgh!' when they feel it, it's like –.] Mmm, it's the initial response, to touch it and go 'Oh it's just horrible!' [Merl laughs], but once you explain like, you know, 'I've got one of these and – and it's very good, and it works!' And that tends to – think that 'Oh well I've got to get one of those!' [laughter] and they buy it then. We – we sell – we'll sell at least one at every party we do. And we do – 'cause, er – 'cause I've got one and FX's got one, so we just say like 'Ooh yeah, it's very very good' [Merl laughs] and they're like 'OK, I'll buy one of those'. [Laughter.] We went – um, we went door-knocking, we knocked on this lady's door and she said 'Have you got any good vibrators?' she said ''cause, like, I've never had one and I want one'. So we was telling her about this one, I said 'It's made of latex, and it's so realistic' and FX said to her [laughs] 'If you see that coming up under the duvet you wouldn't know the difference [Merl laughs] between that and the real thing'. And she was in stitches, she said 'I like youse two, you're very very funny', she said, 'I'm going to buy one'. [Laughter.] So we got her to buy one on the door. (Donna)

In Donna's account of her and FX's (obviously very successful) sales pitch, the 'realistic' nature of Reelfeel is its main attraction – not just in terms of its appearance, but also because of the 'nice feel' of the latex. However the 'feel' of the vibrator is also greeted with considerable ambivalence, and even cries of 'Eurgh!', during kit demonstrations at parties – for some guests the feel is *too* realistic. Similar reactions are provoked by Foreskin, which is always greeted with dismayed laughter as it is passed around the room – but which also appears to sell well, despite the initial dismay:

I hate it. I hate Foreskin with a passion. But you get it out of the box and you can't help but play with it. It – you can't – you can't help it. It's horrible, but you play with it. [. . .] But I hate it, and I – I won Foreskin and Black Prince at the same meeting. [. . .] And I don't like either of them. [Merl: I don't like Foreskin at all. I think it's pretty gross actually.] No, it's hideous. It is horrible. I've sold quite a few of them. And I can't understand why 'cause it's horrible! [Merl laughs.] Disgusting! It's not – it doesn't even look nice. (Joy)

The laughter and ambivalence provoked by Reelfeel and Foreskin recall the reactions to the jelly willies, and I would suggest that this is for similar reasons. As its name suggests, Foreskin is covered with loose folds of 'skin' which move up and down the shaft when rubbed; Reelfeel's latex is a removable outer sheath which, when removed, lies in a flaccid heap. At one party, Dawn even suggested that Reelfeel could be used to 'wind up your partner by flicking the tip of it' – i.e. of the latex sheath – just as Joy had suggested pulling the jelly willy. Both vibrators thus recall the soft, sticky qualities of the jelly willies which, as discussed above, are redolent of the penis rather than the phallus. Nevertheless both vibrators also have the phallic qualities of rigidity and durability. Their initial reception during kit demonstrations is ambivalent because the objects themselves are ambiguous.

Thus the resemblance of 'realistic' vibrators to the (usually white) penis is highly valued by party organisers, partygoers and the Ann Summers catalogue alike ('feel it, believe it!' as the latter says of Reelfeel). But so is their *lack* of resemblance, in that they are capable of feats of endurance and intensity which real penises (of whatever hue) cannot achieve. Indeed vibrators and other phallic sex toys are in this sense quite simply *more phallic* than real penises (Bernheimer 1992). They also potentially threaten the distribution of phallic power within heterosexual encounters in that they are controllable by women who can switch them on and off at will. This means that vibrators in general, and 'realistic' vibrators in particular, have to be carefully handled in heterosexual relationships, both literally and metaphorically.

Joy and Beth reflect on the sensitivities of men around vibrators:

But you tend to find women that are in their mid- to late twenties and a bit older are more open to ideas and they will listen. When you start talking about, like, the Climax Creator and how you use it, they'll actually sit and listen, whereas the teenagers aren't that bothered by it. They actually sit and think 'Well would my other half mind that?' They – they get a little bit more involved in it. (Joy)

I love doing the older parties. Over thirty-five, I would say. They'll do everything and anything. And they'll order the most of the – You get good sales from them. I can just imagine their husbands saying 'What you bought that for? You don't need that, you've got me!' [Laughter.] (Beth)

Joy and Beth are both talking about slightly 'older' women – women in their twenties and thirties rather than teenagers. The significance of this here is that these women are more likely than teenagers to be in long-term heterosexual relationships, and thus are more likely to need to negotiate with partners' sexual anxieties around vibrators. As Joy puts it, older women will spend time considering what their partner would or would not 'mind', whereas the men in Beth's account fear that vibrators will make the men themselves obsolete.

As with the 'lesbian' fantasies discussed at the end of the last chapter, these quotes do not offer any direct data about what men really think or feel about vibrators – they are about what women imagine or expect men would feel. In this sense they are negotiations with *women's* ideas and expectations about masculinity. Given the extent to which feminine gender identification is about being an object of men's desire, women's expectation that vibrators would make men anxious is itself an expression of anxiety on the part of the women themselves – anxiety that men will withdraw their desire from them if they go home with a vibrator. In other words, the anxiety that men might find vibrators threatening is itself another facet of the feminine gender identification which takes place around 'willies' at parties. Whereas the laughter deflates men's claims to have the phallus, the anxiety reinstates those claims: men must not be made to feel inadequate in relation to phallic sex toys, so that women will not lose their status as objects of phallic desire. This also encapsulates the dynamic in which female homosociality serves the interests of women who serve the interests of men. Men retain their claims to phallic privilege in the teeth of all the evidence, and women retain both their own privilege as heterosexual and their access to the various cultural, financial and material benefits of relationships with individual men.

Anxieties and expectations about masculinity can also be used as selling points. Joy sells the Climax Creator to her guests by specifically pointing out during her demonstration that its tiny vibrator (revealed when the attachment is removed) is a good way to introduce your partner to vibrators if he is 'a bit unsure' about them. If you start off with a nine-inch vibrator, she tells them, he might not like it, but if you start with this little one 'he won't be intimidated by it' – and you can then work your way up to bigger and bigger sizes. Thus women's expectations about men's anxieties are reinforced during Joy's kit demonstration, and the solution offered is not to reconsider the definition of masculinity but to buy an Ann Summers product. Not that this is unreasonable in the context of party guests' everyday lives: direct negotiations, and sometimes rows, do take place between actual men and women about vibrators. One guest at Helen's party was reluctant to receive a vibrator as a raffle prize because, she said, the last time she had taken a vibrator home with her it had caused an argument. Nor do I wish to under-emphasise the autonomy of women in choosing or buying vibrators; although women often make their choices with their partners' (actual or potential) anxieties in mind, men's preferences are by no means the only or necessarily the most important consideration. Helen's guest soon decided that she did want another vibrator after all; the (real or imagined) objections of Beth's customers' husbands do not prevent the women from buying the goods in the first place. Indeed in some cases the rivalry, competition and sheer excitement of female homosocial interactions may induce women to order vibrators and other goods regardless not just of men's preferences but even of the preferences of women themselves once they are outside of the homo-social context (cf. O'Neill 1993). It is extremely common for party-goers to order goods at a party and then to decide once the party is over that they do not really want them after all. As Trish put it during her interview, 'Some people order stuff and then send it back afterwards because they don't want to lose face in front of the hostess and what have you. You know like some people, everyone's ordering stuff so they feel obliged to order something.' Many party organisers regard returned goods as the bane of their lives ('untold aggro', in Trish's words).

Nevertheless, the relationship between men, vibrators and penises remains a point of tension at Ann Summers parties, particularly when vibrators are represented as being *better than* penises. Dawn usually begins her kit demonstration at parties with a lively and very funny sales patter, which aims (among other things) to assure party-goers that they will not be stigmatised for buying vibrators at the party: 'no-one will think you're a sad lonely person at home on your own' if you buy a vibrator because, after all, 'we all know that men can't insert and vibrate at the same time, it confuses their brains'. Dawn also recom-mends some of the vibrators, particularly those such as Toad in the Hole which have adjustable rotating shafts, by claiming that 'no man can do this for you, ladies'. These statements are enjoyable variations on the post-feminist theme that 'men are useless', and are always greeted with laughter. On the other hand, vibrators are often presented as additions to the sexual repertoire of heterosexual *couples* rather than just of heterosexual *women*. This is most obviously the case in relation to so-called 'his 'n' hers' vibrators such as the Little Beaver, Climax Creator and Vibromatic Ring, specifically designed to be used during penis-vagina penetration; but it is often also the case in relation to phallic vibrators (both 'realistic' and non-'realistic'):

> Um, sometimes I do, um, for the raffle, I do – I only do three prizes, but it'd be a thong for her, a pouch for him, and a vibrator for both. So sort of like when I get them out I say, like, 'This is for you, this is for him, and this is for both'. (Melanie)

> Although you say you treat yourself, if anything I think the real winners out of – out of the Ann Summers really is the men [Merl laughs], because you – you find, see, they're the ones that get the real enjoyment. We get to feel sexy wearing it, yes. But they get to get the enjoyment of us feeling sexy. So you know, I do think that the men still win more than the women in this – in this business. Unless of course you're buying a vibrator and then it works either way. (Cherry)

Thus although it is always tacitly acknowledged that vibrators may be bought for the purposes of masturbation, the discourses surrounding vibrators at Ann Summers parties assume that they are primarily for use by heterosexual couples. When Dawn assures her party-goers that no-one will think they are 'on their own' if they buy a vibrator, she is subtly asserting that 'on your own' is not their only or even primary purpose. In other words, Ann Summers discourses suggest that 'the man' is 'missing' from the vibrator not because the vibrator has replaced him, but because it is merely intended to *supplement* the man that you already have. Vibrators are to be used as well as, not instead of, real men's bodies.

Ultimately, then, none of the laughter at Ann Summers parties about big phalluses and little penises unyokes the penis from the phallus. This unyoking may occur in some other sexual cultures: Judith Butler, for example, has suggested the possibility of a lesbian phallus, possession of which 'can be symbolized by an arm, a tongue, a hand (or two), a knee, a thigh, a pelvic bone, an array of purposefully instrumentalized body-like things' (Butler 1993: 88). But within the (hetero)sexual culture of Ann Summers, 'purposefully instrumentalized body-like things' such as 'realistic' vibrators very emphatically do not offer any opportunities for imagining a non-penile phallus, no matter how hilarious the penis itself may seem. Nor is there any space within this culture for an erotic appreciation of a non-phallic penis as a variable, responsive and touchingly vulnerable organ (Bernheimer 1992, Smart 1996). On the contrary, as we shall see in the next chapter, the unchangingly phallic, erect, penetrative penis is constructed as absolutely necessary to female (hetero)sexuality as such. Moreover the female homosocial context does not allow even a tacit acknowledgement that vibrators may be used in sex between women: no lesbian phalluses appear at Ann Summers parties in any guise. If the laughter prompted by vibrators, jelly willies and Party Petes mocks the naturalisation of men's power as phallic, the desirability of 'realistic' vibrators, men in uniform and the male gaze simultaneously *depends* upon that naturalisation of power, strength and authority as masculine attributes. In this female homosocial world, being an object of the desire of the powerful is an occupational hazard of life as a woman, and also one of its biggest thrills.

Summary and Conclusion

Male homosociality is characterised by the use of women as conduits or exchange objects for relationships between men. This symbolic exchange of women has a number of effects: it separates same-sex identification from same-sex desire; it positions heterosexual men's relationships with each other as more powerful and important than their relationships with women; it enacts a form of male bonding in which heterosexual men protect and pursue their own power over (some or all) women; it excludes both women and homosexual men from direct access to that power; it acts as a vehicle for intra-group rivalry and competitiveness as well as solidarity. Female homosociality in Ann Summers settings is characterised by the symbolic exchange of men *as exchangers of women* – as socially and culturally powerful. As with male homosociality, this exchange of men separates women's same-sex identification from same-sex desire, but it also treats women's relationships with men as more powerful and important than their relationships with other women. For this reason female homosociality cannot be described as 'bonding' in a sense analogous with the male bonding of male homosociality. It also involves a paradox: women talk about and represent men as if they were hegemonically masculine and phallic, and at the same time acknowledge that real-life men are neither of these things and mock them for their shortcomings. This paradox mirrors that at the heart of post-feminist femininity: 'men are useless but we love them anyway' in this context becomes 'men do not really have the phallus but we'll let them carry on pretending that they do'. Thus the exchange of men in Ann Summers settings enacts a form of gender identification which is post-feminist and which ultimately colludes with rather than challenges heterosexual men's power and privilege.

This analysis of the exchange of men, however, can only be applied with certainty to the specific gender régime of Ann Summers; whether it also applies to other female homosocial gender régimes, in other settings and institutions, will only be established through further research. Ann Summers settings, especially parties, are probably relatively unusual in that they deliberately incite (hetero)sexually explicit talk between women. The sexual content of the talk, representations and interactions between women in Ann Summers settings, and the ways in which they construct (hetero)sexual pleasures and bodies, form the subject of the next chapter.

Feminine Bodies, Feminine Pleasures

As the list in Chapter 3 of 'willies' present in games, prizes and products attests, Ann Summers parties are largely about sex. Women's sexual 'experience' is important to Ann Summers because so many of the games and jokes at parties and meetings revolve around sexual experience and sexual knowledge. As has been noted by many researchers on sexuality, women who have had 'too much' heterosexual experience or knowledge are often stigmatised in our sexual culture as 'slags' (Lees 1986, Holland et al. 1998); indeed many party organisers during their interviews told tales of such stigmatisation, especially while canvassing or 'door-knocking' when men in particular, but also some women, call the party organisers 'slags', 'sluts' or 'dirty women' to their faces. In the homosocial environment of parties and meetings, however, women's sexual knowledge and experience is highly valued, not just metaphorically but also literally. In the points game, for example, players win points for having had certain sexual experiences, and indeed the game actually *deducts* points if the player is a virgin. The homosocial setting of Ann Summers parties offers an alternative to, and perhaps even a space of resistance against, the stigmatisation of women's active sexuality or sexual desire. 'Being sexually experienced' is one of the hubs of gender identification at Ann Summers events: 'being one of the girls' at parties or meetings involves knowing about and liking sex. Indeed the association between sexual experience and Ann Summers parties is so strong that party-goers at their first Ann Summers party are even called 'Ann Summers virgins', and are teased accordingly by the party organiser.

Of course this gender identification encompasses only *heterosexual* experience and knowledge – the lesbophobia inherent to female homosociality demands that no such value is placed on same-sex experience, which is rarely if ever confessed at Ann Summers events. Moreover it is only certain kinds of heterosexual experience or knowledge which are valued: experience or knowledge of bondage-domination/sadomasochism (bdsm) or fetishism, for example, are not so straightforwardly valued, as we see in the next chapter. Nevertheless, even within these normative restrictions, I wish to underline the importance of Ann Summers events as a setting where women's sexual knowledge and experience are not just positively valued but also shared and transmitted, and where women's sexual innocence is greeted not with admiration for their 'purity' but with teasing for their 'naiveté':

> Right, well that girl that's just 'phoned me [laughter], that was the very first party that she'd ever been to an Ann Summers party. [Merl: Oh really?] Yeah. Um, and that was the last party I done, when there was only the five girls there. And she said 'Well I definitely learnt a few things that night' [laughter], she said, ''cause I didn't have a clue what duo balls was or anything else', so she enjoyed herself. [. . .] But I also done, um, the games where you ask the questions? [Merl: Oh yeah.] Yeah? And they have to write down 'true' or 'false', and she actually won that game. So that's what she just said to me on the 'phone, 'They might all think I'm thick [Merl laughs] and not know anything, but I won the game!' So she was pleased with herself. [Laughs.] (Vanessa)

As we saw in Chapter 2, teasing at Ann Summers events is an exercise of power between women which serves to enforce the specific terms of feminine gender identification. When this woman was teased for 'being thick' at the party, her membership as 'one of the girls' was being tested, and the definition of 'the girls' as heterosexually knowledgeable and experienced was being enforced. Her acceptance of these terms is evident both in her laughing along with the teasing ('she enjoyed herself') and in her pride in her sexual knowledge (she won the 'true or false' game). Moreover the party not only tested her existing sexual knowledge, but also equipped her with *new* sexual knowledge to enable her to *become* 'one of the girls' – she was pleased that she 'learnt a few things' at the party. This reveals the extent to which the games, jokes and kit demonstration (e.g. of the duo balls) at the party actively *recruited* her into 'being one of the girls' rather than simply reflecting a pre-existing gender identification on her part. It also reveals the specifically *post-feminist* nature of this gender identification. Just as sexual pleasure is treated by post-feminism as an object of consumerist entitlement, so sexual knowledge and sexual experience are valued for their own sake, as ends in themselves rather than as the means to achieving sexual equality or sexual liberation; indeed this gender identification assumes that sexual experience *is* sexual liberation, that once the knowledge has been acquired the equality has simply been achieved. This chapter explores some of the ways in which the homo-social structure of Ann Summers settings actively recruits women into *bodily* gender identifications and constructs heterosexually feminine sexual bodies, sexual pleasures and sexual experiences.

Several party organisers commented on the surprising openness with which partygoers seem to discuss sexual matters at parties:

> You can get a bit – honestly, the things some people tell you, and you've never met them before in your entire life, and yet they're telling you all about their sex life. It gets a bit embarrassing sometimes, but – [Merl: Do they talk to you like they expect you to know everything there is to know about sex?] Yeah. Yeah, everything. [Laughs.] I'm not – I know as much as the next person, you know? [Laughter.] I'm married with three kids, you know, I – I know as much as anyone else. I must do, some of the things that people tell me I think 'Oh, I didn't know you could do that!' [Merl laughs], you know. (Sarah)

There is some evidence that talking in groups enables women to be more rather than less open about their sexual experiences, which would suggest that parties and meetings, if not interviews, may offer more accurate pictures of women's sex lives than one might expect (Frith 2000). Moreover, as suggested in Chapter 1, post-feminist 'confessional culture' fostered by talk shows, women's magazines and self-help texts suggests that being open about one's sex life is good in itself: as Beth commented in previous chapters, such openness 'makes you a better person' because 'you're not living a lie'. But it is also the case that women may lie, exaggerate, conceal or misrepresent various aspects of their sex lives, whether intentionally or unintentionally. This may be particularly the case in homosocial settings where gender identification is so much at stake: saying the wrong thing, being the wrong kind of woman, can have disastrous consequences for one's status as 'one of the girls'. We have already seen some of the ways in which those who transgress the boundaries of Ann Summers gender identification are punished: with bitching or teasing, with lesbophobia, or with open confrontation and anger such as occurred with Sarah's lesbophobic guest.

Nevertheless, these very misrepresentations are themselves revealing, because they both shape and are shaped by everyday assumptions about sexuality – about, for example, what can or cannot be discussed with others, what is or is not 'normal', or (as Sarah's words suggest) the association of 'sexual experience' in general with heterosexual, married, reproductive experience in particular. The analysis of talk and represent-ations about sex therefore often focuses on what sociologists call discourses:

> [A] discourse is a "regulated system of statements". However, a discourse is not necessarily written down in any one place; its level of articulation is social [. . .]. A discourse in this sense is shared by a social group of speakers and actors. It involves more than language, indeed it also organizes meaning and action. (Gilfoyle et al 1992: 210).

Discourses are not just individuals' ideas or prejudices; they are sets of beliefs and assumptions which shape the way social groups understand the world. Indeed, for some theorists, the body itself is the product of sets of discourses, insofar as our body image, our mental maps of the workings of our bodies, the ways in which we organise, classify and interpret physical organs and sensations, are all shaped by discourses about sexuality, gender, race, dis/ability and so on (Butler 1993). As such, discourses are never neutral: they are always intimately connected to power relations – indeed, they are themselves the sites of power struggles over definitions of, for example, heterosexuality/homosexuality, or masculinity/femininity, or normal/abnormal (Foucault 1984). One famous example of a discourse about female sexuality is that of vaginal orgasm: this discourse, widely propounded by psychologists and sexologists during the first half of the twentieth century, insisted that clitoral orgasms were 'immature' and/or weaker than 'mature' or stronger vaginal orgasms – or even that clitoral orgasms did not exist at all. Thus many women classified (and some still do classify) their experiences of clitoral pleasure as irrelevant to, or less significant than, vaginal orgasm; and many women regarded themselves, and were regarded by others, as 'frigid' because they did not experience vaginal orgasm, regardless of their experiences of clitoral orgasm. This discourse was subsequently attacked and rejected by feminists and others from the 1960s onwards, and replaced with the assertion that, on the contrary, the clitoris was the primary if not the only site of female orgasm – which in turn led many women to reinterpret and reclassify their vaginal and clitoral pleasures (Segal 1994, Maines 1999). The 1980s and 1990s saw a similar debate about the Graefenberg spot (G-spot) (Blank 1989). Indeed, for some scholars, discourses not only regulate the interpretation and classification of bodily experiences, but also shape the body itself (Martin 1989, Laqueur 1992). The discourse of the G-spot, for example, does not just re-organise the relative meanings of clitoral and vaginal pleasure; it posits the existence of a whole new body part. Thus the analysis of discourses can reveal important information not just about the ways bodies and sex are talked about in public, but also about the ways they are understood and experienced in private – and about the ways they are implicated in relations of power. This of course does not mean that bodies are *only* discourses: they are also physical entities. As former medical student Thomas Laqueur (1992) recalls, theories of the body as discursively constructed do not erase the daunting corporeal reality of the body in the operating theatre.[1]

In effect, then, there are several kinds of bodies present at parties, meetings and interviews. There is the body as discursively constructed, and the body as physical entity. These bodies are not separate, but are profoundly, inseparably connected to each other: discourses both shape and are shaped by our understandings and experiences of both our own bodies and those of others; bodies both inform and express our positions in relation to those discourses (does your body tell you that you do or do not have a G-spot – or has it yet to make up its mind?).[2]

Alongside this discursive/material body there is also another doubling: the female body as sexual or, as I shall be terming it, as erogenous; and the female body as homosocial. These too are profoundly connected to each other. They are both heterosexual bodies: the homosocial is heterosexual by virtue of its structural position (in relation to men) and its gender identification; the erogenous is heterosexual by virtue of its specific organisation around particular organs, body parts and erotic practices. I have chosen the term 'erogenous' to refer to the sexual organisation of the female heterosexual body for two reasons. Firstly, to use the term 'sexual' would simply become confusing, because it would result in a proliferation of similar terms (sexual, heterosexual, sexuality, sex). Secondly and more importantly, the term 'sexual' is too vague, as are many of its alternatives (such as 'erotic' or, even worse,

---

1. The nature and location of the boundary between the discursive and the physical is the subject of heated academic debate. See e.g. Laqueur 1992, Butler 1993, Ramazanoglu 1995, Jackson 1999.

2. This is not just a question for female readers. The 'male G-spot', supposedly located in the prostate gland and stimulated through anal penetration, has itself become the nexus of sets of discourses about male embodiment, masculinity, (homo)sexuality and pleasure.

'sensual'). In using the term 'erogenous' I am referring not just to sexual pleasures in general, but to very specific organisations of those pleasures.

'Erogenous' is probably most familiar in everyday usage in the term 'erogenous zones', used to refer to specific parts of the body which are (a) supposed either to provoke or to experience erotic pleasures and (b) distinct and distinguishable from other, non-erogenous body parts. So-called erogenous zones are situated at the intersection of the material and the discursive: the real physical body experiences the pleasure and/ or the desire such zones elicit; but the designation of some body parts as erogenous and others as non-erogenous is shaped by sets of discourses about gender, sexuality and so on. To take an example which will be discussed in more detail below, everybody has an anus, but not everybody experiences the anus as an erogenous zone: as we will see, the sexual discourses in circulation at Ann Summers parties are heavily invested in defining the anus as non-erogenous, unlike, say, some male homosexual discourses which locate the anus as an epicentre of erotic pleasure.

Thus when I write about the 'erogenous body' or 'erogenous zones' in what follows, I am not quite using the term in its everyday sense, because I am suggesting that the erogenous as such is shaped by *discourses*: rather than just being a natural physiological or even psychological attribute of human bodies, the erogenous shapes the body according to organising principles which are themselves deeply embed-ded in power relations. In the homosocial setting of Ann Summers events, heterosexual practices are constantly represented but never actually performed. This means that the female erogenous body – which, as heterosexual, is ostensibly oriented toward men – is in fact being represented at such events *to other women*. In fact I wish to argue that these representations of the female erogenous body elicit gender identification. Having (or claiming to have) a particular kind of body, which experiences particular kinds of pleasures in particular kinds of organs, is one of the most important facets of gender identification at Ann Summers events. It is also one of the most insidious pathways for the circulation of power at such events. As discussed in Chapter 3, being desirable in the right way to the right kind of (i.e. phallic) men is an important feature of gender identification at Ann Summers events. The representation of the erogenous body at such events extends the grounds of this gender identification to the body itself and its erotic pleasures. In other words, 'being one of the girls' is not just about attracting (or wanting to attract) the 'right' kind of man; it is also about performing (or wanting to perform) the 'right' kinds of sexual practices, and experiencing the 'right' kinds of pleasure with him once you have him. The diversity of women's sexual experiences, fantasies and desires is elided at Ann Summers events in favour of a homogeneous erogenous organisation whose form and pleasures are always predictable. Thus the demands of gender identification smooth over differences between women's bodies and women's pleasures, and replace them with a single normative vision of female sexuality.

Like the erogenous body, the homosocial body is also located at the intersection of the material and the discursive. The homosocial body sees, feels, eats, drinks (and indeed gets drunk), laughs and makes other kinds of noises, both verbal and non-verbal. There is a highly complex relationship between the homosocial body and the erogenous body at Ann Summers events, insofar as the representations of the erogenous body are *made by* the homosocial body. One might say that the homosocial body is 'ghosted' by the erogenous body, in the sense in which atmospheric interference produces the 'ghosting' or doubling of images on a TV screen. The erogenous body's orgasms (or lack of them) ghost the homosocial body's voice; the erogenous body's sensations ghost the homosocial body's skin. But the homosocial body also has organs and actions which exceed the terms of the erogenous body. These include sexual organs and actions which are not contained within the proper boundaries of erogenous zones. For example, 'fanny farts' are a source of homosocial humour at Ann Summers parties, and also a source of gender identification in that such humour is based on women's supposedly shared knowledge about the eccentricities of a supposedly shared female anatomy. However, while obviously located in the genitals, 'fanny farts' do not form part of the erogenous repertoire as such – they are not represented as a source of anyone's erotic pleasure.

In what follows, then, I will attempt to outline some of the contours of the erogenous and homosocial bodies in Ann Summers parties, meetings and interviews. In doing so I am necessarily mapping a female heterosexual body; but this of course does not mean that I am mapping *the* female heterosexual body. There are many other versions of heterosexual femininity and embodiment circulating under different gender régimes: the body described here is not just culturally and historically specific, but also highly specific as to class, ethnicity, dis/ability, age and so on. The body mapped below will not be the same for all heterosexual women – indeed, it may not always be the same for the specific women who participated in this research, who move between different gender régimes, including work, leisure and familial-domestic régimes, not just within their own lifetimes but within the space of a single day.

The Heterosexual Female Erogenous Body at Ann Summers Parties

The erogenous body at Ann Summers events is not encountered directly, then, but is represented in games, jokes, anecdotes, images (including catalogue images) and other ways. As such it is always *filtered through* the homosocial: the things women say or show about their sex lives at meetings or parties may not necessarily give a precisely accurate picture of the erogenous body and its sexual practices. However I wish to avoid the implication that there is a genuine or authentic erogenous body (i.e. the one that has sex) which is present in the bedroom but absent in the meeting or party. Two important factors must be borne in mind here. Firstly, the erogenous body itself may not always be fully present in the heterosexual bedroom, in the sense that women themselves may not confess their fantasies, desires or masturbatory practices to their male partners (or indeed to themselves, if one takes into account the workings of the Unconscious). Secondly, despite the tacit rules and injunctions which may induce party-goers to lie about or misrepresent their own sex lives in ways discussed above, Ann Summers parties rely heavily on a discourse of 'honesty' in which it is taken for granted that women are almost always telling the truth. This discourse is an essential precondition for successful gender identification: 'being one of the girls' revolves around what is said and done at Ann Summers events; one must therefore maintain the fiction that what is said and done is real and truthful, otherwise the very grounds of the identification fall away. Party organisers often insist that women are honest about their sexual selves at parties, and that parties are an environment where women can be just as 'rude' or 'natural' about sex talk as they are with their partners:

> I quite like the hostess game, you know. But I – I do it a different way, sort of like sometimes, like, I will get – like you've got your list of questions, and the list when they've got to answer them back, well I'll get the whole lot of them to do it. So sort of like when it asks, like, specific questions, like 'How old was you?', you know, sort of like, and it goes round, all right, people can lie, you know, but nine times out of ten they don't. You find that they don't lie, you know, and sort of like – and then, like, they're with their friends, and, like, you just sit there, and everyone's falling about on the floor laughing 'cause this one's just told them she lost her virginity in a bike shed! (Melanie)

> 'Cause I used to be – if it was just me and my husband here I was all – always said what I wanted to say, I could be rude and whatever. But I

would never do it in front of anybody else. But as you go to the parties and you find they're making witty comments, you think 'Well, if they're being themselves, why can't I?' And then you just – and then in the end you don't even think about it. (Beth)

I mean, like, even up to when I got married I was just the quietest person. I mean, I'd have a little giggle and that with [my husband], like, I'd have a laugh with him, but with anybody else, I mean, I just wouldn't open up or nothing. Now I just say it naturally, I just sort of – if I'm going to say something I just say it, and I have people in fits because I'm just so natural. (Cathy)

This discourse of 'honesty' appears all the more powerful because it persists alongside party organisers' admissions that they themselves sometimes lie about their own sex lives, especially about their experience (or lack of it) with sex toys where 'personal recommendations' of specific products may boost sales:

I mean, whether I should say this or not, whether you'll put in your book [laughs], that I actually lied and said 'This is good, I've used it in the bath and massaged myself and all that with it'. Although I had used it, but I haven't actually used it in the bath. Yet again, three girls ordered one that night with the [Bath Massage] Ball. (Vanessa)

But if I go to a party, I mean, someone asked me about – I – I've never in my life used a vibrator, but if someone asks me at a party 'What's –', 'Oh that's brilliant' I tell them [laughter], 'I've used that before'. But I haven't. I know people that have, but if I say 'Oh yeah, someone did' or 'some –', they think 'Oh right', you know. [Laughs.] But if they know and think that you've used it yourself and you think it's good, then they'll think 'Oh yeah'. (Laura)

Paradoxically, party organisers' deliberate lies about their own sex lives actually work in accordance with the discourse of 'honesty' rather than in contradiction with it. As Laura points out, party-goers expect their party organisers to make recommendations from a position of knowledge and authority; and they also assume that knowledge and authority about sex spring directly from personal experience. The fact that Laura's friends have told her that the vibrator is good is not enough; she has to pretend to have experienced it herself. Conversely, in hostess games and points games played at parties, tales of one's sexual experience are taken as indicators of one's sexual knowledge, such that 'naiveté' means both inexperience and ignorance. Thus the things that are said at parties are placed within a discourse of 'honesty' in which 'knowing what you are talking about' means having had personal experience of it. In this discourse, the erogenous body is the source of the homosocial body's 'knowledge' about sex, and the homosocial body tells the 'truth' about that knowledge.

The discourse of 'honesty' in this way enables gender identification at parties. It smooths over the real differences between women's sexual experiences and sexual practices and suggests that the female erogenous body is always the same for all women. It also turns the post-feminist investment in sexual openness into a new pathway for the circulation of power. Although (as discussed in Chapter 3) Beth and other party organisers celebrate the fact that doing Ann Summers has made them feel more able to talk openly about sex, some party organisers experience this not as freedom but as pressure. In this context, *differences* between women in terms of their willingness to be sexually open, or to use sex toys and other products, become difficult, embarrassing or even threatening. For party organisers such as Laura who have not used some of the products in which party-goers take an interest, the choice is to lie and retain one's status as 'one of the girls', or to tell the truth and put one's status – and one's sales – at risk. Diane does not lie, and suffers the consequences:

> I've had somebody embarrass me! [Laughs.] [Merl: How did they do that?] Well, I – um, it was actually showing all the vibrators, and, um, it was – I was, like, passing them around, and they were saying, like, um, 'Oh what does this one feel like, have you tried it?' And of course I – I got embarrassed at that. Um, and I just went, 'No, I don't need to, my sex life is all right thank you, I don't need toys'. [Merl laughs.] And that's how I got out of it, but I knew I'd got embarrassed 'cause I could feel myself getting red. (Diane)

This little moment of crisis in gender identification reveals a two-way power struggle between Diane and 'the girls' at her party. Their power over her is visible in her embarrassment; her attempt to exert power over them is visible in her attempt to stigmatise the use of vibrators – which is itself an attempt to redefine the usual post-feminist terms of Ann Summers gender identification. All of this suggests that claims about openness and honesty at Ann Summers parties and other female homosocial settings are not to be taken at face value: they may themselves reinforce normative gender identifications.

Technique and interior zones

Many previous researchers on female heterosexuality have used discourse analysis of tales of sexual experience and sexual knowledge to build a picture of the meanings and dynamics of heterosexual encounters (Gilfoyle et al. 1992, Hollway 1984, Roberts et al. 1995). In many ways my analysis of parties, meetings and interviews confirms the findings of such research. In particular, my participant observation and interviews confirmed the prevalence of the 'male drive' discourse analysed by Wendy Hollway (1984), which asserts that men have a natural and largely uncontrollable urge for heterosexual sex: 'they think about it every six seconds', as Helen assured me during her interview. The 'permissive discourse' (Hollway 1984), which asserts that sex is a natural urge for both men and women and as such should not be repressed, was also very prevalent; and as several commentators have pointed out, this apparently egalitarian discourse is not without its drawbacks for women. By positing that sex is a *natural* urge, this discourse subtly implies that it is somehow 'unnatural' or abnormal for women to say no to sex. Indeed the rise of post-feminism since Hollway's original research has arguably exacerbated this situation: the post-feminist trumpeting of women's sexual liberation as already achieved, and the valorisation of women's sexual pleasure as an end in itself, has subtly shifted the terms of the permissive discourse, such that saying no to sex is not just 'unnatural' but also repressed, self-oppressing and downright uncool. Many women at parties and meetings negotiated with this dilemma by joking about finding 'excuses' not to have sex. Jokes along these lines were extremely common at parties even amongst young and/ or single women. A popular raffle prize at a party by Joy which I observed was a coffee mug listing several 'excuses' not to have sex (such as 'the children will wake up'), which was greeted with appreciative laughter even by a childless nineteen-year-old guest who in other respects was keen to represent herself as something of a 'girl about town'. Party organisers also joke about such 'excuses' during kit demonstrations, and these jokes often include hostility or aggression against men and their non-phallic 'willies' as described in the previous chapter. For example, Sarah describes items from the men's novelty underwear range (Figure 4.1) as 'a good excuse not to have it, when he walks in the bedroom wearing that you won't be able to stop laughing'.

One of the most prevalent discourses at Ann Summers events, and perhaps even more significant of the erogenous body than either the male drive discourse or the permissive discourse, is what Gilfoyle et al.

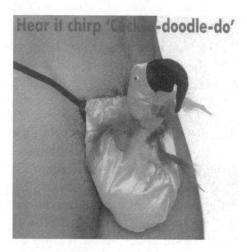

Figure 4.1 Cockerel Pouch, from the Ann Summers catalogue autumn/winter 1999

(1992) call the 'pseudo-reciprocal gift discourse'. This discourse frames heterosexual intercourse as an exchange: women 'give' sex (or, in some versions, 'give' themselves) to men, and in return men 'give' women orgasms. A good example of this discourse in women's party talk occurred at a party organised by Cathy, at which one of the younger guests told her friends that she was angry with her boyfriend and was therefore refusing to 'give' him sex – 'he's not getting any', she said. According to Gilfoyle et al, the giving is 'pseudo-reciprocal' rather than really reciprocal because it is not an equal exchange: it positions women as passive objects which are both received (or 'taken') by men and 'acted upon' by them. Drawing on Gilfoyle et al.'s analysis, Roberts et al. (1992) go further to suggest that one of the consequences of the pseudo-reciprocal gift discourse is that men's orgasms are regarded as the inevitable and 'natural' outcome of sex, whereas women's orgasms are more difficult to achieve: men have to 'work' at giving their partners orgasms, and this in turn may lead men to experience heterosex as a test of their sexual technique. In this context, women's 'failure' to achieve orgasm signifies men's 'failure' of technique; this stress on 'technique' thus means that 'women's orgasm is not pleasure for pleasure's sake, but is used to prove the quality of men's technique' (Roberts et al. 1992: 526). Another consequence of this is of course that orgasm becomes the endpoint and primary purpose of any heterosexual encounter.

Roberts et al.'s analysis suggests that the discourse of 'work and technique' is more prevalent in men's talk about sex than in women's, and they contrast this with the discourse of 'love and relationships' found in women's talk. However this distinction did not appear in my research with Ann Summers. The post-feminist injunction that women should enjoy sex just as much as, and even on the same terms as, men seems to have short-circuited the 'love and relationships' discourse, which was *not* very prevalent either during participant observation or in interviews. Unlike Roberts et al.'s interviewees, 'the girls' at Ann Summers parties do not spend much time talking about the importance of love or relationships as such; they lay claim to sexual pleasure as theirs by right. They do so however in ways which leave the pseudo-reciprocal gift discourse intact. In other words, sexual pleasure is women's right, but it is still men's responsibility to give women that pleasure through effective work and technique. In what follows I want to argue that the erogenous female body at Ann Summers events is fundamentally a body which is acted upon: it receives pleasure in general, and orgasm in particular, as the result of 'successful' sexual technique. The only contribution which women make to this work is in 'getting him going' in the first place, as discussed in Chapter 3; the female erogenous body arouses desire and pleasure in men's bodies not through technique, but through the use and consumption of Ann Summers products.

As described above, the erogenous body is not just a free-flowing body of undifferentiated pleasure: it is by definition zoned, classified and organised. Indeed, at Ann Summers events the organisation and classification extends not just to the erogenous body but also to its sexual practices. Hostess games and other similar question-and-answer games routinely ask, for example, 'what is your favourite sexual position?' This question demands, and almost always receives, a simple one-word or two-word answer: 'sexual positions' are understood as part of an organised, codified repertoire, where each discrete 'position' is known and named. Indeed, this question, routinely asked, routinely receives one of two replies: 'on top' or 'doggy-style'. I only once heard a hostess give any other answer to this question: tellingly, she also found it difficult to name the sexual 'position' in terms which would be 'known' or understood by her guests. Rather than simply naming a pre-given option from the (apparently very narrow) repertoire, she could only say that she didn't know what it was really called but that she called it 'spoons'. All of her guests said that they had been expecting her to say either 'on top' or 'doggy-style'. Similarly, the question 'do you like to dominate or be dominated in bed?' routinely receives the thoroughly post-feminist reply 'dominate' – even, in one case I observed, when the party-goer claims moments later during the same game that her favourite sexual fantasy is to be 'tied up'. Again, I encountered only one party-goer who said that she liked to be dominated, much to the surprise of her fellow partygoers. These replies – so narrowly limited and yet apparently given quite spontaneously – reveal the extraordinary power of normative gender identification in such games, which ruthlessly smooth away differences between heterosexual women.

Moreover all of these attitudes and positions ('spoons' included) are ones in which penis-vagina penetration takes place. As we saw in the previous chapter, Ann Summers is profoundly phallocentric; it is hardly surprising that this phallocentrism is the core organising principle of the erogenous female body, and that penis-vagina penetration is regarded as 'the' sexual act. The importance of the clitoris to women's sexual pleasure is constantly highlighted at Ann Summers parties, particularly by party organisers while demonstrating their vibrators; but when asked 'what is your favourite sexual position?', no-one at an Ann Summers party is likely to say 'sitting on the edge of the bed with his face between my thighs'. It is 'obvious' and even 'natural' that sexual position means position during penetration.

This is one of the central organising principles of the erogenous female body – and, by implication, of the erogenous male body – in Ann Summers: *female bodies are penetrable*. This penetrability is located in three discrete zones: the vagina, penetration of which is represented as both permissible and desirable; the mouth, represented as permissible but not desirable; and the anus, represented as neither permissible nor desirable.

In all three cases penetration is paradigmatically phallic, in the form of either an erect penis or a phallic vibrator: penetration by hands or fingers, although clearly part of the heterosexual repertoire, is often discursively positioned as secondary to and/or a substitute for penetration by a phallus:

> 'Cause it tells you [on the box containing the Tickler Set] where they're supposed to go. 'Cause a lot of women look at the little black one and think 'That's not going to fit over his dick', and they don't realise it's supposed to go on his finger. So that's why I say 'It's at the back, it tells you where they go', and 'Oh, so it's on your finger! Didn't realise that!' [Laughter.] I'm like, 'I know they stretch, but they're not going to stretch that much!' (Joy)

As this tale of the Tickler Set demonstrates, it is always assumed that penetration is penile unless one is specifically informed otherwise.

It is similarly taken for granted that the vagina is the main point of entry into the penetrable erogenous body. Phallic vibrators, whether 'realistic' or otherwise, literally embody this principle. But even the non-phallic 'his 'n' hers' vibrators such as the Vibromatic Ring, Little Beaver and Climax Creator are organised around vaginal penetration: all three are designed to fit around the penis so as to provide clitoral stimulation during intercourse (Figure 4.2). In fact only two of the vibrators in the catalogue for autumn and winter 1999 are explicitly not intended for vaginal penetration: the Bath Massage Ball and the Heart Throbber (Figures 4.2 and 4.3). The status of the former as a sex toy is ambivalent: many party organisers during their kit demonstration describe it primarily as a simple massager which can *also* be used as a sex toy. As for the Heart Throbber, I never once saw this item demonstrated at parties, even by those who had it in their kit, nor was it ever picked up

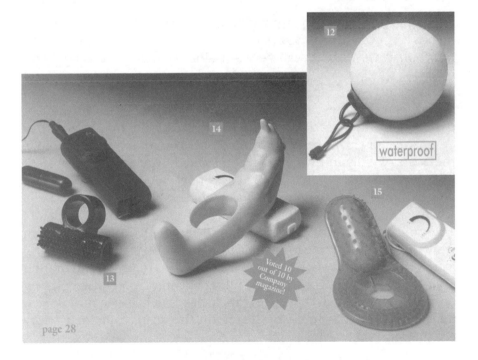

Figure 4.2 (Top R) Bath Massage Ball and (bottom L-R) Climax Creator, Little Beaver and Vibromatic Ring vibrators, from the Ann Summers catalogue autumn/winter 1999

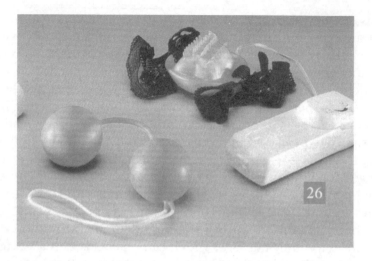

Figure 4.3 (L-R) Jiggle Balls and Heart Throbber, from the Ann Summers catalogue autumn/winter 1999

or commented upon by party-goers. In any case, the catalogue recommends that even this vibrator, so obviously oriented around the clitoris rather than the vagina, 'can be worn alone *or during intercourse*' (my italics).

Some party games make explicit references to or representations of the vagina: these reveal a construction of the vagina as an inert or passive hole into which the phallus is inserted, rather than as an active or muscular organ. At parties organised by Dawn or Cathy, for example, the game of willy-in-the-cup is accompanied by the party organiser's joking commentary that 'now you know how your old man feels when he gets home from the pub, he has trouble getting it into the hole' whereas 'we have the easy part, we just lie back and think of England'. The candle-in-the-bottle game similarly represents the vagina as an empty receptacle waiting to be filled by a phallic object. (Even the party games which do not make such obvious allusions to sexual penetration or to the genitals often involve the filling of empty receptacles: picking up and dropping small chocolates into a cup from between one's knees, for example.) The vaseline game represents the vagina as an inert, sticky receptacle:

> What you do is you blindfold someone, you pick on someone basically, and you ask the other girls who can take a joke, who can take a really sick joke. And um, you blindfold them, and you give them different items

and you get them to guess what they are, right, and what you do is, you make the items really easy so that they really go for it, they really know what they're talking about, they get really confident. And then you ask them to think of the dirtiest part on their body, which is only one, really. You ask them to stick their finger out, and you ram their finger in a pot of vaseline. And their face! [Merl laughs.] Their jaw hits the floor, they're like 'Eurgh! What's that?' and they're, like, trying to get the blindfold off so they can see what it is. And I'm going 'Calm down, it's only vaseline!' you know. (Cherry)

The erogenous body's vagina, then, is constructed through what one might call the discourse of the passive vagina. Any pleasure experienced by this vagina is passively received rather than actively taken: in other words, it depends on the phallus, and on the technique with which it is wielded. One of the forfeits often given during party games is to 'describe the worst sexual experience you have ever had'. The tales told for this forfeit are of course never tales of rape or sexual coercion – the light-hearted party context rules out such tales as inappropriate. 'The worst sex you've ever had' in this context is always (a) penis-vagina penetrative sex and (b) sex ruined by failures on the part of the man, either because his penis was insufficiently phallic ('he didn't have much', as one partygoer put it) or because his technique was faulty ('he finished much too quickly', as another party-goer put it). In other words, because the passive vagina is neither expected nor able to actually *do* anything during sex, 'bad sex' is always the man's fault. Tales of 'bad sex' thus fit into the post-feminist discourse that 'men are useless' discussed in previous chapters. They also provide an opportunity for gender identification which both smooths over differences between women – it is taken for granted that *anyone* who receives this forfeit will tell the same kind of tale, indeed will have a tale to tell at all – and offers an opportunity for solidarity, comfort and consolation in the face of male uselessness and sexual disappointment. Like the laughter at 'willies' discussed in the previous chapter, tales of 'bad sex' simultaneously enact gender identification between women and express disappointment with, and aggression against, men.

This construction of the 'passive vagina' extends to the use of vibrators. Where vibrators are used by a couple, men's technique (or lack of it) is again regarded as the key to women's pleasure (or lack of it). At a training session for party organisers, Dawn 'performed' a kit demonstration during which she recommended the Purple Pulser because it was 'soft and bendy' and so was 'good if your man's never used a vibrator before' because he wouldn't have to worry about pushing it in, 'it goes round the U-bend'. Even when men are not present the vagina is still constructed as passive: discussions about whether particular vibrators 'work' (or, at one party, the claim by one rather drunken guest that even 'candles work') puts the onus of work, technique and activity on the vibrator rather than on the female body.

The only exception to this discourse of the passive vagina arises in relation to the duo balls (sold in the catalogue as Jiggle Balls (Figure 4.3)). Party organisers' sales pitch for the duo balls invariably includes a recommendation that they are good for the pelvic floor muscles and are thus particularly recommended after childbirth. This recommendation tacitly constructs the vagina as a muscular, active organ rather than just a passive receptacle. Tellingly, however, the duo balls are always greeted with confusion when demonstrated at parties: being neither phallic nor a vibrator, they are simply incomprehensible to many guests (including Vanessa's guest as discussed above) until the party organiser explains them:

[S]he was going 'Well what do you do with these duo balls?', you know, and she just looked at me. I said 'Well they're not gobstoppers, love!', you know. [Merl laughs.] She said 'Oh, right'. She said, 'but surely I can't put them inside me, can I? Will I lose them?' I'm saying 'No, you won't lose them, you've got a bit of string there'. (Vanessa)

And we were saying, you know, 'These are the duo balls, you insert them inside yourself', and this foreign lady's saying 'What? What? Me no understand, where – where you put them? What you do?' So well [makes an illustrative gesture], 'You insert them inside yourself' [Merl laughs], and we're trying to do the actions but she just couldn't grasp it. [Merl: Oh God. [Laughs].] And this went on for a while. And she said 'No no, me no understand, what you do? Where they go? What you do?' [laughs], and everyone's getting the hump then, they're like, 'Oh for God's sake, you know, she's showing you where you put them, you must understand', and then this granny that was sitting next to her went, 'Oh for God's sake woman, you shove them up your fanny!' [Laughter.] (Justine)

Thus the discourse of the passive vagina is so powerful that many party-goers are literally unable to comprehend the only sex toy designed for an active, muscular vagina. It is also significant that the vagina is understood as active primarily in relation to childbirth and its aftermath (i.e. exercising the pelvic floor muscles), rather than simply in relation to women's sexual pleasure. There is never any discussion, for example, of using one's pelvic floor muscles as a technique to enhance one's own pleasure during sex, or indeed to enhance that of one's (male) partner.

In fact the penetrability of the vagina in general is closely linked to the female body's fertility. This appears in a common discursive equation where sex = penetration = (actual or potential) pregnancy, jokingly expressed in the idea that Ann Summers parties and/or products can make you pregnant:

> Um, and [one of my regular hostesses] is five months pregnant this time. [Laughs.] I walked in, she had one of the Ann Summers dresses on. I went 'Hello FX, how are you?' 'Oh yeah, fine', blah blah blah blah blah. And, er, she turned to the side and I thought 'Oh!' She's only tiny! [Laughter.] 'Oh! She's got a bit of a pot – pot belly there!' But she said 'Oh I'm five months pregnant'. So obviously from the last party – it's obvious she's having too many Ann Summers parties. [Laughter.] It's working on the children side – she's already got five children. (Dawn)

> Um, and within the first year of [joining] Ann Summers I was actually pregnant again. [Laughs.] [Merl: There you go!] And er, that was down to – well, what I was told it was down to was the Sex Blaster that they sell! [Laughter.] 'Cause I – I actually tried it out! [Merl: And it worked!] Yeah! [Laughter.] And I – I can't deny that, 'cause it actually did work! [Laughter.] So that was – yeah! [Laughter.] In fact people say to me, when I – they say to me 'Oh what's that?' when I show them the Sex Blaster, I talk to them about it and they say 'Do you think it works?' and I just say 'Well, I have a daughter now!' [Laughter.] (Laura)

Thus the penetrability of the vagina is part of a discursive construction of the female body as *interiority* – a body which receives, holds and ultimately expels things from its inside.

The erogenous female body's second port of entry is the mouth. Fellatio is often referred to and represented at parties, both implicitly and explicitly; it is represented as something which most party-goers will have experienced but which none will have enjoyed. When playing the points game, for example, Dawn routinely gives her guests mock apologies before asking questions about fellatio: the question 'have you ever given a man a blow job?' carries thirty points but really, she tells them, it ought to carry more; during the hostess game she apologises for even asking the question 'do you spit, swallow or gag?'. Similarly, during the name tag game at one party Lucy joked that she would have to remember to remove her 'Sucking Sindy' name tag before going home 'otherwise he'll think his luck's changed'. Despite the popularity of games (the gobbling game, the blow job game – involving sweets and balloons respectively) and forfeits (e.g. putting a condom on a vibrator using only your mouth) which refer to fellatio, there is no discursive space at parties or meetings for women to say that they *enjoy* performing fellatio. Even products such as the raspberry-flavoured Willy Drops, or the Banana Dick Lick which is always greeted with enthusiasm at parties, imply that fellatio in itself is distasteful – and that ways should be found to conduct it nevertheless.

One of the consequences of this is that there is never any discussion of fellatio as a matter of *women's* action or technique; this discourse constructs fellatio as something to be endured as best one can, rather than as the practice of an active female mouth on a passive penis. Thus even in fellatio the female mouth is constructed as passive, just as the vagina is constructed as passive during penetrative sex. In fact the female mouth and the vagina are often explicitly linked by games, forfeits and jokes, so that they sometimes appear to be almost inter-changeable (cf. Coward 1984). For example, Cathy often jokes during her kit demonstrations that crotchless knickers should not be worn out of doors, 'otherwise you'll get chapped lips'; the quote from Vanessa's interview above links the vagina with the mouth in the image of duo balls as 'gobstoppers'. In some cases this ambiguous relationship between the mouth and the vagina is part of the fun:

> There are all these silly little things that are absolutely brilliant. Like, I haven't got any at the moment, the, er, sexy dice? [Merl: Oh yeah.] They are wonderful. Um, and I always – I always manage to get a laugh, 'cause I – you always say 'It tells you what you do and what you do it to', and I say 'For God's sake, girls, if you buy them and use them and he keeps getting "Kiss lips", "Fondle lips", don't just think about these [points to mouth], think about the other ones! 'Cause you'll get "Blow willy", "Kiss willy", "Fondle willy". He'll be getting all the pleasure, and he'll get "Kiss lips", and he'll go [kissing sound], "Fondle lips" and he'll just play with them. Like, think!' (Joy)

Here again, the lips of the female mouth and those of the vagina are equally passive – recipients of men's activity (because he is following the instructions of the dice which tell him 'what you do and what you do it to'). Moreover, Joy's instructions to her partygoers to 'think about the other ones' continues the discursive zoning of the vagina rather than the mouth as the main locus of female sexual pleasure.

The anus is a far more problematic zone of the erogenous female body than either the vagina or the mouth. Two of the vibrators listed in the catalogue – the Squirmy Elephant and the Little Beaver – include anal stimulators, and the catalogue also lists a separate Anal Stimulator vibrator. However, party organisers and party-goers alike strictly exclude anal penetration from any discussions of sexual activity, and on the few occasions when it is mentioned the possibility of anal penetration is quickly closed down. As mentioned in the previous chapter, Dawn simply ignored the cries of 'stick it up yer bum!' with which a group of men greeted the game of vibrator relay, although she readily replied to their other comments; similarly, when during a game of truth or dare at a party organised by Cathy one of the guests asked her friend 'is your bum a virgin?', the question was simply blanked, both by the friend in question and by everyone else. The Little Beaver's anal stimulator is similarly ignored and/or unnoticed by most party guests, whereas the anal probe attached to Squirmy Elephant is often greeted with incomprehension – and party organisers themselves often do not explain what it is during their kit demonstrations.

The Anal Stimulator itself, however, is less easily glossed over: if it appears during a kit demonstration the subject of anal penetration simply has to be discussed. In fact I only observed two parties at which the Anal Stimulator was part of the kit demonstration, and on both occasions it provoked a mixture of anxiety and distaste (both of which were expressed through laughter). The first of these occasions was at a party organised by Helen. Helen assured her guests that, despite its name, the Anal Stimulator did not have to be used 'for that' but could be used for 'other things'. The disingenuousness of this attempt to present the Anal Stimulator as a non-anal toy was revealed when one of the guests asked Helen if she had ever used it herself: her reply of 'No I haven't!' was extremely indignant. On the second occasion, at a party organised by a different party organiser, there was no such attempt to disguise the Anal Stimulator's primary purpose. Tellingly, at this party one guest asked 'isn't that for gay men?' – a question which goes to the root of the 'problem' of anal penetrability. What is at stake in this 'problem' is the most fundamental discursive construction of both female and male erogenous bodies: where heterosexual female bodies are penetrable, *heterosexual male bodies are impenetrable*. According to the logic of heterosexuality at Ann Summers parties, male bodies and female bodies both have anuses; if the anus of one can be penetrated then so can that of the other; thus neither is penetrable.

Moreover the anus is problematic in a way that the mouth is not, because anal stimulators by definition construct the anus as a potential source of pleasure. As the discursive construction of fellatio outlined above suggests, oral penetration is not supposed to include the mouth itself as a site of pleasure – hence the absence of any discourses of women's enjoyment during fellatio; in fellatio the only physical pleasure on offer is phallic rather than receptive. In any case the strict heterosexuality of Ann Summers clearly precludes the possibility that any phallic object might enter a male mouth, to such an extent that even the willy-shaped chocolates are only permissible in female mouths:

> Too much chocolate [gets eaten at parties]. [Laughs.] I mean, I think I've gone off it after all [laughter] – seeing all this chocolate and doing melted chocolate and making willies out of them and – my son comes in, 'Can I have one?' I think 'Oh God!' But the thing is, like, it's all right, you see women eating chocolate willies, but a bloke eating a chocolate willy [laughter], no, it doesn't work! (Laura. Laura's son was four years old at the time of the interview.)

However, products such as the Anal Stimulator or Squirmy Elephant inescapably situate the anus as a site of pleasure, and so raise the possibility that the heterosexual male erogenous body might be organised around non-phallic pleasures – indeed, might be organised around receptive, interior pleasures. This possibility is taboo: the anus is coded as an erogenous zone for gay men only (cf. Maddison 2000).[3] In fact Ann Summers events sometimes use the power of this taboo and turn it back on heterosexual men as a way to cope with, or even to take revenge for, their sexual demands. Although Helen's guests were disturbed by the Anal Stimulator during her kit demonstration, earlier in the party they had happily joked about the rubber washing-up gloves

3. This also reveals an element of homophobia (i.e. against gay men) which is perhaps endemic to female homosociality in Ann Summer settings and elsewhere. On the one hand, on the surprisingly rare occasions when gay men are referred to in Ann Summers settings, they are treated, benignly if condescendingly, as endearingly non-phallic and hence – because Ann Summers definitions of sex are overwhelmingly phallocentric – as non-sexual. Helen, for example, while speculating about Ann Summers parties for men during her interview, said that she thought that gay men, unlike heterosexual men, *would* play party games and giggle along like 'the girls'. On the other hand, gay men's *sexual* bodies and activity are reduced to penetrative anal sex and as such regarded with revulsion (cf. Storr 2001). Insofar as homosocial femininity is articulated around signifiers of hegemonic phallic masculinity, sex *between men* appears to figure as an excluded Other, which threatens the heterosexual configuration of masculinity, femininity, penetrability and the phallus.

she distributed as part of one of the party games, which they greeted with cries of 'Bend over, boyfriend!' Similarly, in conversation with her female friend and me after her formal interview, Melanie told us that when her partner, who openly dislikes her being a party organiser, nevertheless says that he wants them to try out all the items in her kit, her standard retort is 'Bend over then, we'll try them out on you first'. Both of these homosocial jokes involve the play between identification (with women who are expected to 'get' the joke) and aggression (against men) familiar from other jokes about 'willies' and 'bad sex'. They also figure anal penetration not as bodily pleasure but as psychological punishment. Moreover, part of what makes them *jokes* is precisely the element of taboo. If feminine gender identifications at Ann Summers parties were to countenance the penetration of men (with finger, hand or sex toy) as a part of the erogenous female body's repertoire, then the idea of getting one's partner to 'bend over' would be neither hostile nor funny.

These 'zones of penetrability' of the erogenous female body represented at Ann Summers parties – mouth and vagina, the latter connected to fertility – are about depth and a *receptive interior*. The erogenous female body represented at Ann Summers parties also has other zones – primarily the clitoris and the breasts, especially the nipples – which are to be stroked or rubbed rather than penetrated, and which are about surface and a *receptive exterior*. These too receive their pleasure from the technique and activity of men and/or vibrators.

Technique and exterior zones

The clitoris is afforded a privileged position in female sexuality: party organisers often refer to it as 'the most sensitive' or 'most important' part of the (female) body. Many party organisers place great emphasis on the clitoris, especially when passing round the vibrators during their kit demonstration. Party-goers and party organisers alike sometimes also express scepticism about men's competence to use effective techniques on the clitoris: for example, when one of Cathy's party-goers revealed that her favourite sexual fantasy was 'lesbian sex', another guest immediately responded that this was hardly surprising because 'you know that a woman will find the spot' – i.e that men are unable to 'find' the clitoris. Once again, 'men are useless', and jokes about their uselessness enact identification between women as well as hostility against men.

As we have already seen however, this focus on the clitoris does not displace the centrality of penis-vagina penetration as *the* sexual act. This poses a dilemma for the erogenous body itself: how to reconcile the intense pleasurability of the clitoris with the centrality of vaginal penetration? To challenge the centrality of vaginal penetration would of course be to challenge the centrality of the penis – and hence to challenge its alignment with the phallus; it would also be to challenge everyday assumptions about men's 'natural' desires for penetrative sex as constructed by the male drive discourse; indeed, given some women's complaints that men cannot find and/or adequately stimulate the clitoris, it might potentially challenge the role of men in women's pleasure altogether. Ann Summers does not issue such challenges. The Ann Summers solution to this dilemma is rather to accept penetration as 'natural' and to find ways of stimulating the clitoris *as well* – to position clitoral pleasure as supplementary rather than central to heterosex for women, despite its status as 'the most sensitive part of the body'. Thus, as we have already seen, vibrators with clitoral stimulators are either intended for use during penis-vagina penetration, or else they have clitoral stimulators as well as, rather than instead of, a phallic shaft, in which case the vibrators are designed so that clitoral stimulation can take place at the same time as vaginal penetration. In any case, not all party-goers share party organisers' estimation of the importance of the clitoris: some party-goers are quite uninterested in the clitoral stimulators attached to phallic vibrators, for example, or even consider them to be 'in the way'. Indeed one guest at a party organised by Sarah did not know what the clitoral stimulators on such vibrators were for, and an explanation from her friends that they were 'to go at the front' apparently left her none the wiser. Needless to say, no party-goer ever displayed ignorance of, or lack of interest in, the vagina as an erogenous organ.

The last of the heterosexual female body's erogenous zones is the breasts – or, to be more precise, the nipples. Importantly, men's nipples do not feature at Ann Summers events as erogenous zones of the male body: in this discursive world, only women have erogenous nipples. These too are the recipients of pleasure through men's technique, specifically through men's hands or mouths, and the Ann Summers product range includes some products intended to enhance this pleasure: the autumn and winter 1999 catalogue included raspberry ripple flavoured Nipple Lick ('you pour, he licks!!'), Tutti Frutti Booby Drops and Pleasure Gel. It is worth noting that the latter is described in the catalogue as intended to 'enhance *penile* sensation and orgasm' (my emphasis), but that party organisers tend to place equal if not greater emphasis on its use for the clitoris and/or the (female) nipples.

Joy in particular always makes a point of demonstrating the Pleasure Gel's potential for female erogenous zones:

> And then the Pleasure Gel is another good one, 'cause I always get – I always try and get at least one person to try it on their nipple. 'Cause one tries it, and then they say 'I can feel it tingling' and they're all like 'Ah, let me have a go, let me have a go!' And you're guaranteed you're going to get at least one or two orders for it. Whereas if you just say about it in the book [i.e. catalogue], they don't try it and they don't buy it. Whereas if you've actually got it and someone tries it and they go 'I can feel it tingling', 'Ooh yes look, mine's gone hard!' [Merl laughs], everyone else tries it. That always gets a reaction, I love that. (Joy)

At the party organised by Joy which I attended, many guests did indeed try the Pleasure Gel by rubbing some onto their own nipples under their clothes. The sensation produced was interpreted by party-goers through the prism of male technique: one guest described the sensation as being 'like someone's mouth's there', and later as 'like someone's going like this', making a gesture with her fingers. The importance of men's mouths for this erogenous zone is also reflected in the very frequent jokes about breastfeeding, particularly in relation to the peep-hole bra which forms part of the Kizzy lingerie set. Cathy routinely joked of this set that 'it's good for breastfeeding but it depends who you want to breastfeed'; party-goers with small babies also sometimes joked about using Kizzy as a nursing bra. Just as comments and jokes about the duo balls are the only occasions when the vagina is figured as active, so these jokes about breastfeeding are the only occasions when the breasts are construed as actively *doing* something rather than as having things done to them; and again, just as with the duo balls, this activity is posited in relation to childbirth and its aftermath rather than in relation to female pleasure as such. Indeed, the implied activity of the breasts is undercut in such jokes by the fact that of course they *are* only jokes: no-one is really going to use Kizzy to breastfeed anyone. I have no doubt that the real breastfeeding of adult men (as offered, for example, by some specialist sex workers) would be regarded as completely beyond the pale of feminine gender identification at Ann Summers events.

Erogenous functions

Thus the heterosexual erogenous female body as represented at Ann Summers events is primarily organised around its breasts, mouth and genitals. This is not to say that no other body parts are permitted any erotic role or potential. The various kinds of body paint and massage oil (including perfumed, 'lickable', edible and/or heat-sensitive products) certainly suggest more diffuse, whole-body kinds of erotic practice; but such practices, framed as 'massage' or other kinds of 'foreplay', supplement rather than disrupt the very specific locations of the erogenous zones.

The defining characteristic of this erogenous female body is perhaps its *receptivity*: it has both a receptive exterior and a receptive interior. One of the notable features of this body's erogenous organisation is that the interior and exterior are strictly discrete and separate: the female body has an 'inside' and an 'outside' which are separately described, experienced and subjected to technique:

> I had one lady that bought a vibrator, phoned me up a week later and said 'Beth, I don't know if you can help me, I've bought this vibrator, what do I do with it?' And I just went 'What?' She said 'What do I do with it?' I said 'Whatever takes – whatever turns you on, love! [Laughs.] You put it up, in, out, whatever you want to do with it!' [Laughter.] [. . .] She said 'Can I use it inside, outside?' I said 'Use it wherever you want, that one, love', so she went 'Oh right, that sounds fun then'. (Beth)

In particular, as illustrated by Beth's list of 'up, in, out', the clitoris and the vagina are both represented and experienced as two quite separate organs, located on the outside and the inside respectively. References to female genitals in terms which might encompass both clitoris and vagina, and/or which might locate genital pleasure within different erogenous boundaries such as the vulva, are so rarely encountered as to be almost negligible in Ann Summers discourses; even the frequent references to 'lips' discussed above tend to construe the labia as the lips *of the vagina* rather than as embracing vagina, clitoris and vulva all together. This way of talking about clitoris and vagina as separate organs is so taken for granted today in everyday discourses of female sexuality that it appears 'natural'. However, as discussed above, the very recognition of the clitoris is the outcome of many discursive struggles; and the discreteness of the clitoris from the vagina, such that the former is represented and experienced as a wholly external organ and the latter a wholly internal one, is also discursively constructed. Some sexological and/or feminist models of the clitoris suggest that a greater and more significant proportion of its structure is internal than our everyday discourses allow (Phillips & Rakusen 1978, Laqueur 1992). This suggests not just that the specific erogenous zones of the female (and indeed male) erogenous body are discursively constructed, but that the very possibility of discrete zones is itself at least partly so.

Moreover the existence of these zones is frankly functional. Under this organisational régime, the erogenous body as a whole is represented and experienced as having one ultimate goal: orgasm. As we have seen in this chapter, Ann Summers discourses and products offer all kinds of ingenious ways in which heterosexual woman can achieve clitoral orgasm without disrupting the centrality of penis-vagina penetration to heterosex as such. If my analysis in this chapter has both implicitly and explicitly issued a challenge to the centrality of penile penetration, it is also important to challenge the centrality of orgasm too – clitoral or otherwise. Many critiques have been made of popular sexological texts, from sex manuals to TV documentaries, which insidiously suggest that spectacular orgasm is not just a right but also a duty; that insufficiently intense or frequent orgasms are a kind of deficiency which must be remedied, whether by sex therapy, self-help or simply obtaining more and more 'information' about sex (Heath 1982, Segal 1983). That the goal of sex is orgasm is so 'obvious' that it is never actually stated at Ann Summers parties: in this post-feminist world it is taken for granted that women's sexual liberation and equality with men is legible in the quality and quantity of their orgasms. But it is precisely this 'obviousness' which makes it such a powerful discourse, especially in relation to sex toys and vibrators, the whole point of which is to ensure and/or improve the quantity and quality of female orgasms. It also underlies many of the pleasures of the *homosocial* body at Ann Summers parties.

The Female Homosocial Body at Ann Summers Parties

The erogenous body mapped above is not necessarily that which is experienced by individual women during their heterosexual encounters, but is rather the body which is represented *to other women* in the homosocial setting of Ann Summers events. The gender identification which is an essential component of homosociality as such includes identification with this particular version of the female erogenous body. Making the right kind of gender identification at Ann Summers events includes identification with an appropriately gendered erogenous body, defined as receptive and functional, with its erogenous zones in the 'right' place experiencing the 'right' pleasures (or displeasures). Being 'one of the girls' requires one's participation in specific discursive constructions of bodies, organs and pleasures.

Homosocial and erogenous bodies are therefore in a complex and dynamic relationship with each other at Ann Summers parties. The homosocial body plays games, makes jokes, eats and drinks at parties – and in doing so it also represents the female erogenous body to other women. Indeed, insofar as this particular version of the female erogenous body serves the purposes of group identification with other women rather than of sexual pleasure with individual men, the whole *point* of the erogenous body is precisely *to be represented* by the homosocial body. The erogenous body 'ghosts' the homosocial body at parties: the activities, expressions and above all the pleasures of the homosocial body at parties trace some of the outlines of the erogenous body. But the homosocial body is not simply a polite or social mask for the erogenous: as discussed above, it also has its own autonomous life and pleasures. In this section I shall try to show some of the most common examples of the 'ghosting' of the homosocial body by the erogenous body.

The homosocial body's oral pleasures

Far and away the most prevalent of the homosocial body's pleasures are the oral pleasures available at parties. These obviously include drinking, especially drinking alcohol, which is itself an important part of the whole party experience both for the guests themselves and from the point of view of the party organisers:

> It also helps if they've had a drink. If they're sitting there drinking tea it doesn't work quite as well. Um . . . So – yeah you know, when people have a drink they tend to loosen up a bit. [Merl: Have you had any where they just sit there drinking tea then?] Yeah. Yeah, I've had a few like that [inaudible]. You notice the sales are nowhere near as high, and you know – I don't know, they're just a bit quiet. I mean, I tend to ask if they've got a bit of music on in the background and things, because otherwise you just sit there in silence. And um, there's nothing worse than that. And yet – you're desperately trying to perk them up, and you just can't, you know, 'cause there's none of the giggles or . . . that you get when people have had a bit of a drink. It's definitely better if they've had a drink. [Laughs.] Not – I mean, not everyone drinks, I know, but . . . [Merl: It's just the atmosphere though isn't it?] Yeah, that's right, yeah. I mean, you know, they tend to only have, like, the lower alcohol ones, only, like, the – the lower wines and all that. But it's just like a night out. I think if they get that atmosphere, a night out atmosphere, it's the best way. (Sarah)

Alcoholic drinks were also the focus of several promotions on offer to party organisers and their guests during my research, particularly sweet drinks such as Sheridans chocolate liqueur. For many guests these boozy oral pleasures are supplemented by cigarettes, which are usually consumed in great numbers at parties.

Many party hostesses often prepare and/or supply food for their guests: this is usually finger food, such as crisps, nuts, sausage rolls and sandwiches, rather than a formal meal. Indeed a formal meal is regarded as thoroughly inappropriate to Ann Summers parties, partly because it disrupts the informal and dynamic use of space:

> 'Cause I went to – the biggest house I ever went to was somewhere like [North London] [. . .] And [the hostess]'d done a big meal on a big table at the other end of the room, and they all vanished up there, so I packed my bags and left. That's the only party I've walked out of. (Lucy)

However, even sausage rolls and sandwiches are often left largely uneaten at the end of parties. The food around which Ann Summers parties revolve is not savouries but sweets, and in particular chocolate:

> Um, we buy the, um, the Cadburys minis, you know the mini bars? [Merl: Oh yeah.] We – we buy those [as prizes] and we find they go down quite well actually, 'cause girls love chocolate. [Laughs] [Merl: This is very true.] That goes down very very well, we give a lot of those. (Donna)

> That's the mad thing about Ann Summers, for some reason everybody loves chocolate. [Laughs] [Merl: I know, the amount of sweets people buy before they go to a party, it just amazed me the first – the first time I saw it.] Mmm, yeah, yeah. Oh yeah. I mean, I'm doing, um, a party on Friday, and [the hostess] said 'Don't forget your Celebrations!' [Laughter.] I said 'Why?' She said 'Oh that's how I'm getting everyone here!' [Merl: She promised them chocolate!] [Laughter.] Yeah! It's quite good actually, 'cause – I mean, we give out – give away the little prizes, like the little willies, sticky willies, and key rings and things like that, but instead of doing that all the time, 'cause, like, they're – if – if they're are repeat group with you then they sort of like – they've all got one of those [laughs], they've all got this and – and you bring chocolates and that and they 'Ooh [laughter], can we have a chocolate?' and so 'Yeah, yeah, all right'. But I try and play games with the sweets as well. Like I had, um, balloons, load of balloons blown up, and they had to bend – like, crouch down, pick the balloon up between their knees, run over and get this chocolate willy and eat that, and then the next one comes along and does it. And it was – they loved

that as well. So the more chocolate the better! [Laughter.] I don't know, this fetish about chocolate and Ann Summers, it just – [Merl: And it's got to be chocolate, no other sweet will do.] No, no. I've tried taking different sweets, but they're just like 'Oh, didn't you bring any chocolate?' [Laughter.] (Laura)

The consumption of chocolate is almost compulsory at Ann Summers parties. The hostess at a party organised by Melanie not only disliked chocolate but actually suffered from migraines after eating it. Nevertheless she still took part in chocolate-eating games. Indeed, sweets and chocolates are so prevalent in party games and prizes that to refuse to play such games would almost be tantamount to a refusal to participate in the party – and in the gender identification it enacts. If you want to be 'one of the girls' at an Ann Summers party then you have to like sweets: the discourse that 'girls love chocolate' practically defines femininity as such.

Indeed the female homosocial body is constructed at Ann Summers events as a body with an insatiable sweet tooth. In addition to sweet-eating games already discussed so far, such as the Walnut Whip game, the gobbling game, the Kit Kat game, and the game of dropping chocolates into a cup from between one's knees, there are many other popular eating games including:

- Bouncing bollocks. Each player fills her mouth with sweets and then says the phrase 'bouncing bollocks bouncing bollocks bouncing bollocks' with her mouth full. The player who can hold the greatest number of sweets in her mouth and still speak intelligibly is the winner.
- Maltesers and cream. This is usually a race between two players. Each player has a paper plate on the floor in front of her, and each plate contains a number of Maltesers (or other sweets) hidden under a pile of 'squirty' cream (i.e. canned whipped cream). Players must eat the Maltesers from the plate without using their hands.
- The Polo game. Players are given a Polo mint on a piece of string. The party organiser tells them to hold the end of string in their mouths and then instructs them to eat the Polo without using their hands.
- Smarties and die. A plate of Smarties is put into the middle of the room and players are given a die. Each player rolls the die in turn. When the die lands on a six, the player who threw it then has to pick up as many Smarties as she can using a pair of tweezers (or in

some variations a teaspoon) until another player throws a six, at which point it becomes her turn. The winner is the player with the largest number of Smarties at the end of the game.

- The Opal Fruit game.[4] This is usually a racing game between two teams. Each player must unwrap an Opal Fruit while wearing a pair of rubber washing-up gloves. Once she has unwrapped her sweet she passes the gloves onto the next team member who then does the same. The last team member to unwrap her sweet must then blow up and burst a balloon.
- Juggling balls and chocolate willies. This game is usually played as a race between two teams. Each player has to pick up a juggling ball in her mouth without using her hands, run to the other end of the room and put the ball down again; she is then given a 'bootlace' sweet with a chocolate willy tied to the end, and has to suck up the bootlace and eat the willy without using her hands.

As has often been noted, food in general and sweets in particular often have the allure for women of the 'naughty but nice' (Coward 1984, Gamman and Makinen 1994; cf. Probyn 2000). As Gamman and Makinen (1994) note, the 'culture of plenty' of late capitalist societies like the UK positions women in a peculiarly tense and even eroticised relationship with food:

> Most Western women experience food as a site of struggle. They have easy access to food to accommodate the means of survival, as well as pleasure from eating. But they also know from cultural messages about what it means to be a woman, that they must exercise restraint around food. For many women, then, food appears to provoke more compelling fantasies and conversations than sex and is perceived as just as alluring and dangerous. (Gamman and Makinen 1994: 148)

'Calorific sweets' in particular are the object of such fantasies and desires: both sex and sweets are 'sinful' for women, and 'the pleasure of eating sweets is [coded as] a sexual experience' in advertising and other popular cultural forms (Gamman and Makinen 1994: 151)[5].

4. Opal Fruits are now sold in the UK under the name Starburst, but were always referred to by their former name at parties.

5. This circuit of sin, chocolate, sex and pleasure is neatly expressed for example in the Cadburys 'Wicked' chocolate selection box. I was unable to resist buying these chocolates as parting gifts to unit organisers at the end of my research – after all, what could be a more perfect gift for Ann Summers party organisers to share at their unit meetings?

Concern about the size and shape of the body – including changes wrought by childbirth and its aftermath – constitutes a kind of background radiation at Ann Summers events, so taken-for-granted as a condition of heterosexual femininity that it is almost as naturalised as heterosexuality itself. But 'girls love sweets' is also naturalised, and women at Ann Summers parties and meetings enthusiastically tuck into chocolates and sweets despite their protestations about putting on weight – indeed, in the double bind of the 'naughty but nice', their enthusiasm is *fuelled* by the fact that the sweets will supposedly make them fat. This eroticised tension between pleasure and denial is actively fostered at Ann Summers parties: during kit demonstrations, and especially the trying on of lingerie sets by party-goers, I sometimes observed women literally eating chocolates with one hand while holding a tape measure in the other. The tension itself is a site of gender identification: being 'one of the girls' means precisely experiencing the tension and sharing it with others. This aspect of feminine gender identification around sweets can perhaps be summed up as 'feel the ambivalence and eat it anyway'.

Moreover, many of the party-goers and party organisers are also the mothers of young children, and as such are used to providing sweets and chocolates for children (indeed this was a common strategy to keep pre-school-age children quiet during my interviews with party organisers in their homes). Eating sweets at parties is perhaps an opportunity for women to experience a kind of treat which they are used to dispensing to others in everyday life. Many of the sweet-eating games, such as the Smarties and die game, are originally children's party games (or variations on children's games): perhaps then the games themselves are also a form of 'fun' and pleasure which party-goers are used to providing or organising for others than themselves.

As has already been discussed above, the mouth is a key zone of penetrability for the erogenous female body. The centrality of oral pleasures, particularly of eating sweets and drinking alcohol, also locate the mouth as the most important organ of the homosocial body at parties. It is hardly surprising therefore that the homosocial mouth is persistently ghosted by the erogenous mouth. This is most obviously the case with the chocolate willies (discussed above) often given as prizes, but many games and jokes also allude fairly explicitly to fellatio. The bouncing bollocks game is all about how much one can fit into one's mouth; similarly during the game with juggling balls and chocolate willies, when players ask (ask they frequently do) whether they are allowed to pick up more than one ball at a time, party organisers and/

or onlookers often respond with jokes along the lines of 'she's used to getting two balls in there!'. This kind of joking and teasing about fellatio both represents and polices the erogenous body: as we saw above, the erogenous mouth is discursively constructed as performing fellatio without pleasure. Games and jokes which refer to fellatio enact a gender identification (we have all done it) while enforcing the female erogenous body's normative boundaries (none of us has liked doing it). Moreover they ensure that this gender identification remains compatible with the service of men's interests (we all dislike it but we do it anyway because men like it). In this context the homosocial body's insatiable demand for sweets and chocolates appears more than a little over-determined by the erogenous body's reluctant servicing of men's sexual demands. The sense that eating chocolate at Ann Summers parties and meetings is an illicit pleasure (if not a downright guilty one, particularly for the many women on slimming diets) is fuelled by the coding of the erogenous female mouth as an organ dedicated to *men's* rather than women's pleasure.

Edible or 'lickable' products also play on the ambiguity of the mouth as zone of both erogenous penetrability and homosocial pleasure, particularly when party organisers allow their guests to taste such products during kit demonstrations:

> Um, the Lust Dust is brilliant. [Merl: What is that?] It's literally lemon sherbet, but it's really, really sour [laughter], literally. But everyone seems to like it. Everyone seems to like it. I mean, places like Athena, down the high street, they sell it as well. [Merl: Oh do they?] Yeah. But um, like, they just seem to buy it – oh they love it. It's just 'Oh have you got that on you?' It's like 'No', because everyone eats it at the parties! [Laughter.] I've been through about four tubs of that, and I'm not doing it any more! [Laughs.] 'Cause they literally sit there like [makes an illustrative gesture]. [Laughter.] Like the um – the Banana Lick Dick [*sic*], I sell a lot of that. (Laura)

> Um, get good reactions from things like the Banana Dick Lick. That always brings a smile, they're like 'What?' [Merl: Is it the name?] Yeah. And then they try it, and they're like 'Oh that's nice'. 'Yes, don't use it on a dick, put it on ice cream! Put it all over the top, all over ice cream. Lovely!' [Merl laughs.] (Joy)

Tasting sessions such as these during kit demonstrations are a form of homosocial pleasure which is deliberately and explicitly ghosted by the erogenous body since, after all, it is to the latter that the products as such are addressed. Conversely these products invoke an unusual ghosting of the erogenous body by the homosocial, in that the supposedly unpalatable act of fellatio is made acceptable, if not enjoyable, for women by dousing the penis in sweet-tasting Willy Drops and Dick Licks.

Because it does not involve any contact with another woman, this sensual ghosting of the mouth through sweets and Ann Summers products is relatively 'safe' in that it is unlikely to stray too close to the lesbophobic boundary between homosociality and homosexuality. The lesbophobic boundary means that certain rules are observed about what can and cannot be put into the mouth. Not only can no part of any other party-goer's body be allowed to enter the mouth, but there are also rules about more indirect forms of oral contact between party-goers. This rule is so 'obvious' and taken for granted that it only becomes visible on rare occasions: one such occasion did occur however at a pub party organised by Diane, at which she decided to play the game with the juggling balls and chocolate willies:

> And I played one with – with balls, but um, what happened was normally they have to pick the balls up with their mouth, but I didn't think that was fair, 'cause I didn't have enough balls for everybody. So what I done is I got half of them to take it to one end of the room and the other half taking them back. Well, I didn't think that was fair to actually have them put it in their different mouth. So we got a spoon, and they had to pick this ball up off the floor with a spoon and take it to the end. [Merl: In their mouths or in their hands?] No, in their hand. They was only allowed to use one hand and the other hand had to be behind their back. (Diane)

As Thorogood (2000) argues, rules about the intimate space of the mouth construct physical and symbolic boundaries of our bodies and identities. Diane's concern with hygiene at this party – it is not 'fair' to ask a party-goer to put into her mouth a ball which has already been in another woman's mouth – also expresses a concern about intimacy: one would usually only expect to share a spoon or a toothbrush, for example, with a person with whom one was extremely intimate – usually one's child, one's parent or one's partner. Occasional jokes about lickable products also reveal this rule prohibiting oral contact between party-goers, such as when one of Sarah's party guests spilled some of the Edible Body Paint and her friend jokingly told her 'well, I'm not licking that off *you*!'

The only exceptions to this 'no oral contact rule' occur when friends kiss each other, either during the party itself or when saying goodbye at the end of an evening. Unlike other kinds of oral contact, kissing one's friends is not just permissible but sometimes even desirable as an aspect of feminine gender identification – where, for example, kissing one's friends is regarded as an appropriately feminine, emotional expression of affection. Thus for example, during their dispute with the lesbophobic guest at Sarah's party discussed in Chapter 2, party-goers explicitly stated that it was acceptable to greet a female friend with a kiss under certain circumstances. There are of course widely understood if rarely stated rules about the differences between intimate and non-intimate kissing: guests do not normally kiss each other on the lips, for example. Thus the lesbophobic guest vehemently insisted that kissing a female friend was not the same as 'snogging' her – and none of her adversaries in the dispute disagreed with her on this point. (A similar distinction between kissing and 'snogging' is implicitly drawn by the hostess game question about 'kissing another woman sexually'.) Kissing is also in a somewhat anomalous position at Ann Summers parties in that the erogenous body as it is constructed at Ann Summers events is not a *kissing* body: neither the products themselves nor the games, jokes or conversations at parties pay any attention to practices of erotic kissing, and the mouth is constructed as an erogenous zone insofar as it is penetrable by penises and/or phalluses rather than by tongues. This maintains the boundary between homosociality and homosexuality at parties by distinguishing between the female homo-social body and the female erogenous body as represented to other women. The homosocial body kisses its female friends – in a non-erotic way; but the female erogenous body does not kiss at all – and so there is no danger of kissing a female friend 'erotically' by mistake. The elision of kissing from Ann Summers discourses of the erogenous body also ensures once again that the erogenous female mouth remains a source of pleasure for men rather than for women: women's oral pleasures in this construction are located in sensations of taste, especially sweet tastes, rather than in tactile sensations.

These contradictory rules, pleasures, elisions and prohibitions make the mouth the most highly charged of the homosocial body's organs. Moreover the mouth is not just an organ into which food, drink and body parts are taken; it is also of course an organ of communication, both verbal and non-verbal (Falk 1994). The uses of the female voice are another vitally important source of homosocial pleasure at Ann Summers events.

The homosocial body's vocal pleasures

Homosocial bodies at Ann Summers parties are extremely noisy. Indeed, just as Ann Summers places value upon women's sexual experience in a culture which usually stigmatises it, it also places value upon women's 'loudness' in a culture which usually stigmatises 'loud' women as unladylike, unattractive and vulgar:

> When they're with their husbands it's all 'Don't you – you shouldn't say things like that, you're a lady' or 'Don't do this' and 'You shouldn't tell people what we get up to'. So obviously when they're out they're like 'Right, I'm telling them everything [Merl laughs] and I'm going to do everything!' And I find – I love doing the older parties. Over thirty-five, I would say. They'll do everything and anything. (Beth)

This too is a site of gender identification: being 'one of the girls' is about being 'loud'. Moreover the terms of this gender identification are not simply reducible to the demands of conventional heterosexual femininity, as Beth's comments about being 'a lady' in relation to husbands attests. Like other aspects of female homosociality, the opportunity to be 'loud' at Ann Summers parties offers respite from the demands and conventions of everyday gender régimes – but without going so far as to challenge them.

Alongside the gales and even shrieks of laughter accompanying games and jokes, there is also a lot of shouting, cheering, sexual swearing and generally raucous behaviour at Ann Summers parties. Party organisers actively encourage party-goers to shout or cheer, especially during games, as it builds up a sense of excitement and high spirits – which may in turn boost sales and/or increase the likelihood of future party bookings. As discussed in Chapter 1, party organisers routinely divide themselves, each other and potential recruits into 'quiet people' and 'loud' or 'bubbly' people; they similarly talk about 'loud' or 'quiet' parties, and will direct a great deal of attention to achieving the right balance of 'loudness' in their party-goers. Although party organisers generally dislike parties which are too rowdy to control, they also dislike parties which are too quiet and expect poor sales from such parties:

> So when you walk through the room you're listening to them. If they're saying – if there's hardly any conversation going on you know it's going to be really hard work. You know that you've got to try and find games that are going to break the ice first of all, you know, it's – it's – it is, it is hard. (Dawn)

'Loudness' or 'bubbliness' is also an important quality for party organisers themselves, and one which some party organisers actively 'put on' at parties:

> I can be very shy [laughs], but I'm different when I'm at a party, I tend to be – I'm, like, a totally different person when I do a party, I'm very upfront and very loud. [Laughs.] And it helps! (Donna)

> I get myself geared up, from the moment I get in from work, if I've got a party I start getting into Ann Summers mode. [Merl: What is Ann Summers mode?] Loud. [Laughter.] Basically. Um, loud, bubbly. (Joy)

Indeed, unit organisers and area managers put almost as much effort into encouraging a noisy atmosphere at meetings as party organisers do at parties, particularly on those occasions where meetings are also celebrations of individual or group achievements. When one of the unit organisers 'won' her company car, the presentation was made at an area meeting: the car keys were hidden inside one of balloons festooning the meeting room, and the unit organiser had to burst all the balloons until she found them; her area manager exhorted everyone to shout and cheer encouragement as she did so. The noisiest Ann Summers event of all was the catalogue launch, at which party organisers and unit organisers alike were encouraged to shout, cheer, scream, thump the tables and even sing until it was literally impossible to hear what was being said by those on stage, despite their microphones; as discussed in Chapter 3, when the male strippers made their appearance at that event the noise from the audience was truly amazing – and was an important enactment of gender identification between the women. The vocal pleasures afforded by being able to swear, shout and laugh freely are very important aspects of the homosociality of Ann Summers events in general, not just at parties.

Forfeits given at parties include many 'loud' behaviours:

> It's the one who's done the most who gets the forfeit is normally the one who's got the most to say [. . .] So normally they are up for it. And especially with their friends and everyone else, like, edging [sic] them on, 'You've got to do it now, go on, you've done it!', like, you know, things like that. Um, but no, I've had them standing out in the middle of the street shouting out 'I love sex, I love Ann Summers, I need a big vibrator tonight [Merl laughs], come and help me!' You know, things like that. (Trish)

Other similar forfeits include going outside to shout 'I used to be sexually frustrated until I bought a vibrator from Ann Summers', or standing in the middle of the room singing 'I've got a lovely bunch of coconuts' while holding up one's breasts. They also sometimes involve going outside and talking to men – usually strangers encountered by chance in the street – in a far more directly sexual way than is usually permissible: some forfeits, for example, require party-goers to give a condom to the first man they see, or to interview a man in the street using a vibrator as a microphone. Going outside to play games also provides opportunities for party-goers to shout at, heckle and/or reply to men in ways that would probably be impossible outside of a female homosocial group, as discussed in the previous chapter.

Some of these vocal homosocial pleasures are very insistently and even deliberately ghosted by the erogenous body. This is clearly the case, for example, in the use of sexual swearwords, and indeed in sexually explicit talk generally at parties. Some games actively foster this: in the alphabet game, for example, party-goers shout out as many 'rude' words as they can think of beginning with particular letters of the alphabet. However the most intense ghosting takes place during the extremely popular game of orgasm bingo. Orgasm bingo is not just a noisy game in itself, but is also often used as an 'icebreaker' at the beginning of parties to encourage noisy participation at the party as a whole. As Joy told me during her interview, 'I always do the orgasm bingo to start with, 'cause that helps break the ice, 'cause you get everyone making silly noises and doing silly things.' Orgasm bingo is like 'ordinary' bingo: everyone has a grid containing nine numbers (guests are usually instructed to draw these grids themselves and fill in their own choice of numbers before the game begins), and then the party organiser calls out randomly selected numbers; the first person to have all of their numbers called is the winner. The 'twist' with orgasm bingo is the winner does not shout 'bingo' or 'house' (as with ordinary bingo), but instead has to 'fake an orgasm'. Moreover, every time one of their numbers is called the players have to moan, sigh or make some other noise indicating an approaching 'orgasm'. This basic form of orgasm bingo also has some variations:

> [. . .] Orgasm Bingo which is a good one. That's the same as normal bingo but instead of – well, as well as crossing off the number they've also got to shout out what's on a card that I give them. And that can be – I mean again I sort of judge it a bit. They do choose it, so it's [not] just totally random, um, but if I know it's a really good crowd and, you know, they're

not ashamed of saying anything then, you know, I obviously give the right cards out. And that can be anything from standing up and shouting 'Faster! Faster!' or 'My fanny farts!', 'My fanny needs a fondle!' [laughs] and [Merl laughs] – and things like that [laughs]. So every time they cross off a number they've also got to stand up and shout out what's on the card. [Laughs.] Then when they get to their last number, instead of calling 'house' they've got to fake an orgasm. (Justine)

[. . .] There are lots of variations on it. You can do it where they just start off have an orgasm and then build up and build up, or my favourite one is when they put their favourite animal. Or there's one that – one that I used right from the beginning, I'd forgot about it until I reminded the other day, where you get them to write down their – either their pet name for their partner or something – they just scream and shout abuse or whatever, you know. Oh like, I had one party where I called out a number and someone was going 'Harder, harder!' and another one shouted out 'Rub my tits!' [Merl laughs] and oh, it was like – things like that. (Lucy)

In the 'favourite animal' version to which Lucy is alluding here, players are asked to write down their favourite animal (*before* they are told what game they are about to play) and then have to make the sound that animal would supposedly make while having an orgasm.[6]

This is an outstanding example of the ghosting of the erogenous body. Not only is no-one really having an orgasm during such games; no-one is really *faking* an orgasm either insofar as no-one is trying to convince anybody that they really are having an orgasm right then and there. The noises are being made for the benefit of the other women present rather than for a male partner, and as such are being made by the homosocial body. But both the game itself and the ways in which it is introduced and explained by party organisers demonstrate that *really* faking orgasms is an activity performed by the heterosexual erogenous female body – indeed, according to many jokes at parties, is a very frequent activity. Dawn, for example, explaining the rules of this game, usually tells her party-goers that 'when you get to the last number you go into your full orgasm, like in [the film] *When Harry Met Sally*, and I don't want to hear anyone say they don't know how to fake it,

6. Taylor (1978) records a similar games of bingo, including animal bingo, being played at Tupperware parties in Britain in the 1970s. Winners of the Tupperware version do not of course 'fake' an orgasm at the end of the game, but just shout 'Tupperware!' instead of 'Bingo!'

we've all had to fake it some time or other'. At a party organised by Cathy, the winner of orgasm bingo put on a truly amazing performance, at which her friend commented 'you obviously fake it a lot'. As Roberts et al. (1995) have argued, heterosexual women's practice of faking orgasm is itself a response to the discourse of 'male technique' discussed above: heterosexual women are aware that heterosexual men may feel anxious or inadequate if they cannot 'give' a woman orgasms, and so women fake orgasm to reassure their partners that their technique is effective (cf. Duncombe and Marsden 1996). Faking orgasm is therefore fully congruent with other discourses of the erogenous body at Ann Summers parties, the various zones of which are recipients of technique in ways discussed above. It is also congruent with the post-feminist discourse that 'men are useless but we love them anyway', in that it posits that all women will have had at least one male partner whose technique was not up to scratch. Thus when Dawn tells her party-goers that 'we've all *had to* fake it' the 'having to' has a dual force: we will have 'had to' fake it because of poor male technique ('men are useless'); and we will have 'had to' fake it because we take responsibility for sparing the feelings, and the phallic illusions, of both the man in question and heterosexual men as a group ('we love them anyway'). In this way 'faking' orgasm at Ann Summers parties expresses both gender identification (we've all done it, haven't we girls?) and disappointed aggression against men. By turning this (apparently inevitable) disappointment into a joke, it also simultaneously helps women to serve men's interests by defusing the potential challenge both to phallocentric penetrative sex and to men's illusions of their own phallic proficiency.

The specifically *vocal* quality of faked orgasms and of orgasm bingo is also important. As has often been noted (perhaps especially in relation to pornographic film and video), representations of sexual pleasure are almost always phallocentric, and male sexual pleasure and orgasm are therefore easily represented, signified through the visual forms of penile erection and ejaculation. Women's pleasure is far less 'visible' within the terms of phallocentrism, and thus tends to be signified through vocal performance (Williams 1989). This discourse – that men's orgasms are visible and women's are audible, that 'men make a mess and women make a noise' – is widely circulated not just in pornographic representation but also in other everyday contexts of heterosexuality (Jackson and Scott 2000). Games such as orgasm bingo clearly participate in this discourse. In doing so they are actively locating female orgasm within a phallocentric context – the discourse of 'audible' female orgasm fundamentally presupposes that female genital pleasure is not 'visible' because it is not phallic.

In fact, there are some occasions on which Ann Summers parties can and do acknowledge that women 'make a mess' too. Cathy and Helen routinely joke to their guests during kit demonstrations that the thong underwear with certain outfits such as Fifi is convenient because 'you don't have to wash them, you can just scrape the bits off'; the vaseline game described above by Cherry also recalls the 'mess' of the female erogenous body, specifically the vagina. However all of these instances code this female mess as dirty, whether explicitly (Cherry talks of 'the dirtiest part on their body') or implicitly ('bits' to be removed by washing or scraping – Dawn's description of the curve of the vagina as 'the U-bend' may also be said to link female mess with germs or dirt). Thus although there is some acknowledgement that female erogenous bodies can make a mess *as well as* a noise, the noise is acceptable and even expected, while the mess is very clearly unacceptable. Conversely, the 'mess' of male orgasm may be represented at parties through games with canned whipped cream (usually referred to as 'squirty cream', and significantly another opportunity of sweet oral pleasures at parties) and jokes about wet patches, but there is never any allusion to male erogenous bodies making a noise *as well as* a mess. This mess/noise dichotomy might be compared with the impenetrable/penetrable dichotomy organising heterosexual male and female erogenous bodies respectively – particularly as it is men's penetration of women which is paradigmatically supposed to produce both the mess and the noise.

However, although vocal pleasures are one of the central homosocial pleasures in Ann Summers settings, and despite the general popularity of orgasm bingo as one of many party organisers' favourite games, 'faking orgasms' at parties is not necessarily experienced as 'fun' by partygoers themselves. Many party organisers reflect that some women find it extremely embarrassing to 'fake orgasms' at parties:

So I mean, there – there have been girls that, when I do pass the parcel, when there's a forfeit in between each layer, some of them don't put a lot of effort into it, where if they've got to fake an orgasm and they're a bit quiet, they just say 'Oh, ooh-ooh', and then I'll let them have that because, you know, that's fair enough, if that's what they want to do. Whereas you get the other women that go on for ten minutes giving all the 'Aaaaaah!' [Merl laughs] and yeah, that's fine, you know [laughs], each to their own, it depends how much they want to get involved, but they have – I do stress that they've got to do something, even if it is just that tiny bit of effort. Otherwise they shouldn't have been there. [Merl: So you insist that everyone does something.] Yeah, mmm. I mean if they don't necessarily want to do that particular forfeit then they've just got to model something, and they can do that over their clothes, and I'm sorry, you can't be that shy. You can just put on the bra over your top and that's it, it's done. (Justine)

It is tempting at this point to link this embarrassment to the structure of homosociality, and to suggest that some party-goers find 'faking orgasms' difficult or impossible to do because it strays too close to the boundary between homosociality and homosexuality: sitting in a room full of women making orgasmic moaning sounds might feel like too risky an activity for some women. Pretending to fake an orgasm may also blur other boundaries and provoke other anxieties. Alongside Dawn's and others' jokes that 'we've all had to fake it', such games are also accompanied by joking comments that 'now you know what your friend sounds like when she's having an orgasm' (or even, in the case of past or present flatmates, that they know already because they've heard each others' orgasms through the walls). Such jokes and comments highlight the stylised nature of the performance: not only do all 'faked orgasms' performed at parties sound the same, but they apparently also sound the same as real (or real fake) orgasms overheard by flatmates. As Jackson and Scott (2000) suggest, the fact that the cries and moans which accompany heterosexual women's orgasms tend to sound the same and to follow the same vocal pattern in itself suggests that we are dealing here precisely with a *performance*: the way in which orgasm is represented to one's male partner is not simply a spontaneous outburst of pleasure but is a ritualised and codified expression, even when the orgasm itself is genuine. Knowing the 'right' noises to make to 'fake an orgasm' is itself a site of homosocial gender identification, and one which paradoxically acknowledges the artificiality of the supposedly 'natural' practices of the female erogenous body. In this sense 'faking an orgasm' for the entertainment of one's female friends is more 'real' than faking an orgasm for one's male partner – and throws into question the 'real-ness' of the sounds one might make for one's partner while *really* having an orgasm.

The homosocial body's tactile pleasures

The tactile pleasures available at parties can be broadly divided into two main groupings: physical contact between party-goers, and physical contact with Ann Summers products, chiefly during the kit demonstration. Perhaps more than any other kind of pleasure, physical contact between party-goers is located right at the border between the homosocial and the homosexual. As we saw in Chapter 2, party-goers can often be very physically affectionate with each other, especially when they are drunk: in Sarah's words, 'most of the time they all mess about sort of kissing and cuddling each other and, like, getting on top of each other, you know, that – they go over the top with it.' Many popular party games also require physical contact between players. Several games, for example, involve teams of players dressing each other in silly outfits, whether these be 'sexy' outfits made out of dustbin liners (the supermodel game), baggy old underwear sets complete with stockings and suspenders (the scarecrow game), or pairs of old tights (the tights game):

> Um, you have two teams, and they each have a pair of tights, and going down the line in order they've got to put the tights on, over their shoes, over their clothes, and basically as long as it – they can get it to their knees and they stretch it the rest of the way, it's just got to go over their hips, and then take them off, pass them to the next one, and on and on. Um, the only rule is they can't sit down, but they can help the other members of their team as much as they like. So you've got one woman holding her up and the other one pulling them up and [Merl laughs] it's – it gets really funny [laughs]. And the state of the tights at the end you don't want to know! [Laughter.] (Justine)

However, this physical contact can also be a source of lesbophobic anxiety at parties. For example, the eruptions of lesbophobic anxiety discussed in Chapter 2 were either prompted by physical contact between guests (the Walnut Whip game at Helen's party) or prevented such contact in subsequent games (the orange-under-the-chin game at Sarah's party). At a party held in North London, Dawn gave her guests a forfeit to do *en masse* and even before she had told them what it was she reassured them that it would not involve 'touching anybody else'. Given that the erogenous female body is constructed at Ann Summers parties as the recipient of male technique – and in particular that its external zones are stimulated by stroking or rubbing – these anxieties not only stem from the nature of the homosocial-homosexual continuum, but more specifically reveal the (actual or threateningly potential) ghosting of the homosocial body's tactile pleasures by those of the erogenous body.

This ghosting is at its most intense however during physical contact not with people but with products – especially the sex toys, oils and lotions which play such a key role for the erogenous body. Vibrators cause particular difficulties: they are so obviously *sexual* in design and purpose that many party-goers are embarrassed or anxious during encounters with them – specifically about *touching* or *handling* them:

> Some are [embarrassed], you know, and they're sort of like – they sit there [Merl laughs] and they go [gesture/facial expression] and they go 'Oh no, I can't touch that!', you know. [. . .] [Laughter.] You know, 'Oh I can't touch that, I don't want to touch – oh, it's horrible!' [Merl: So they just don't want to like touch it?] But it's sort of like – I went to one, I hadn't been doing it long, I went to one and there was this girl there, well, girl, she was – I'd say she was about thirty, thirty-five, 'Oh! I couldn't go and touch a vibrator!' [Merl laughs.] And in the end she was sitting there playing with it all night for about an hour! (Melanie)

> Some people, they're like 'Ooh, this is nice', and they 're, like, putting it on all different parts of their body and then pass it round. Some of – you get a crowd, and it's like a relay. They'll sort of hold it, and without even looking, pass it to the next person. [. . .] But yeah, sometimes, they – they pass it round quicker than I can get batteries in the next one. (Lucy)

Demonstration of these products at parties therefore poses a peculiar problem: these products above all others are addressed directly to the erogenous body as such, and yet they must be demonstrated, described and even in some sense 'tried out' in a homosocial setting. Indeed some party organisers simply choose not to demonstrate any vibrators at parties because of the difficulty and embarrassment they can cause: Cathy, for example, rarely demonstrated any vibrators, even though she was widely regarded by both party-goers and fellow party organisers as unusually adventurous and uninhibited in relation to games and forfeits. At many of the parties I observed, demonstrating and 'trying out' vibrators consisted solely of looking at them while they were switched on, and usually (though not always) of touching them with one's hand or, more often, just with one's fingertips. Some party organisers also find ways to introduce their customers to physical contact with working vibrators by using them in party games:

> Um, then we played, um, pass-the-vibrator between their legs while it was turned on. And they all thought that was incredibly weird. Because

I don't think any of them had actually felt a vibrator when it was on. And, um, so that was good. I sort of did it with the vibrator between their legs, and then they had the massage ball that I've got between their neck because it's very fluffy and very easy to pass. Um, and that turned on full blast is really, really strong. (Cherry)

In this way Cherry's customers are able to feel a working vibrator – if not on the erogenous zones, then at any rate near them.

However, some party organisers negotiate with this tension between the homosocial setting and explicitly sexual products with an ingenious tactic which deliberately brings about the ghosting of the homosocial body by the erogenous body. (Indeed, guests who have been to Ann Summers parties before will sometimes make this suggestion themselves if their party organiser does not do so.) The most common form of this is the deliberate ghosting of the nose by the clitoris: the only time I observed Cathy demonstrating any vibrators at a party, she instructed everyone to try the vibrator by holding it against the tip of their nose because 'they say that the sensation you get on the end of your nose is the same as the sensation you get down there'. The acceptability of the nose for trying out vibrators at parties is of course precisely predicated on the fact that the sensation is *not* the same: the nose is a homosocial rather than an erogenous body part, as this quote from Lucy indicates:

I mean, the last party I did, this woman – I was telling them to put it on the end of their nose. I always say to them 'Put it on the end of your nose, that's the second most sensitive part of your body'. And I say like 'Obviously we don't want you to put it on the first sensitive part of the body'. And then, like, the woman that's sitting at the end, I say, 'Because by the time it gets round to [her], it's going to be – you know [laughs], she's not going to want to know'. Like, they normally find that quite funny. But the last one, she was putting it on the end of her nose, then she was putting it in her armpit [laughs]. (Lucy)

Just as the nose is deliberately ghosted by the clitoris, so the armpit is deliberately ghosted by the vagina. This use of the armpit is far less common than that of the nose. It should also be noted that even this attempt to contain the embarrassment or anxiety through deliberate tactics is not always successful, and it is not uncommon for some party-goers to find even this kind of physical contact with vibrators excruciatingly embarrassing. All of this is of course predicated on the smoothing over of differences between women by representing the erogenous body as the same for everyone – sexual pleasure always means having the same sensations in the same places.

There is one interesting variation on this deliberate ghosting which I encountered during my participant observation at a party organised by Joy. This occurred not with vibrators but with the Pleasure Gel, some of the reactions to which on the part of Joy's guests have already been discussed above. The sampling of this product by using it directly on one's own nipples is the only example I encountered of the direct use of products on an erogenous zone at parties. Insofar as the Pleasure Gel can also be used for clitoral massage, this may even be an example of one erogenous zone (the nipples) being ghosted by another (the clitoris) in a homosocial setting. However, during this kit demonstration Joy told an anecdote of a pub party she had once organised where one of the guests, to Joy's amazement, tried out the Pleasure Gel by putting her hand down the inside of her own knickers. This guest had quickly announced 'oh, that works!' and had spent the rest of the evening fidgeting around in her seat. The gales of laughter which greeted this anecdote were a clear indication of the outrageousness of such behaviour. It is also worth bearing in mind of course that both the nipples and (in this isolated and outrageous case) the clitoris are kept firmly hidden under the clothes during these kit demonstrations: the pleasure may be verbally reported to other party-goers, but the erogenous zones themselves are kept very strictly out of sight.

The homosocial body's visual pleasures

There are many visual pleasures available at parties, to be found both in looking at the catalogue and also, much more interactively, in looking at and being looked at by other party-goers. Many feminist theorists and cultural critics have noted that heterosexual femininity is closely bound up with relations of looking – that femininity, in Laura Mulvey's famous phrase, connotes 'to-be-looked-at-ness' (Mulvey 1975). It has also been widely noted in film and media studies that the visual is a primary medium of identification. Many film and media critics have drawn upon the psychoanalytic theory of the 'mirror stage' (Lacan 1989) to suggest that, just as a baby sees itself *as* a 'self' for the first time when looking into a mirror, so adults unconsciously 'see' themselves in film or photographic images with which they identify. Both the baby and the adult are of course mistaken: the 'baby' in the mirror is not really 'me' as a baby, any more than the image in the magazine is really 'me' as an adult. In both cases the image is more perfect, more complete, and altogether less messy, disorganised and untogether than my own inner experience of myself. My recognition of 'self' in the image is always a *mis*recognition, and an idealised one at that. Given that femininity as such is also about being visible, the play of identification and idealisation in looking at images may be particularly intense for women looking at other women (Doane 1987, Winship 1987).

Party organisers usually put some time aside during parties for party-goers to spend looking at the catalogues. Indeed catalogues are constantly looked at and referred to throughout the kit demonstration and are often returned to intermittently throughout the evening. The glossy photographic images of women in Ann Summers lingerie invite readers' identification in the same way as images of women in everyday advertising and magazines. These images are often of women in 'seductive' poses, pouting suggestively at the camera and giving a 'come hither' look which might suggest that they are actually addressed to a heterosexual male rather than a female gaze (Figures 3.1, 5.1, 5.2, 5.3, 5.6). But in inviting female readers to identify with the image, the catalogue is inviting them to 'see' themselves *as* the heterosexually attractive, seductive woman – as the object of male gazes and male desires, the importance of which for feminine gender identification in Ann Summers was discussed in Chapter 3.

However, when these catalogues are looked at during parties – that is, in a homosocial setting rather than by a lone individual – identification with these idealised images is in some respects offset, or even disrupted, by the homosocial identification with the other women in the room. Party-goers often discuss catalogue images amongst themselves and criticise the images of women as unrealistic or artificial. For example, one of Dawn's party-goers in North London commented that 'there's enough lip gloss in here [i.e. in the catalogue] to sink a battleship' – drawing attention to the artificiality of the feminine glamour on display. It is extremely common for party-goers to comment on the 'boobs' of models in the catalogue, specifically on their obvious silicone implants – again drawing attention to the fact that their large breasts 'aren't real'. As a form of 'bitching' about the models, these comments help to cement the gender identification of party-goers as 'real women' with 'real' figures.

This does not mean, however, that party-goers manage to sustain this critique of catalogue images or to resist the tyranny of impossible body ideals more generally, especially in relation to weight and body size. Just because the images are not 'real', this does not mean that party-goers and party organisers do not wish that they *were* real, and indeed that they might attain those impossible ideals themselves. Instead the homosocial awareness of the 'unreality' of catalogue images is caught in tension with a continuing identification with them as ideals. A neat example of this tension occurred during one of Dawn's unit meetings, during which Dawn referred to the flame-red Siren (part of the Glamour range of Ann Summers clothing) as 'that fantastic dress' (Figure 4.4). One of the party organisers replied to this that if she were to wear Siren she would 'look like a string of sausages' (because she would be too thin for it), and Dawn then added that if she were to wear it herself she would 'look like Mr Blobby gone wrong' (because she would be too fat for it). Everybody laughed along with these comments – but neither comment dampened any woman's enthusiasm for the dress.

Party-goers often take photographs of each other at parties, and on special occasions such as hen nights may even make video recordings. Photographs and video recordings also feature at special events for party organisers themselves, all of which usually also involve some form of 'dressing up'. The most important example of this is the catalogue launch, which is always a fancy dress event; many party organisers and unit organisers lavish vast amounts of care and planning on their costumes, and admiring, being admired for and taking photographs of the final costumes are among the chief pleasures of the launch itself; as Joy said of a previous catalogue launch, 'you could have stood on stage and looked at all the costumes for hours'. A training workshop I observed around Hallowe'en was also a fancy dress event, as well as an opportunity for party organisers to observe and participate in different ways to 'dress up' one's party guests in Ann Summers lingerie. Many party organisers regard this 'dressing up' of party-goers as an essential selling technique:

> [Merl: So it sounds like the best – or maybe not the best way, but a really good way to get things to sell is to have them and get people to try them, rather than just look at them in the catalogue.] Yeah. It's like the – with the underwear, the silver range, when they brought that in in July, um, I ordered it straight away. 'Cause I'd saw it at the catalogue launch, and I saw it in the book [i.e. catalogue], and in the book it looks nothing compared to when you've actually got it in your hand. 'Cause you can see how nice the material is, you can see it glitters, and if you've just got a picture of it, it's flat, you can't see the beauty of it. So it – it does help if you've got the stuff there that they can look at. Especially if it's nice, it's like the, um – the silver and the zebra – zebra print. If you've got them people can see them, actually pick them up and have a look at them and feel them, and they know that they're good and they look nice. (Joy)

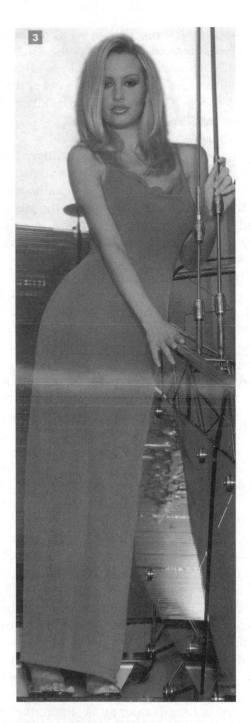

Figure 4.4 Siren dress, from the Ann Summers catalogue autumn/winter 1999

[. . .N]ow I've started just ordering a few of the men's pants and bits, you know, 'cause nobody's ordered that yet, so I thought 'Well why aren't they ordering that? Is it 'cause they can't actually see it?' So I'll order some of them. [. . .] I'd like to get a lot of the things out of the catalogue so I can actually show people. 'Cause as I say, I do definitely think you earn more out of it that way. (Vanessa)

The 'modelling' of Ann Summers clothing and lingerie is therefore often one of the most important features of parties, and occurs in the context not just of games and forfeits but also of kit demonstrations. Sometimes this modelling is formalised: for example, at the student union party Dawn had already arranged for a number of volunteers to dress up and model certain items on stage; Cathy's home party also featured a pre-arranged modelling session with volunteers dressing in and showing certain items to the other party-goers. Sometimes party organisers may use themselves as models in a semi-formal way, as we have seen with Helen in Chapter 2. However by far the most frequent occasions for modelling are much more informal. Party organisers often invite and actively encourage party-goers to try on items of clothing or lingerie during kit demonstrations, and also often have their guests put on items of lingerie – usually over their clothes – as a part of games or forfeits. Thus as we have already seen, Justine says that when some women are too embarrassed to 'fake an orgasm', she will let them off with the lighter or less difficult forfeit of wearing some Ann Summers lingerie over their own clothes. Dressing up and 'modelling' at parties is regarded as a relatively low-risk form of homosocial fun, particularly when the lingerie is worn over one's own everyday clothes. Indeed, paradoxically it is lingerie which is most often worn over the clothes when modelled by party guests, whereas the dresses and other clothing outfits in the Glamour range are more likely to be worn 'properly', with guests withdrawing to bathrooms or bedrooms to change into the outfits and then coming back to the party to show themselves to other guests. This distinction between dresses and lingerie is drawn during modelling sessions at parties not just by those doing the modelling but also by onlookers. One party organiser at a party I observed in south-east London explicitly instructed her guests to try on the dresses and other Glamour items 'properly' rather than over their clothes. In the case of the lingerie modelled over the clothes, much of the party-goers' conversation revolved around whether *husbands and boyfriends* would like them; in the case of the Glamour range, the conversation was about whether the *women themselves* liked them.

This makes clear that the reason lingerie must be worn over the clothes by party guests is that a homosocial body wearing lingerie is closely ghosted by an erogenous body in the same outfit. As described above, the heterosexual female erogenous body's own sensations are organised around the breasts, mouth and genitals; but the erogenous body's *visibility to others* as such is organised around a heterosexual male gaze, and this gaze may focus on body parts which are not necessarily important to the female erogenous body's own pleasure. Thus for example the female erogenous body locates pleasure specifically in the nipples, but the male heterosexual gaze is interested in the breasts in general rather than just the nipples in particular. Hence of course the concern with breast size – whether of catalogue models or 'real' women – a topic which has nothing to do with the erogenous sensations of the nipples and everything to do with the preferences of a (real or imagined) heterosexual male gaze: as Beth told me during her interview, 'anything, basically, any sort of bra that makes their boobs look bigger than they are [will sell]. That's what I normally find, they go 'Cor that'd make my boobs look big, here, what do you reckon?'' The male gaze is also interested in body parts which do not feature in the female body's erogenous zones at all: a discussion at Helen's party of whether particular Ann Summers bras would enhance 'your boobs' was brought to a close when one guest wryly commented that 'if you're wearing suspenders they don't really pay much attention to your boobs', even though the female erogenous body represented at Ann Summers parties does not organise its pleasures around its legs or thighs at all.

One of the consequences of this is that the homosocial pleasure of trying on and admiring lingerie at Ann Summers parties is ghosted by this heterosexual male gaze, such that when guests are asked for comments or advice on items being modelled by their friends they are implicitly being asked to look with a heterosexual male gaze *as well as* with a female homosocial gaze. When partygoers ask each other 'Cor that'd make my boobs look big, here, what do you reckon?' or wonder aloud whether each other's husbands or boyfriends will like particular items, the homosocial gaze is being ghosted by a heterosexual male gaze, and the homosocial body's visibility being ghosted by that of the erogenous body. This grants women power to judge one another's feminine appearance and attractiveness in terms of its 'market value' to men. Insofar as such modelling and judging is about finding outfits to look heterosexually attractive – i.e. to look nice for the benefit of men – it is a key example of female homosociality helping women who serve men's interests. A further consequence of this ghosting is that modelling and looking at lingerie often strays close to the boundary between homosocial and homosexual. This can be the prompt for a great deal of laughing and joking, such as when one of Joy's party guests, modelling a revealing top for an appreciative audience, asked 'do you fancy me?' and everyone burst out laughing. It can also be the cause of anxiety: as we saw in Chapter 2, when the homosociality at Helen's party 'went wrong' during one of the party games, Helen felt that she had to issue the proviso that 'I'm not a lesbian or anything' before modelling any lingerie for her guests. In fact the idea of women at Ann Summers parties modelling lingerie for each other is one of the lesbian spectres which Helen tries to exorcise by attributing it to men:

> [. . .E]very man wants to go to [an Ann Summers party], don't they? They want to be a fly on the wall at one. [. . .] [Merl: What is it about it – what do you think they want to go for? [. . .]] They want to see the underwear. And I – I suppose they think that we model it. I reckon they do. Yeah. (Helen)

The irony which Helen has not spotted here is that of course women do 'model it' – indeed Helen herself often models lingerie for her guests. Women dressing up for each other at Ann Summers parties is *not* just a male fantasy, but a powerful and important site of feminine gender identification. Helen's description of it *as* a male fantasy can be read as an attempt on her part to disavow the homoerotic implications of this common homosocial pursuit.

Thus if the sex toys, lotions and potions listed in the Ann Summers catalogue are oriented around the erogenous female body's *sensations*, one might say that the lingerie is oriented around its *visibility* to a heterosexual male gaze. There is little if any conversation about the *feel* of the lingerie, of whether it is soft and silky or rough and scratchy, for example: lingerie is regarded as a source of men's visual pleasure rather than of women's tactile pleasure:

> But um, you know, but – most of the stuff is all right. There's – as I say, there's a couple of things that I personally wouldn't wear, but you can see that other people would for a laugh or, you know, *for their husband or their partner* or whatever, you know, they – you could see that they would. (Sarah. My emphasis.)

Diane even says that 'men like – know what they like to see their ladies in. And you normally get the women ordering what their men have told them to order'.

This does not of course mean that lingerie is simply bought with men's preferences in mind: the display, choosing and consumption of lingerie in Ann Summers settings is in fact far more complex than Diane's statement implies. The role and significance of lingerie for women themselves as well as for their menfolk are the basis of the discussion in the next chapter.

Summary and Conclusion

Gender identification in Ann Summers settings includes corporeal identification, such that being 'one of the girls' means having particular bodily knowledges, experiences and pleasures. Bodies are multi-faceted things, at once physical entities and discursive constructions. Female bodies in Ann Summers settings are also both erogenous and homo-social, and these two facets of the body interact and exist in tension with each other. The female erogenous body is constructed as fund-amentally receptive and is organised around a small number of erogenous zones: the receptively interior zones of mouth and vagina, and the receptively exterior zones of nipples and clitoris. The homosocial body is organised mainly around the senses of sight, touch and taste and around the use of the voice, with the mouth being the most privileged homsocial organ. The mouth is also the site of the most intense ghost-ing of and by the erogenous body through use and representations of sweets (especially chocolate), fellatio and orgasm, although such ghosting also occurs at other sites. All of these senses and pleasures are fractured by the lesbophobic boundary of female homosociality, such that visual pleasure in other women, for example, is available only by identifying with a real or imagined heterosexual male gaze. Moreover both the erogenous and the homosocial body serve the interests of men as well as, or sometimes instead of, those of the women themselves. In the case of the erogenous body, this includes the preservation of phallocentric definitions of sex, whether penetrative vaginal intercourse or fellatio, despite their apparent inadequacy for clitoral orgasm or oral pleasure. In the case of the homosocial body, it includes the containment of women's aggression against men or disappointment with men in the form of the 'affectionate' post-feminist joke that 'men are useless but we love them anyway'.

The point at which homosocial bodies and erogenous bodies defin-itively converge in Ann Summers settings is of course the point of sale, when the homosocial body hands over its cash or credit card to pay for items to equip the erogenous body. As we saw in Chapter 3, heterosexual women's paradoxical status as both subjects and objects of desire includes the use of 'sexy' consumer goods such as lingerie to initiate men's sexual activity by 'turning him on'. Thus if the female erogenous body's pleasures are produced by male technique, then 'the girls' can incite and even improve that technique through the judicious use of products such as 'his 'n' hers' vibrators to stimulate the clitoris during vaginal intercourse, or Pleasure Gel or Booby Drops to enhance erotic sensations in the nipples, or lingerie and fantasy outfits just to 'get him going' in the first place. The consumerist ethos of post-feminism has a particular piquancy in the case of Ann Summers, where the sense of entitlement to sexual pleasure as a consumer good takes on a strangely literal form. Men's sexual 'equipment' is the phallus, or at any rate their pretensions to it; 'the girls" sexual equipment is their Ann Summers collection.

Classy Lingerie

five

> Sexual properties are as inseparable from class properties as the yellowness of a lemon is from its acidity [. . .]. This is why there are as many ways of realizing femininity as there are classes and class fractions. (Bourdieu 1984: 107–8)

We saw in Chapter 2 that the homosocial gender identifications involved in being 'one of the girls' are also ethnic identifications, and that to be 'one of the girls' is also to be white. Chapter 3 also explored some of the ways in which this whiteness is played out in homosocial talk about, and preferences for, 'realistic' sex toys. This chapter unravels some of the complexities of *class* identifications in Ann Summers settings, and some of the ways these are played out in talk about, and preferences for, lingerie and other consumer goods. The first part of this chapter discusses the inseparability of class and gender, and the ways in which social class infuses the femininity of Ann Summers party organisers and partygoers, particularly through distinctions of taste. The chapter then moves on to a more detailed examination of the place of class in the women's consumption decisions and taste preferences during Ann Summers parties. The world of Ann Summers is a world of taste distinctions: as we will see, femininity is as inseparable from class in Ann Summers settings as the blackness of a basque is from its polyester.

Peeling the Lemon

Any discussion of class in Ann Summers settings faces an immediate problem: to what social class do Ann Summers party-goers and party organisers belong? Class is notoriously difficult to define, despite the evident inequality and stratification of contemporary society. How many classes are there, and how do we decide who fits into which class?

177

Is your social class decided by your occupation, your income, the type of housing you live in, your educational level, the opportunities and 'life chances' open to you, your leisure pursuits, some combination of these, or something else entirely? These questions may be even more difficult for women, particularly for those whose main occupation is unpaid labour in the home. Two thirds of the women interviewed for this book had no paid work other than party organising. Are party organisers, housewives or full-time mothers skilled, semi-skilled, unskilled, or professional workers?

These difficulties of definition and criteria are reflected in interviewees' responses to the question 'What class would you say you belong to?' (see Figure 1.3 in Chapter 1). As we saw in Chapter 1, only six of the fifteen interviewees felt able to identify themselves unequivocally as either middle or working class. Others chose a category after some hesitation and/or prompting from me; some came up with their own self-descriptions, such as 'normal' or 'common' or 'never got any money'; Joy and Laura resisted self-classification altogether. Superficially this may appear to mirror the interviewees' reluctance and/or difficulty in recognising themselves as white or as heterosexual; as discussed in Chapter 1, no sociological categories of any kind seem to feature very prominently in most interviewees' self-perceptions. The crucial difference, however, is that failure to recognise oneself as white or heterosexual is a manifestation of relative social privilege. Both whiteness and hetero-sexuality, as privileged social categories, are treated as 'normal', defined against a pathologised or stigmatised Other; they are so taken for granted that heterosexuals and white people often find it hard to conceive of themselves as even having a sexual orientation or an ethnic-ity at all (Dyer 1997, Frankenburg 1993). But interviewees' difficulty in recognising their class location – indeed, in some cases, in recognising even that they may have a class location – does not come from a position of privilege.

To take one of the most common criteria of class positioning, that of type of accommodation, for example, only five of the interviewees were owner-occupiers; most of the others lived in council or housing association accommodation. To take another criterion, that of occup-ation, two of the five owner-occupiers had no paid work other than party organising: both were married and financially dependent upon their husbands, who worked in the jewellery trade and as a public utility shift worker respectively. The remaining three worked as either secretaries or hairdressers. Of those who lived in council or housing association accommodation, only one was in current paid employment as an office worker; the others' previous paid jobs had been as dancers, nursery nurses, packers, shop assistants, bar workers, factory workers and bank clerks. Whatever self-designation the interviewees make in terms of social class, clearly none of them does so from a position of material wealth, professional status or class privilege. 'Middle class' at most here would seem to mean *lower* middle class. In this respect the class profile of interviewees chimes with existing sociological discussions of direct selling, including catalogue selling, as the province of 'working- and lower-middle-class women with time on their hands, little money and a network of other women living in similar positions with whom they could use the catalogues to gain friends' (Edwards 2000: 116) – although exactly how much time such women really have 'on their hands' with small children at home is rather debatable.

This raises the question of why working-class and lower-middle-class women should be unable or unwilling to pinpoint their own class positions as such. I would suggest two possible and related explanations for this. Firstly, as Beverley Skeggs's (1997) ethnographic work with working-class women has suggested, the label 'working-class' may be particularly problematic for women because of its highly stigmatising gendered and sexual connotations. Skeggs suggests that the label 'working-class' was originally applied to women (and men) as an act of surveillance by the middle classes during the nineteenth century. The 'working classes' were those who needed to be watched, restrained and 'civilised'; working-class women were regarded as ignorant, dirty and irresponsible, a stigmatisation which persists today in public debates about single mothers, national or moral decline, and the so-called crisis of the family. Thus to be identified as a working-class woman still risks associations with being a 'slag' and/or a bad mother, and Skeggs argues that the working-class women in her study paradoxically refused to recognise their own class position while at the same time struggling to define themselves against it:

> [T]he label working class when applied to women has been used to signify all that is dirty, dangerous and without value. In the women's claims for a caring/respectable/responsible personality class was rarely directly figured but was constantly present. It was the structuring absence. Yet whilst they made enormous efforts to distance themselves from the label of working class, their class position (alongside their other social positions of gender, race and sexuality), was the omnipresent underpinning which informed and circumscribed their ability *to be*. (Skeggs 1997: 74)

Secondly, and as this quote from Skeggs suggests, there is a distinction to be drawn between social class as a category – usually imposed by others from the outside – and social class as a lived experience. This is best illustrated by Joy's response to the question 'What class would you say you belong to?':

> Oh God knows! [Merl: Everyone says that! [Laughs.]] [Sighs.] Well, I'm definitely not upper class. [Laughter.] Definitely not upper class! Um . . . [Merl: 'God knows' could be the answer, that's a perfectly acceptable answer. You don't have to say one if you don't know . . .] I don't know. I don't really know what the – the, um – how they work out what class you are supposed to be in, or what class you are in. (Joy)

'What class you are in' for Joy is something 'they' work out, rather than something that *she* lives. And yet Joy's everyday life is no less saturated by class than that of any of the other interviewees. She and her partner (a shift worker) live in a council flat, and both of them take casual night work as well as holding down full-time jobs – indeed, if one includes Joy's party organising she actually has three jobs. Her position in terms of wealth, income, living conditions, leisure time and social status in this sense certainly informs and circumscribes her ability to be.

There are also other, less categorical and perhaps even more intimate ways in which class infuses Joy's everyday life, her sense of self and her relations with others. Although Joy struggles to place herself in any of 'their' *categories*, she is, like all the interviewees, an expert on the everyday *processes* of class distinction and class identification, and especially on the inseparability of class from gender. Mere moments after our discussion of class, my final interview question ('Where would you like to be in five years' time?') elicited a fluent description of the niceties of class distinction and 'proper' femininity:

> Hopefully [I'll be] married with a house. [Laughter.] [. . .] Talking to my dad, and like – 'cause my step-sister's getting married on Saturday, and he's like 'Well when are you going to get married?' 'When we can afford it'. He said 'Why?' I said 'Well are you going to pay for it?' He went 'No', I said 'Well then, when we can afford it!' But it's going to cost a fortune, 'cause I've seen the dress I want. [Merl: Oh God, that's fatal.] [Joy whispers something and Merl laughs.] I took one of my friends to see it, well it was actually my other half's best mate's girlfriend at the time. Um, we walked in – it's in a wedding shop over at [a shopping mall]. And we walked in there, and there's all these lovely flouncy frilly things which

aren't me. Um, and I've pulled this dress out [laughs] and I've gone 'That's the dress I want!' She's looked at it and she went 'You wouldn't wear that'. I went 'I would'. 'No you wouldn't'. 'Oh yes I would!' Um, it's black and white zebra print fur material bodice, white net skirt with black bows all over it [Merl: Oh it sounds amazing], and she's gone to me 'You wouldn't wear that'. I'm like 'Yes I would, I'd wear it just for the reaction I'd get from my family!' 'Cause they'd be like 'Oh what is she wearing?' 'Cause they'd all expect me to go, like, frilly and loads of lace, and that's not me. But this dress is just like – [Merl: It's everything – I can definitely see you in one of them.] Oh yeah. This dress is like 'Wow!' I've already thought out what he's going to wear. Black trousers, um, hopefully black velvet three-quarter length coat, and a zebra-print cravat. And I've also had the idea of maybe having the photographs in – or some photographs in black and white. And I mean, I was thinking, I said to [indecipherable] maybe saying to all the guests 'Come in black and white'. [Merl: That'd be nice.] But I don't think most of them'd like it. [Merl: Oh really?] Yeah. 'Cause I – I know most of my – well, FX'll be fine cause she wears black anyway. [Merl laughs.] Um, but know a lot of people don't – they like wearing colours for weddings. [Merl: Yeah, that's true, and they like to get the old hats out and stuff don't they?] But I'm thinking about what flowers do I go for, do I have black and white flowers? Can you have black and white flowers for a wedding? And I think, 'Well why not?' [Merl: Course you can.] And um, it's do I have my hair up, do I have my hair down, or . . .? Loads – loads of things like that. But the amount of people I've said about the dress, they're like 'You wouldn't wear [inaudible]?' 'Oh yes!' [Merl: Oh yeah, I know that you would. I don't need to be told twice. I can see you wearing it. Definitely.] [. . .] But I think it'll be the zebra print. Either that or some lairy colour. [Merl laughs.] They've got some really nice lilac and purple dresses, I'm like I could go really mad and go for purple. But then I think my mother would kill me. [Merl laughs.] The zebra dress – the zebra-print top have got it – it – the first time I saw it I was like 'Ah, want it!' [Merl laughs.] Seven hundred pounds. [Merl: Oh wow.] And it's gorgeous. It – it is *the* dress. So hopefully this time within five years I'll have worn it. [Merl: And have it in your wardrobe, stashed away.] Yeah. I'll never get rid of it. I'll never get rid of it. Keep it forever. (Joy)

A wedding dress is saturated with meanings. It connotes heterosexuality, femininity, respectability, social status, adulthood, glamour, romance and fantasy, not least the aspirational fairy-tale fantasy of being 'princess for a day'. It is also for most brides the single most expensive item of clothing they will ever possess, and constitutes a substantial proportion of the overall cost of the wedding (Ingraham 1999, Friese 2001). Joy's discussion of her wedding dress – which she has picked out before the wedding date has even been set – betrays the ways in which class informs and circumscribes her life. She cannot yet set a wedding date because she and her partner cannot afford a wedding, despite having five jobs between them. Joy also takes it for granted that her wedding dress will be shop-bought rather than custom-made, and indeed that it will be bought in a shopping mall rather than in Knightsbridge or Mayfair: these material conditions of the wedding plan are so taken for granted that they do not even register *as* conditions in Joy's description. But Joy's description does register the subtleties of what she can and cannot get away with in relation to her friends and family, especially her mother. The dividing line between the acceptably outrageous and the unacceptably lairy is fine indeed, but Joy negotiates it with aplomb: furry zebra print is on one side (just), but purple is definitely on the other. The demands of a respectable working-class wedding, represented by her family's tastes – lace, frills, 'nice' colours – are weighed against Joy's desire for a working-class fashion statement, and she negotiates between them to find the right note for her own brand of 'un-frilly', (hetero)sexually liberated femininity without going *too* far in the direction of the unrespectable.

In fact Joy is relatively unusual in that she likes to play with working-class codes of feminine respectability with her fashion sense more generally. She would often tell me with great relish of the disapproval which regularly greeted her tattoos and mini-dresses at office parties, and of the deliberate 'tackiness' of her catalogue launch outfit. In effect, Joy challenges the conventions of class and gender by flouting them, deliberately wearing outfits which risk association with the unrespectable or even the vulgar. Her excited anticipation of her family's shock at the zebra-print wedding dress is yet another challenge to working-class convention. Paradoxically, of course, such challenges only work because they take place *within* a working-class context: in the extremely unlikely event of its being worn by, say, a society lady or media baron's daughter, that £700 mall-bought zebra-print furry dress would be a very different kind of classed and gendered fashion statement.

Social class, then, infuses women's (and men's) everyday lives, and there is a certain kind of 'know-how' of class according to which we all make judgements about what to wear, how to speak, how to behave, and about other people's dress, speech and behaviour. In Pierre Bourdieu's famous phrase, 'Taste classifies, and it classifies the classifier' (1984: 6). In other words, our everyday tastes and preferences mark out our class

status to other people, and other people's judgements about our tastes
mark out their class status in turn. This is most fruitfully understood
as a process: tastes do not simply reflect a fixed or pre-existing class
position, such that one can simply 'read off' a person's class status from
her favourite TV programme; tastes rather *make* class distinctions – and
indeed form the basis of certain kinds of class conflict.[1] Thus for
example a certain kind of hairstyle does not simply reveal that one is
already 'common', but actively *makes* one common in the eyes of those
who consider themselves socially superior or more culturally 'savvy';
and conversely, other people's judgements of one's hairstyle as 'common'
may lead one to judge those people in turn as 'snobs' or 'pretentious'
(cf. Gimlin 1996). Designations of oneself or (more likely) others as
common or snobbish do not constitute systematic sociological classific-
ations, but they are nonetheless a very acute form of what Bourdieu calls
the 'practical mastery' or 'practical "science"' of class in everyday life:

> The practical mastery of classification has nothing in common with the
> reflexive mastery that is required in order to construct a taxonomy that
> is simultaneously coherent and adequate to social reality. The practical
> 'science' of positions in social space is the competence presupposed by
> the art of behaving *comme il faut* with persons and things that have and
> give 'class' ('smart' or 'unsmart'), finding the right distance, by a sort of
> practical calculation, neither too close ('getting familiar') nor too far
> ('being distant'), playing with objective distance by emphasizing it (being
> 'aloof', 'stand-offish') or symbolically denying it (being 'approachable',
> 'hobnobbing'). It in no way implies the capacity to situate oneself
> explicitly in the classification (as so many surveys on social class ask
> people to do), still less to describe this classification in any systematic
> way and state its principles. (Bourdieu 1984: 472)

Ann Summers meetings and parties are heavily freighted with these
processes of class differentiation through tastes and preferences. Indeed,
the remainder of this chapter will argue that tastes and preferences form
the basis of homosocial class identifications which are inseparable from
feminine gender identifications in Ann Summers settings. But as many
readers (particularly British readers) will doubtless already be aware,

1. In fact Bourdieu (1984) has been widely criticised for producing exactly this kind
of static, deterministic analysis of the relationship between taste and class in his empirical
work on the subject, despite the stress on process and dynamic play in his conceptual
discussion (e.g. du Gay 1996, Gronow 1997, Skeggs 1997).

these class distinctions are not just made within the world of Ann Summers; Ann Summers itself, as a brand name, is saturated with connotations of taste and class. Some examples from my own field notes will illustrate what I mean here:

1. I am having a conversation with a friend who is asking me how the research is going. This friend is a fellow academic, a white lesbian in her forties. I tell her that I hope to go to a lot of Ann Summers parties during the next few months. She remarks, in tones of heavy irony, 'You'll meet a nice kind of people like that!' (October 1999)

2. I am having a conversation with a white gay male friend, a fellow academic in his late twenties. He tells me that an Ann Summers shop has recently opened in his local area, and that as he was walking past it one day recently he overheard a giggly conversation between two women who were daring each other to go inside. One of the women had wanted to go into the shop; the second woman had said she couldn't possibly go in because someone might see her; the first had replied that she shouldn't be so silly, no-one was watching to see who was going into the Ann Summers shop. The women walked past the shop without going inside. As he is telling this story my colleague and I laugh at the silliness of these two women. I then ask him if he has been into the shop himself. He replies that he has, but that he did not linger to look around because it would lower what he calls his 'cred' in all kinds of ways if anyone were to see him in an Ann Summers shop. (February 2000)

These taste judgements, which party organisers would doubtless regard as snobbish and pretentious respectively, also demonstrate the inseparability of class from sexual connotations: they position Ann Summers as a vulgar ('nice kind of people') and unsophisticated (no 'cred') brand of *heterosexuality*, in implicit contrast to the sophistication, cultural savvy, political self-awareness and intellectual credentials of academic lesbians and gay men. My friends were simultaneously making both a class distinction and a sexual distinction between themselves and the women who go to Ann Summers shops and parties. As this chapter argues below, sexual judgements are equally closely bound to taste judgements *within* Ann Summers settings. But my own milieu in terms of class and sexual cultures, represented here by my queer academic friends, casts judgement from the outside on the whole of Ann Summers as unsophisticated, unstylish, 'uncred'-ible, cheap, common – as, in a word, *naff*. Such judgements are not simply made from fixed positions of class privilege – both of these friends, like me, have working-class or lower middle-class origins and attained their current middle-class status through higher education and the academic profession – but rather actively *produce* class distinctions as taste distinctions. One of the things that separates us from our working- or lower middle-class roots is our current disdain for Ann Summers (and perhaps this also separates us from our heterosexual 'roots', insofar as many lesbians, bisexuals and gay men regard themselves as heterosexual by default during childhood until they 'discover' their sexuality (Plummer 1995)). In my own case I feel the separation to be particularly precarious: both of my sisters have been Ann Summers party organisers; if higher education had not separated me from my class origins I might well have done the same. I felt this very acutely on the rare occasions during participant observation when I attended parties as an invited guest rather than simply as a researcher. On the one hand, I simply did not want to order any of the products, particularly the fashion and lingerie items, because they were not to my current taste. On the other hand, I knew how rude and even hurtful it might be to my research participants to say so. And underneath all of this was the dimly audible note of my teenaged, heterosexual, lower middle-class self who probably would have liked to buy something after all.

'Taste classifies, and it classifies the classifier.' My classification of Joy and other interviewees as working-class or lower-middle-class is inseparably bound to my own stake in distinctions of class, sexuality and femininity. This is perhaps even more the case in relation to the parties I observed where, in the absence of formal interviews or classification data, my judgements of party-goers' class status were based entirely on my own 'practical mastery' of class through accent, interior décor, dress and behaviour. This has caused me many anxious moments, not least because I know that some participants will think that I am not merely wrong to call them working-class, but actually *rude* to do so. To call a woman 'working-class' on the basis of her tastes, appearance and conduct is potentially hurtful, precisely because of the connotations of the vulgar, the common and the unrespectable which deters many women from naming themselves working-class in the first place. This is what Skeggs calls 'the emotional politics of class' (1997: 90).

Homosocial Underwear

Strictly speaking, nobody *needs* underwear. In fact underwear as we know it today, in the form of underpants, knickers and bras, did not develop until the nineteenth or, in the case of the bra, early twentieth centuries: undergarments before then had mainly been stockings and shifts, worn by both sexes for warmth and comfort (Steele 1985, Wilson 1985, Craik 1994, Wilson-Kovacs 2001). In this sense, as Elizabeth Wilson (1985) points out, underwear is useless clothing, worn purely for the purposes of adornment; what is significant about women's underwear is not so much what it *does* as what it *means*.

Wilson makes this suggestion in the context of a wider argument about fashion and its relationship with capitalism and modernity. For Wilson, fashion is essentially ambiguous:

> For fashion, the child of capitalism, has, like capitalism, a double face. [. . .] We live as far as clothes are concerned a triple ambiguity: the ambiguity of capitalism itself with its great wealth and great squalor, its capacity to create and its dreadful wastefulness; the ambiguity of our identity, of the relation of self to body and self to the world; and the ambiguity of art, its purpose and meaning. (Wilson 1985: 13-15).

Not all commentators share Wilson's conviction that fashion as such is always or necessarily the child of modernity (e.g. Craik 1994), but nevertheless many studies of fashion and dress chart the ambiguities embodied in clothes and our relationships to them. In the case of underwear, several sets of ambiguities have been traced. For Wilson herself, 'the distinction between underwear and outerwear reflects the distinction between the public and the private [. . . and] parallels the late twentieth century ambiguity surrounding privacy, intimacy and sexuality' (1985: 107). Underclothes are simultaneously private (hidden under the clothes) and public (intended to be seen and admired). Indeed, certain fashion styles and leisure pursuits involve the wearing of underclothes as outerclothes: party-goers often debate whether particular bras or basques might be worn to parties or nightclubs, and this is such a common expectation around certain garments that Ann Summers has responded with a specially designated range of 'clubbing' wear (introduced after my participant observation was concluded). Other commentators have suggested that underwear also plays on the ambiguities between concealment and display; between seductiveness and respectability; between eroticism and romance; between the feminine and the sexual; and between the luxurious and the 'cheap' (Steele 1985, Craik 1994).

There have been few if any studies however of the ways in which women negotiate these ambiguities in their everyday practices of choosing and buying underwear. Such practices and negotiations are the subject of the discussion that follows. In the specific context of Ann Summers parties, they are of course homosocial practices and negotiations; and, like all taste judgements, they are also class practices and negotiations. In negotiating these ambiguities, then, women are doing something much more substantial than just choosing a bra or a pair of knickers: they are forging identifications of class, (hetero)sexuality and femininity, and defending their own positions against the judgements of others.

The girls go shopping

The 'girlie shopping trip' is perhaps one of the most common, and most enjoyable, forms of homosocial leisure for women. When Joy chose her wedding dress, she took a female friend with her to see it. The friend's amazed reaction ('You wouldn't wear that!') confirmed that the dress would have the meaning and effect Joy intended, and ratified her taste judgement of the dress as an impressive fashion statement (rather than as, say, pretentiously lavish, or intolerably vulgar). Moreover this ratification was made not in a straightforward act of agreement – Joy's friend does not seem to have *liked* the dress – but in a more complex dynamic of self-recognition and differentiation. Taste judgements and shopping decisions are formed not by isolated individuals, but through group identifications (and dis-identifications) *between* women; the heterosexual meanings of clothes in such contexts are received, decoded and exchanged not between women and men, but amongst women themselves. Party organisers know this very well, and have to develop tactics to deal with it when it threatens to work against them:

I find that if one person buys something then somebody else will. [Merl: Oh right, so they all kind of follow each other.] Yeah. I had a party the other week where, you know the leopard skin bra one, the Wild set, I ordered seven sets of those [laughter]. I mean there was eighteen ladies there but I ordered actually seven of those. And at another party I wouldn't even order one. So they sort of, yeah, they do [Merl: That's really funny!] – they follow on. (Justine)

You get some things that people will look at and just say 'Yuk! [Laughs.] Eurgh! It's red, eurgh, red!' [Merl: [Laughs.] Really, they don't like red things?] No, a lot of people don't like red. But then you'll go to another

party and they'll like – they will all be into the red and they'll all buy
Vamp. It's, um – it's just depends on the individual I suppose. And you'll
find as well that if one person says 'Oh I don't like that – that', you can
see someone looking at it and sort of half liking it, and they'll go 'No, I
don't suppose it is all that'. [Laughs.] I think other people put them off.
So then, you've got to step in and do your sales bit. (Beth)

(Wild and Vamp appear in Figures 5.1 and 5.2 respectively.)

Figure 5.1 Wild lingerie set, from the Ann Summers catalogue autumn/winter
1999

D & DD cups
available in
'Vamp'

page 6

Thong & Brief available

Figure 5.2 Vamp lingerie set, from the Ann Summers catalogue autumn/winter 1999

Although Beth here claims that 'it depends on the individual', all of her examples demonstrate the extent to which taste judgements at parties are formed through group dynamics. It must also be borne in mind that even these group judgements are not made in an aesthetic vacuum, and that Ann Summers parties constitute a whole world of taste and class distinctions. Some markers of taste are provided by the hostess and party-goers themselves, from interior décor to clothes and make-up, from references to popular films and TV shows to choices of background music, and from types of food to types of alcohol. Many other markers of taste are provided by Ann Summers – not just the kit items and catalogues themselves, but also the many competition prizes and promotions, which during my participant observation included a Mediterranean holiday, weekend breaks in Paris and at a Pontins holiday camp, day membership of a health club, Freemans mail order catalogues, and gifts of alcohol such as Sheridans chocolate liqueur, Lambrini sweet white wine, and cinnamon-flavoured cider. Sweet flavours, beauty treatments, romantic destinations and thrifty clothes or holidays are gendered as well as classed, distinguishing working-class and lower middle-class femininities as variously hedonistic, aspirational and domesticated. In effect such prizes and promotions offer opportunities for subtle differentiations (Pontins versus Paris, Sheridans versus cider) within the boundaries of working-class and lower middle-class tastes (Ann Summers is unlikely ever to offer a bottle of Veuve Clicquot or day membership of the Institute of Contemporary Arts). Party organisers themselves – many of whom were already choosing and buying Ann Summers products as party-goers before joining the party plan – implicitly stake out these boundaries with the claim that the Ann Summers product range offers 'something for everybody':

'Cause, like, whenever I've been invited to one, I might not have been invited by the hostess, I might have been invited by the hostess's friend and I've attended. But I've always ordered something, you know. I don't feel obliged to order, but I always want to order something, something new from Ann Summers. You can't go away with not buying anything from Ann Summers. (Helen)

I mean, you go to some parties and everyone will be ordering vibrators and sitting there, like, 'Oh, what one are you getting?', 'Oh I'm getting the all singing and dancing one', and 'Oh I'm just going to get, like, this one to start me off' sort of thing. You know, and – and then you go to other ones where people are just concentrating on the underwear. So it all – you know, 'cause there's – that's the good thing about it, it's got something in the book [i.e. catalogue] for everyone. So um, you know, if people are not interested in the toys then the underwear is really top quality, lovely. (Lucy)

[. . .W]ith the Ann Summers there's new stuff coming out all the time. It's clothes, people like clothes, people like novelties, they like games and toys and things, so there's always something – no-one can say there is nothing they want from Ann Summers, 'cause there's always something for everybody in it. (Laura)

These superficially rather bland statements are also of course acts of identification and exclusion: 'everybody' means not everybody in the whole world, but everybody who counts as 'one of the girls', a grouping which enacts distinctions and exclusions of class as well as of gender, ethnicity and sexuality. 'You can't go away with not buying anything from Ann Summers' is not just a description, but an instruction – part of the 'practical mastery' of homosocial classification at Ann Summers parties.

This then is the context in which partygoers negotiate the ambiguities of lingerie. The ambiguities themselves are multi-layered, and can be presented rather schematically as a list of binary pairs which map onto and interlock with each other, such as:

public	private
sleaze	respectability
display	concealment
luxury	utility
eroticism	domesticity
perversion	normality
sex	romance

Given the extent to which these sets of ambiguities are interwoven, singling out particular themes for discussion is a somewhat artificial task: one may analyse them separately, but they are *lived* simultaneously and often confusedly. For the purposes of analysis I will focus on luxury/ utility, sleaze/respectability, and eroticism/domesticity; but many other pairs of ambiguities inevitably follow in their wake, both practically and analytically.

Luxury/utility

It would be a mistake to assume that the relationship between social class and fashion tastes is simply about buying what one can afford. As Tim Edwards (2000) points out, for example, many unemployed working-class young men in the 1980s considered it important to wear designer label clothing; a similar argument could be made for working-class fashions in trainers in the 1990s. The purchase of non-essential and perhaps expensive items as a 'treat' is a regular feature of everyday shopping practices for working-class and middle-class people alike: according to Daniel Miller (1998), treats are usually bought for a particular individual, often (but not always) the purchaser herself, and are thus distinguished from the ordinary shopping which women usually carry out as part of their unpaid domestic labour for partners and/or children. As we saw in Chapter 2, many party organisers use their sales commission to treat themselves or their families to clothes, holidays, new household décor or other kinds of gift; and when it comes to treating themselves, many party organisers buy themselves clothes, including lingerie or other items from Ann Summers.

> I've always liked Ann Summers underwear, and I've always had quite a lot from parties I've been to. But now I just seem to have an awful lot! [Laughter.] Which is one of the perks of the job. [Laughs.] [Merl: Yeah, definitely. [Laughs.]] Actually having bra and knickers what match! [Laughs.] [Merl: Oh my God! What luxury!] Yeah. [Merl: It is though isn't it?] It is! [Laughter] 'Cause before I done this I had the odd little suit, but it was basically, you know, the washed-out bra and the knickers with all the holes in where you've just like [Merl laughs] – you've had them for, like, six years. [Laughter.] Now I have nice new sets! (Donna)

Party-goers too regard Ann Summers parties as an opportunity to treat themselves to a non-essential purchase; indeed the meaning of the purchase is precisely that it *is* non-essential – that it is a luxury. The expense involved in such luxury purchases is an important part of what defines them *as* luxuries. There were regular complaints throughout my research from party-goers and party organisers alike that much of the Ann Summers lingerie was expensive, but this was by no means always a deterrent:

> [. . .Y]ou get some that will sit there going 'Yeah, well I can get that down the market, and I can get that wherever'. But, um, I know there is stuff that you can get in the high streets or in the shops that are similar to Ann Summers wear, but the prices aren't that much different any more, because they are – the shops – some of the shops are actually dearer than Ann Summers. Whereas you used to be able to get, like, the little padded bras and things cheap in the shops, now they're all glam – glamorised and they're a lot more expensive. But the ones like that, you try and sort of curb them, because it does stop people from buying because they think 'Oh I'll go down the market'. But when they've been down the market they notice they don't get it much – much cheaper, and it's not the same stuff. (Laura)

But, um, we've had quite a few comments about the underwear being a bit too expensive. [Merl: Oh really?] Yeah, we've – we've had quite a lot of comments about that. [Merl: Do you think that's true? Do you think it is a bit expensive?] I think some things are a bit too expensive. Some things are. I mean, I bought – me personally, I bought the Vamp suit, the red velvet bra and knickers? [Merl: Oh I know, it's nice that one.] I bought that for myself for Christmas, and um, I think it cost me thirty-two pound. And my step-mum bought one as well, and then two days later she went down [to Essex] and they had one exactly the same in [the] market for nine-ninety-nine for the suit. And she said 'I've just paid thirty-two pound for that!' [Laughs.] A very big difference. [Laughs.] Obviously it was not Ann Summers, but – Er so, I said – I just said to her 'Well, you – you pay for the name, and you pay for the quality'. [Laughs.] That's what we – if anyone comments about it being expensive, we just say 'There's no – you can't put a price to quality underwear, and Ann Summers is quality underwear'. And er, they tend to shut up when you say that [laughter], I don't know why. (Donna)

[Younger party-goers]'re just out for a laugh and a giggle. And they tend not to have as much money either to spend on themselves. They don't want to spend, say, thirty pound on products. Whereas older women, you know, they've had kids or whatever as well, you know, they want to find, like, a nice bit of quality lingerie, you know, so . . . rather than the usual cheap bits from down the road, you know. They don't mind spending money. (Sarah)

Sarah's account makes a subtle shift of emphasis: although she starts by saying that younger party-goers cannot *afford* to spend money, she goes on to imply that what distinguishes older party-goers is their *willingness* to spend money rather than their actual disposable income. Sarah, Laura and Donna are all aware that lingerie can be bought more cheaply on the high street than at parties, but they are equally aware that Ann Summers' relative expensiveness is itself a mark of distinction: that it signifies 'quality'. What you buy on the market or down the road is 'not the same stuff'. Indeed, the relative expensiveness of Ann Summers lingerie may be particularly overburdened as a signifier of 'luxury' and 'quality' because there is none of the fancy packaging which often comes with expensive underwear and which usually does much of the work of such signification: all goods are delivered to the hostess sealed in the same black and red polythene bags, so as to preserve the confidentiality of each partygoer's purchase. Moreover, Ann Summers' status as 'quality' and 'a treat' also functions to define ordinary underwear purchases ('the usual cheap bits from down the road') as non-treat, that is, as essential rather than luxury purchases. Thus even though no-one *needs* underwear for purposes of warmth or protection from the elements, 'ordinary' underwear is defined as a necessity in part because other kinds of underwear are defined as luxuries.

The status of lingerie as a treat or luxury is also intimately connected to the homosocial context in which lingerie is bought at parties. Insofar as treats are distinct from 'ordinary' shopping, they are also impulse or 'unplanned' purchases. Thus for example if a supermarket shopper treats herself to a sweet or pudding or piece of 'luxury' fruit, its status as a treat is marked by the fact that 'treat' never appears as an item on the shopping list even though she buys it every time she goes to the supermarket (cf. Miller 1998); part of what makes it a treat is the sense that it has been selected on the spur of the moment. (This may partly explain why no-one ever talked about buying themselves a sex toy as a 'treat' at parties – the 'treat' was always lingerie or clothing; buying a sex toy, despite all the laughing and giggling that may be involved, may nevertheless be too meaningful a *sexual* a decision to be treated so casually, particularly in light of vibrators' connotations of the penis and phallus discussed in Chapter 3.) In the case of lingerie, party-goers rarely come with a clear idea of what, if anything, they are going to buy:

> A lot – a lot of the girls say, like, they come basically just to play the games, just to have a laugh and a girls' night out. But nine times out of ten we get them to order something [. . .T]hey tend to buy more if they see it modelled, so . . . (Donna)

> But I think they come for a laugh. I don't so – know so much about the underwear, because I think they buy that when they see it, because they like it. But, I mean, there's so many shops now that you can get nice underwear, I don't – and plus a lot of people have said 'Oh, I think it is expensive, some of the things'. You know, in the underwear. So I don't think they come for the underwear. [Merl: Yeah. So they come mainly for just the fun of it?] Yeah, I think they come for the fun of it and having a laugh. [. . .] I think more to have a laugh, and I think once they're there having a laugh and then they actually see the things, then they will buy. (Vanessa)

Treating oneself is part of the fun of Ann Summers parties, the culmination of the girls' night in. From the party organiser's point of view, getting party-goers to order is of course the point of the games, laughter and homosocial fun of the evening (although even here we should not underestimate the other, non-financial pleasures of party organisers at parties – several interviewees told me they still thought parties with low sales were 'good' parties as long as everyone had 'had a laugh'). But as we saw in Chapter 3, it is not uncommon for party-goers to order goods they cannot really afford, only to cancel the order afterwards:

> Um, and the Instinct, you know the black and white zebra-type thing? [Merl: Yeah.] Quite a lot of them I've sold, but then I've had quite a few returns as well. [Merl: Oh no.] Yeah, so . . . [Merl: Did the people say why they were returning them?] Didn't like the, um, quality. [Merl: Oh dear.] Mmm. But then I think that's just an excuse. Some people order stuff and then send it back afterwards because they don't want to lose face in front of the hostess and what have you. You know like some people, everyone's ordering stuff so they feel obliged to order something, and instead of sticking to their limit, they go above it, and then either haven't got the money when it's time to deliver it, or they get their money round there for the hostess and then at a later stage there's an excuse that they don't want it, it don't fit right or they didn't like it, you know. (Trish)

Of course it is the case that many party-goers quite simply cannot afford to buy lingerie or other goods from Ann Summers. Experienced party organisers make a point of listening out for conversations to this effect at parties, and then target potential hostesses by telling them that if they book their own party they may be able to buy themselves a more expensive item with their 10% hostess commission; thus even overt statements of poverty can be turned by a skilful party organiser into pretexts for poor women to buy themselves luxury lingerie.

All of this may sound as if the status of Ann Summers as luxury lingerie is aspirational: that working-class and lower middle-class women's tastes in Ann Summers lingerie represent class aspirations to high fashion and glamorous attire. One could argue that the homosocial identifications involved in choosing and buying 'luxury' lingerie, as both class and gender identifications simultaneously, involve fantasies of being a 'lady of leisure', based on a middle-class heterosexual division of labour in which husbands in full-time employment earn enough money to be able to support their wives and children, and wives do not need to engage in paid labour of any kind. As many feminist historians and sociologists have pointed out, this middle-class division of labour, often popularly regarded as the 'traditional' family form, is in fact the product of the ways in which class and gender hierarchies were reconfigured by the Industrial Revolution (e.g. Phillips 1987); this historical period is not only that in which lingerie as such began to develop, but is also explicitly evoked by Ann Summers items such as the popular corset-style Fever basque (Figure 5.3) (cf. Faludi 1991, Workman 1996, Juffer 1998). This kind of analysis of tastes as class and gender aspiration is congruent with the argument of Bourdieu (1984), for whom taste and fashion among working-class and lower middle-class people are driven by an impulse to imitate and assimilate what are perceived to be the more refined or prestigious tastes of the middle and upper classes.

Figure 5.3 Fever basque, from the Ann Summers catalogue autumn/winter 1999

Although there are certainly aspirational elements to the allure of 'luxury', however, the gender and class dynamics are also more complex than this. For one thing, of course, many party organisers and party-goers *are* supported by their husbands in real life, and the 'traditional' domestic arrangement is therefore not a likely subject of fantasy – although the idea that this arrangement is about leisure and glamour, rather than unpaid work and drudgery, may be so. This kind of 'luxury' lingerie may therefore embody a fantasy in which prevailing hetero-sexual inequalities can be compensated for and even enjoyed without being challenged. But in any case the idea that party-goers' choices may suggest an aspiration to more middle- or upper-class tastes is greatly complicated by the fact that homosocial identifications in Ann Summers settings often explicitly exclude those tastes as unacceptable, inappro-priate, stuffy and boring (cf. Skeggs 1997). Posh women can't be 'one of the girls'. At my very first Ann Summers event, an area meeting of unit organisers, I was told by a group of women that parties for posh women are never any good because they won't part with their money, whereas 'if you live in a council house you don't care what you spend'. This apparently paradoxical claim was made again and again through-out my research. Party organisers made it abundantly clear that parties for posh women were unpleasant or unprofitable, and usually both. The following interview quotes are selected from many:

The worst one I've ever done was where – it – there were twelve people there, and I got sixty pound in sales. [Merl: No! That's like three pence each or something!] But – but – Yeah, the, um – the actual hostess ordered thirty pound and the next [inaudible] ordered [inaudible]. And that was it. And – and that was from an affluent area. [Merl: Do you find that happens often?] Yeah. If they've got money they don't pay up. [Merl: I have heard that.] Yeah. [Merl: Why do you think that is?] Probably that's how they got their money, by keeping hold of it. [Merl: By being mean?] Yeah, yeah. [Merl laughs.] I don't know, they just seem to – I don't know. I think it may be as well that they don't want people knowing that they've bought things from Ann Summers. [Merl: Oh really?] Yeah. [Merl: That's weird, then why do they have the parties?] I don't know. They just want a bit of fun, like girls together, and — [Merl: So what was the actual party like, did they play games and things[. . .]?] Well, they did a bit. Not really, not a lot. [. . .] So you – you do tend to avoid the more richer areas. [Merl: Really?] Yeah, if you can. 'Cause you know – you know that they just don't spend. I mean, like, obviously you're going to get the odd one that does, but the majority of them don't. I don't know why. They just don't.

They've got the money and they don't. [Merl: So does that mean that the better parties are in poorer areas?] Yeah. Yeah, like the council estate areas and – and all that. People that are, you know, ticking by and just want to treat themselves every now and then. That's what seems to be the thing. Definitely the poorer areas, like middle sort of areas. But um, yeah, if they've got a lot of money they tend not to sort of spend as much. [Merl: Yeah. I guess if Ann Summers is a treat then if you've got a lot of money you can treat yourself all the time really?] Yeah, that's right. They don't need to – to worry about that, you know. But yeah, I don't – I – I don't like doing parties with people that have got a lot of money. [Laughs.] Sound funny, but, um . . . Not that you want to sort of take the money off the poorer people, but you know that they're treating themselves and it's just – you know, it's – it's that much better for them, I think. And that – it – they're just much more fun as well. 'Cause the ones sort of that come from the richer areas are sort of, you know, a bit stuck up sometimes, they don't want to get involved, 'Oh no, I'm not doing that', you know. And you're not really asking them to do anything much, and, er, you know, they won't even try items on over the top of their clothes and things like that. (Sarah)

I think the posher they are, the – the less they're going to buy. [Merl: Really?] Yeah. 'Cause I went to – the biggest house I ever went to was somewhere like [North London], and I walked out of there with no sales. [Merl: None at all?] None. [Merl: How did that happen then?] They [laughs] – no-one would buy any raffle tickets. I walked out! [Merl: They wouldn't buy any raffle tickets?] No [Merl laughs], and they were all very posh. They wouldn't buy any raffle tickets. The hostess was going to buy some, and I told her I weren't bothering with the raffle. She said 'Why's that?' and I said 'Well no-one's going to buy any tickets'. And she went 'Oh'. And she'd done a big meal on a big table at the other end of the room, and they all vanished up there, so I packed my bags and left. That's the only party I've walked out of. [Merl: Had they been playing games or anything?] They played – yeah, they played a couple of games, but I didn't – yeah, they played a few games, but I didn't play that many with them, you know. But . . . Yeah, upset me, they did. [Laughs.] They didn't actually seem to be up for a party. [Merl: How weird.] They were very strange. (Lucy)

'Posh' here signifies many different facets of social class: taste, status and attitude as well as money. Each facet is a point of dis-identification for the party organiser, and a point of contrast with the real or imagined 'ordinary' party-goers with whom by implication she does identify. Posh women are, for example, too 'stuck up' to play games or join in the fun in the way that 'the girls' usually do. Paradoxically too, posh women's class and financial privileges have not refined but blunted their tastes: they are too privileged to be able to appreciate the treats and luxuries offered by Ann Summers lingerie, whereas, as Sarah points out, women on council estates (and she is one herself) understand the real value of a treat. Alongside these active dis-identifications there is also a sense of class injuries received ('upset me, they did'): the sense that Ann Summers products, and by implication the party organiser herself, are not good enough for posh women ('they don't want people knowing that they've bought things from Ann Summers'). And it should not of course be forgotten that posh women who fail to buy are thereby depriving the party organiser of her commission, which in many cases may be her primary or only source of independent income. These micro-levels of class conflict, of attack and retaliation, are played out in the homosocial arena of being, or failing to be, 'one of the girls'.

Ann Summers lingerie, then, carries connotations of luxury which simultaneously mark out the homosocial boundaries of gender and class identifications, and distinguish Ann Summers purchases as treats rather than ordinary underwear. 'Ordinary' underwear purchases are thereby defined as practical necessities rather than as useless adornments. However, there was one notable exception to this discourse of Ann Summers as luxury. For Melanie – who was also, significantly, the only interviewee who had already decided to leave Ann Summers at the time of her interview – the relative expense of Ann Summers lingerie was not a marker of quality, but of impracticality:

I mean they don't do the nightdresses, they don't do the knickers any more, and things like that. And like, people used to buy things like that. [. . .] I mean, I've got a thing from about four years ago, Ann Summers, it's like the boxer shorts and like a little camisole top [. . .] And it's – I think it was only about twenty quid, it was like, under – like, nightwear. And I tell you something – I mean, I don't wear the top so much, but sort of like if I go home and sort of like the kids are in the bath, I might sort of throw them out and then I'll get in, and sort of like it might only be sort of like seven o'clock, and it's just, like, lovely to put it on. You know, I'll put the boxer shorts on with a dressing gown on over the top and that's it. And it don't matter if anyone comes in, 'cause it looks like I've got shorts on, a top on, and my dressing gown. [Merl: But they don't do that any more?] Don't do it no more, no. You know, and then they come out with sort of like some zebra print stuff, you know what I mean, that you think 'Oh my God!' [Merl: [Laughs.] You don't like that one then, even though it sells loads?] I don't mind it. I've got the top. I don't mind it, but it's not – not practical, is it? [Merl laughs.] I mean, where would you in a – wear – wear a leopard-skin bra? (Melanie)

One might equally ask where you *wouldn't* wear a leopard-skin bra, since bras by definition are usually concealed under outerclothes. Melanie's negotiation of the ambiguity between luxury and utility invokes some of the other ambiguities outlined above – notably display/concealment and eroticism/domesticity – and consistently resolves each ambiguity in favour of the second term. This is unusual at Ann Summers, and a significant factor in her decision to leave: she clearly thinks that the product range is not as good – meaning, not as cheap and/or practical – as it used to be. This is reflected in her attitude to lingerie in general:

You know, twenty-three pound for a bra is a lot of money [laughs], you know? I mean, you think if you're going to get the knickers and the suspender belt you're talking, like, forty quid. It's – you know. [Merl: It is a lot.] It's nice if you're going out somewhere special, you know. If – if you've got a special occasion like, coming up to Christmas, say you've got like a dance or – you know, something like that, then yeah. But sort of like for everyday use, when you think a bra only lasts, what, three months at the most. I mean, you've got to have more than one bra! To pay that amount of money, they're quite expensive. (Melanie)

Although even Melanie concedes that expensive lingerie can sometimes be bought for special occasions, her tone of voice at this point during the interview clearly implies that she thinks £23 is a rip-off price. This does not however mean that Melanie does not treat herself or buy herself 'luxury' items. It merely means that the role of 'luxury' is played by other kinds of purchase, in Melanie's case shoes and handbags:

That's my – that is my treat, when I go out – when I go out and buy myself a pair of shoes I feel great pleasure! [Merl laughs.] [. . .] But I'm like it with handbags as well, aren't I? [Merl: Oh my God.] [FX: Ah!] Shoes and handbags. [Merl [to FX]: [Laughs.] Looks like you've been dragged around the shops for weeks on end buying shoes and handbags!] [FX: She's got a bag one day and then by the end of the week she got another one!] [Merl laughs.] Shoes and handbags are my downfall! (Melanie)

Thus even Melanie buys herself 'feminine' and non-utilitarian luxuries during homosocial shopping sprees with her long-suffering friend FX.

Sleaze/respectability

Melanie's concession that expensive lingerie is suitable for special occasions is echoed by Diane:

> [. . .W]omen like underwear. Um, they like to feel good. If they feel good in their underwear, then they feel good anyway. And there's nothing nicer than to see a nice matching set, um – Not just – yes, I mean, they do the sex objects and the – the kinky outfits, but just even the – the, er, bra and knickers and suspender belts, or the body suits, they're comfortable, they're nice to wear, they make you feel good. That's not sex. Sex is – is – I mean, that you – you use that wherever you want to use it, that's personal to you, but your underwear is something that makes *you* feel good. Yes, your man likes to see it as well, but if you've got a nice outfit on, with nice underwear underneath, and you're going out somewhere special, you're going to feel good from the inside out. And I think that's – that's what Ann Summers is all about. Makes you feel nice. (Diane)

Diane here is clearly defining 'nice underwear' as a luxury and a treat. She is also insisting that it is *respectable*: she explicitly marginalises the 'kinky outfits' and distinguishes them from the 'nice underwear' which is *not about sex.*

The acute class and gender politics surrounding notions of respectability are analysed by Skeggs (1997), who identifies 'respectability' as a central term in women's struggles with and against stigmatised and sexualised class status. To be 'respectable' for working-class women is to refuse and/or escape the category of the ignorant, dirty, irresponsible and sluttish working-class woman. The specifically *sexual* connotations of failing to be 'respectable' are of course far more damaging to women than to men – as has often been noted, terms such as 'slut' or 'slag' apply only to women, and there are no male equivalents (Lees 1993, Holland et al. 1998). It is therefore unsurprising that the sleaze/respectability nexus is a site of particularly intense negotiation for party-goers and party organisers. Women perform complex feats of distinction and identification around the sexual connotations of Ann Summers as both a product range and a brand name. Merely to reveal that one is an Ann Summers party organiser is to risk being labelled a 'slag':

I actually went to a party on Saturday, it was my friend's thirtieth, and there was people there that I hadn't seen from school. [Laughs.] [Merl: Oh how weird, oh God I'd hate that. My nightmare, oh my nightmare!] I did as well, 'cause I'm, like, four stone heavier, you know, and you think 'Oh no, I'm four stone heavier and I look a mess [Merl laughs] and blah blah blah'. And they was like 'Oh my gosh!' and they said, like, 'Oh how –' One of them's working in a design agency up London, and one's – they've all got really high-powered jobs. None of them are married, none have got children. And I had my little 'un there, I said 'Oh', I said, 'this is my little boy'. 'And what do you do?' I said 'Oh I'm a manager for Ann Summers', and they was, like, 'We knew you would do something like that! [Merl laughs] We just knew that would suit you!' They were like – but they was, like, completely opposite, they was, like, 'Oh great', you know, 'oh, you're doing really well, we saw you on telly, blah blah blah –' [. . .T]hey was, like 'We knew you would just do that! We knew it suited you so much!' Yeah, and I thought, 'Oh great, you telling me I was a slapper at school or something?' [Laughter.] (Dawn)

As with Sarah and Lucy at their 'posh' parties, Dawn herself is acutely aware of the class distinctions in play between her and her former schoolmates: they have 'high-powered jobs' and no children; she is a lone mother whose career with Ann Summers, although of central importance to her, is often dismissed by others as not even 'a real job', much less a high-powered one (and elsewhere in her interview Dawn puts such dismissals down to 'people's snobbiness'). But in fact, as Dawn's account demonstrates, the risk of being labelled a 'slapper' comes as much from oneself as from other people. Dawn's friends are actually very approving of her obvious success, and pleased that she has found a job that she loves. It is *Dawn* who half-jokingly wonders whether this means that she is a 'slapper'.

To be called a slag is an injury without redress (cf. Lees 1993) – not just a gender and sexual injury but also a class injury. The only woman I ever heard refer to *herself* in such terms was, tellingly, a middle-class party-goer who, on winning the points game, joked to her friend that she used to be a 'slapper' before she was married. As an obviously middle-class, well dressed and well spoken woman this party-goer seemed far less anxious to present herself as sexually respectable than women at most of the other parties I observed – although even she presented herself as respectable now that she was married and had children. Even though Ann Summers games like the points game explicitly value women's (hetero)sexual experience, for working-class and lower middle-class party-goers this never means that one willingly calls oneself a slag, or allows oneself to be called a slag by others. One of the parameters of homosocial identification at Ann Summers events is therefore that those present are *not slags*, and that using this term is an act of bitching which ejects the 'slag' from the homosocial group. In doing so it also reveals the post-feminist contradictions of homo-social identifications in Ann Summers settings, which invest heavily in the idea that 'girls just want to have fun' and that participants are sexually liberated, while at the same time policing those boundaries with the deployment of vicious sexual stigmatisation against other women.

However, party organisers in particular do nevertheless often have to deal with this term – not during Ann Summers events themselves, but at points where admission or recruitment into such events is being negotiated. Many party organisers told tales about their experiences of canvassing for party bookings, for example, in which members of the public had attacked them as 'slags' simply because they were selling Ann Summers products. Party organisers had developed two complementary strategies for dealing with such attacks, both of which used lingerie to negotiate the sleaze/respectability nexus.

The first strategy was to claim that Ann Summers lingerie is respect-able. This sometimes involves an implicit or explicit contrast between lingerie and sex toys, such that party organisers willingly concede that sex toys are sleazy so as to preserve the respectability of lingerie. This strategy marginalises sex toys as a kind of 'side line' to the Ann Summers range and invests lingerie with the 'real' meaning of Ann Summers:

Canvassing in [East London] one day I went up to some lady and said 'Excuse me, love, can I interest you in Ann Summers?' and she said 'No, we're not all slags like you'. [Merl: No!] I said 'Oh right!' Yeah. I went 'Oh right, so you know me well then do you?' [Merl: Cheeky cow!] But I just laughed, I mean, I was in hysterics. And then, um, another woman, same sort of approach, so she went 'I don't buy all that filth', I said 'Oh you don't wear knickers then?' [laughter] and I just walked off. And one of the girls went 'I don't think you should have said that', I said 'Why not? She can be rude to me, I can be rude back'. I said 'I ain't doing nothing wrong, all I'm doing is selling underwear'. [Merl: What is it you think people imagine when they react like that? What do they think it is you're trying to do to them?] I don't know. I think they think – I think some people think you're just trying to turn them into sex maniacs, and – but it's not, it's just all the girls getting together and having a laugh, and if they want to buy something they will, if they don't they won't. But that time when that woman said 'No, we're not all slags like you', I – I mean, I was in hysterics, I just went 'Oh, you know me well then!' [Laughs.] So *she* walked off in a huff, not me! [Laughter.] (Beth)

But I do think when you – when you're canvassing, that's when you discover your negative attitudes, 'Oh no I'm not into that' and they shut the door. [. . .] [Merl: What is it that you think people think Ann Summers is? When they go all funny and say 'Oh no', what do they imagine?] I think – I think they all think that it's just vibrators and kinky stuff. That's what I think. I don't think they actually know that we do nice, decent underwear as well, which we do. (Cherry)

As these interview quotes demonstrate, this strategy also reverses the usual distribution of luxury and utility by implying that Ann Summers lingerie is just 'ordinary' underwear. Beth's retaliation against the woman in East London – 'you don't wear knickers then?' – turns the name slag back onto her by implying that knickers in general, and Ann Summers knickers in particular, are a practical necessity. It also demonstrates that the reason why women 'need' underwear is often because it simply 'means' sexual respectability.

Both of these examples involve conflicts between women – bitching as homosocial aggression. Beth and her adversaries on the streets of East London are warring explicitly over their respective status as 'respectable'. Cherry's encounters are less openly aggressive but like Lucy's and Sarah's posh party-goers, her respondents distance themselves from the status of 'slag' by refusing to engage with Ann Summers, and in doing so implicitly place Cherry herself in the 'slag' position. Although Beth's reaction is aggressive, Cherry's stoical claim that the such people are merely displaying their ignorance about the Ann Summers product range is by far the more common response among party organisers. As Donna put it during her interview, 'It's part of the job, you just laugh it off. [. . .] If you get offended by things like that [. . .] then you're not going to last five minutes'. Homosocial aggression from other women is after all an occupational hazard of party organising.

But the accusation of being a slag often comes from men rather than from women: as Cathy put it, 'sometimes, particularly men, maybe they think you – they've got this idea that you could be an old slag or something'. In such cases women sometimes identify with each other and against the men:

Um, I went canvassing once and I got called 'one of those dirty women' [laughter] by someone's husband. [Merl: No!] I was standing there and I said, like, 'Excuse me, um, I'm from Ann Summers, um, can I take a minute of your time?' and she said, er, 'Oh yeah, no problem'. And er, I said 'I'm just canvassing at the moment to see if anyone would like to see our new catalogue or would like a demonstration in their home', and he went 'You're one of them dirty women, aren't you?' And I said 'Well, no', I said, 'I – I, um – I represent Ann Summers', I said, 'I do sales for Ann Summers', I said, um, 'I'm not actually a dirty woman'. [Laughter.] Er, he said 'You are, you sell those dirty things!' and I said 'No, they're not dirty things', I said, 'they're actually, um, marital aids, if you want to call them anything' [laughs], I said, um, 'we actually refer to them as toys at parties', I said, 'because that's what they are, women's toys'. Um, I said 'Some are men's toys', I said, 'if you don't really want to know about it . . .' and she said 'Yeah, shut up and go away!' [Laughter.] So she sent him away! (Laura)

Interestingly, Laura does not attempt here to claim that the lingerie is respectable, but instead defends the sex toys. This may be because she has quickly forged a homosocial identification with the woman (who is immediately willing to hear about Ann Summers) and so does not need to worry so much about respectability, which as such is primarily of concern to women.

A frequent variation on this first strategy is to claim that the Ann Summers product range used to be 'tacky' or unrespectable but that it has now moved up-market. The explicit yardstick for this move is sometimes Marks and Spencer's underwear, which figures as the epitome of both quality and respectability – and which again, as with Beth's 'no knickers' comment, re-aligns Ann Summers lingerie with utility rather than luxury. These interview quotes are chosen from many:

[Merl: Do you think that Ann Summers has changed in the time you've been with it?] Mmm, yeah, yeah. [Merl: Yeah? In what way?] Um, I think – well, I think that in the same sort of way, but maybe not as drastic as maybe years before. But they're getting more comfortable in their, um, underwear, rather than, you know, just trying to impress or – or look sexy it's, you know, trying to feel the same way as well. More like Marks & Sparks! [Laughter.] No. [Merl: Not quite!] Not there yet! (Justine)

Because then Ann Summers was like – ooh, Ann Summers was quite sleazy [when I was eighteen]. [Merl: Was it actually sleazy, or did you just think it was sleazy?] No, it was. [Merl: I've heard people say that, that it used to quite sleazy.] Well it was. The underwear was very tacky, which I know is an awful thing to say, but it was. I mean, I've got one of the brochures from when I first started Ann Summers back again, it was about three and a half years ago, and I'll show you one of the brochures out there. [Merl: I'd love to see it.] It's like – when you look at the stuff then it's, like, red and black leopard print, like red and black. [Merl laughs.] Not like now it's like the animal print, it's like it was red and black and lots of chains and – and – of course, I mean, now Ann Summers are such a big company, they've got their own quality control, everything gets tested and materials before it even gets in the book. Then they never, and it shows, because obviously Ann Summers underwear had a lifespan of probably about a year then [laughter], you know, if that, if it didn't fall to kind of pieces when you washed it! But it was more like, um – Ann Summers was like 'Ooh!' And even getting the parties in. It was hard getting the parties back then, because it was like 'Oh, Ann Summers, no! That's not for me!' [Merl laughs.] Whereas now you expect someone 'Yeah, OK, good, it's an excuse for a good night in with the girls'. [Merl: So it's definitely toned down a bit you think since then?] Oh yeah! (Dawn)

Dawn's vehement insistence that the old-style lingerie was 'tacky' and the new-style is 'quality' is based on very subtle taste distinctions: black and red leopard-print versus black and brown leopard print, for example. The distance between sleaze and respectability is measured in such subtleties.

The second strategy for dealing with attacks on Ann Summers as 'sleazy' is to turn the 'sleaze' accusation against the accuser – to classify the classifier, not as a slag herself (as in Beth's example) but as a sexually repressed snob:

[P]rime example, last night we went out and, um, the lady we went to see, well it was actually one of her friends, she was flicking through the catalogue, and she said 'Oh well, this is a bit – some of it's a bit dirty, isn't it? I wouldn't really like to see myself doing something like that, I see it as a bit slutty'. I thought 'No, bite your tongue Donna, please do bite your tongue [Merl laughs], 'cause I'm going to say something in a minute'. And FX looked at me 'cause she knows what I'm like. [Merl laughs.] I said 'No, I'm not going to say nothing'. And she pointed out a suit in the book, which is, er, Kizzy, have you ever seen Kizzy, the peep-hole bra and knickers? [Merl: Red one.] Yeah. And she said 'That – only a slut would wear that'. And FX looked at me and burst out laughing, 'cause

I've actually got that suit. [Laughter.] And she says, um – and FX was wetting herself. And I said to her 'Well everyone is entitled to their own opinion', I said, 'my personal opinion is, I've got that suit and I – I happen to like it'. I said 'But you're entitled to your opinion'. And she didn't know what to say after that, she couldn't apologise enough. She said 'I'm really sorry if I've offended you'. I said 'It takes a lot more than that to offend me'. I said, 'I wouldn't worry about it', I said, "cause I'm not offended', I said, 'but obviously you're entitled to your opinion', I said, 'and I'm not going to take offence to that', I said, 'some people live conservative lives, some people don't'. And um, that shut her up! [Laughter.] 'Cause what it – what – I find it quite weird really, 'cause she runs – she has actually got her own business, she runs an underwear shop, like a boutique, she calls it. She's very . . . snobby would be the good word to describe it, she runs a very conservative boutique, and she's – she – she said 'Oh I'd like to see one of your catalogues, just to see what sort of competition I'm – I'm up against'. [Merl: Oh really? And then she found out!] [Laughter.] She found out major! [Laughter.] I don't think she was very pleased! (Donna)

Donna here is negotiating the sleaze/respectability nexus by recoding it as liberated/repressed; she is also drawing on the some of the discourses about 'posh' women used by Lucy and Sarah in the previous section. However this does *not* mean that she accepts or reclaims the woman's labelling of her as a 'slut': her tone of voice throughout this anecdote makes it abundantly clear that, despite her protestations, she *was* rather offended. In aligning herself on the side of 'sleaze' in this way she is not challenging the stigmatisation of the 'slut', merely deflecting it.

Although the name 'slag' can almost never be embraced, there are certain conditions under which it is possible to embrace the 'sleazy' side of the ambiguity between sleaze and respectability: when the 'sleazy' is configured as the 'kinky'. Diane's comments about 'kinky outfits' above is actually rather unusual in that it implicitly designates all the sexual meanings of lingerie as kinky and insists that non-kinky underwear is by definition not (or at least not primarily) sexual. 'Kinky' is far more commonly used to describe particular *kinds* of sexuality rather than sex as such. Moreover it is only ever used to describe forms of *hetero*sexuality: it acts as a term which can be negotiated *within* the homosocial context of Ann Summers rather than as something which must be excluded.

Such negotiations reconfigure the sleaze/respectability nexus as an ambiguity between the 'kinky' and the 'normal'. And although the

Figure 5.4 Fur Love Cuffs, from the Ann Summers catalogue autumn/winter 1999

designation 'normal' in mainstream heterosexual discourse usually has a moral import in relation to sexuality, in the world of Ann Summers it is more ambiguous whether 'normality' is a *taste* distinction or a moral one. This is most clearly seen in relation to products and practices involving forms of bondage-domination/sadomasochism (bdsm). The autumn and winter 1999 Ann Summers catalogue featured a small range of such products, including leather handcuffs, a leather whip, a pvc blindfold, and a collar and leash, as well as their famous Love Cuffs in

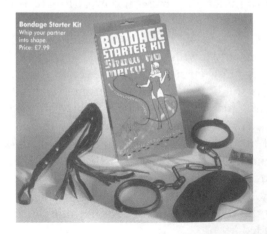

Figure 5.5 Bondage Starter Kit, from the Ann Summers catalogue Christmas supplement 1999

red plastic or pink fake fur (Figure 5.4); the Christmas catalogue also featured a Bondage Starter Kit, containing plastic handcuffs, a blindfold, a phial of massage oil and a cat o' nine tails (Figure 5.5). Clearly the commercial imperative behind every Ann Summers event is a strong disincentive, for party organisers at least, openly to call any of these products immoral or perverted. Instead party organisers will often represent them as 'kinky', and preference for them is treated as a matter of taste rather than of morality:

> What goes on behind people's closed doors ain't – it's up to them isn't it? You know, if they was to order a whip or whatever I'd probably think 'Oh! Didn't think you was into all that', but wouldn't think no more of it, it wouldn't – it wouldn't judge – you know, I wouldn't judge them as a person any differently. (Vanessa)

> I mean, one of the girls [at my last party] was into the pvc stuff. She's not kinky, she just likes it. And I – I don't think anyone that likes pvc is kinky anyway. But personally I wouldn't wear it, but I think that's more because I'm – know I just don't have the figure to wear it. (Cherry)

> Some of it I suppose is a bit – like that – that suit with the boob holes [laughs], that's – that is disgusting. And all that bondage stuff. I mean, it's whatever you're into, I suppose. But they'll always put that in there, 'cause there's always somebody that would like that sort of thing. (Helen)

Even fairly strong condemnations of bdsm-related items are of dubious status in this discourse of 'normality'. Does Helen think the 'bondage stuff' or 'suit with the boob holes' (a rubber body called Provoke) is aesthetically disgusting or morally disgusting? In effect the two are impossible to disentangle: when she says that 'there's always somebody who would like that sort of thing', 'that sort of thing' means both the products themselves and the sexual practices they signify, and both the objects and the practices are matters of taste – a taste which Helen is at pains to stress she does not share.

On the other hand, however, tastes for kinky products expressed by 'the girls' are sharply distinguished from the kinds of 'real' or 'authentic' perversion which go on outside of Ann Summers. 'Real' fetishism, for example, is explicitly ruled out of the homosocial arena of Ann Summers. This was illustrated when Dawn, during a unit meeting, broke off from her presentation to ask the 'girls' in the unit whether any of them had seen a recent item on a TV programme featuring rubber fetishists: 'what's that all about then?' she had asked. (No-one else had seen the programme.) Significantly, she had been reminded of this TV programme by a complaint from the 'girls' about the only item of rubber wear in the Ann Summers range at that time: Provoke, 'that suit with the boob holes' as Helen calls it above. Provoke was the only item in the entire product range which met with universal disapproval – indeed, with revulsion – from all party-goers and party organisers during my research, and was dropped from the spring/summer 2000 catalogue:

> [Merl: So is there anything in the – in the current catalogue that you don't like or that don't sell well?] Yeah, that pvc thing with the holes in the boobs! [Merl laughs.] What is that? Please! My God! [Sighs.] (Dawn)

> [. . .T]he only one I hate is like that rubber suit with the boobs sticking out. Ugh, no, I'm glad we got rid of that. Um, I'd be very surprised if they sold any of that actually at all. I mean, the people that I've met and that I know – [Merl: I've heard of one that's been sold.] One being sold. Oh, I can't even imagine the type of person that bought it. (Cherry)

Provoke was clearly too close to 'real' fetish or bondage gear to be acceptably 'kinky'; as Cherry makes clear, anyone who liked that could not possible be imagined as 'one of the girls'.

'Real' perversion is located by party organisers and party-goers in the sex industry and/or 'bondage'. Interestingly, 'kinkiness' is sometimes defined in contrast to such perversion as a form of 'play' which is in this sense 'inauthentic'. The distinction between inauthentic kinkiness and authentic perversion in particular is often made through subtleties of taste, such as for particular materials – for example, Ann Summers breakable plastic rather than the perverts' cold hard steel. Thus Joy demonstrated the Bondage Starter Kit at a party I observed by suggesting that the handcuffs were plastic because they were 'only to get you started', they weren't for serious or 'real' bondage games. 'Kinky' Ann Summers sex is not *seriously* kinky or perverted, and indeed is perhaps not seriously sexual either. This sets up a rather complex dynamic in which certain Ann Summers products are regarded as 'tacky' because they are not authentically perverted. Justine, for example, distinguishes between plastic and metal in a way which classes the former as 'tacky':

> Nothing [is in the current catalogue] that I really think, 'Oh that is just awful'. Oh, apart from the nipple chain. [Laughter.] [Merl: Which is still

in the new catalogue, I notice.] Yeah. But I did actually order that, just 'cause I wanted to see what it was like [laughter], and it was really tacky, and it's really light, it's not a chain, it's just like, er, silver plastic. And it's not even a proper hook, it's like a little, um, bit of string that you just tighten up. So it's – I thought that was just awful. [Merl: Mmm, that sounds a bit yukky.] Yeah, if you're – if you're into something like that then you'd probably go for a proper chain rather than a silly bit of plastic, but – that's going to snap in two minutes. [Laughs.] Just the weight of your bosoms'll probably snap it! [Laughter.] (Justine)

Justine clearly regards the chain as tacky because it would be inadequate for a real erotic encounter between people who *are* 'into something like that'. This subtly shifts the meaning of the term 'tacky', so that the chain is tacky not because it is too sleazy but because, in a sense, it is not sleazy enough – it is tacky in the way that cheap plastic novelties are tacky.

This classification of Ann Summers as inauthentic and tacky seems very close to the stereotype of Ann Summers that circulates within sexual dissidents' communities, including not just lesbians, gay men and bisexuals (who may dismiss Ann Summers as 'naff' in the way discussed above) but also self-identified 'perverts', fetishists and bdsm practitioners: '"Death to Furry Handcuffs from Ann Summers" – mantra of the Modern Masochistress', as Tiger Miao puts it (1999: 46). But Justine is speaking from a position quite different to that of the Modern Masochistress in terms of both sexuality and class. She is careful to establish that she was not intending to use the chain herself – she is not really 'into something like that', she can only hypothesise about what such a person would 'probably' want. She is thus showing off her sexual knowledge, but it is presented as knowledge about sexual Others rather than about 'girls' like herself. Moreover her condemnation of the chain is similar to Melanie's condemnation of the leopard-print bra: it is tacky because it is impractical. The Modern Masochistress's horror of Ann Summers' Fur Lovecuffs, on the other hand, is not about their impracticality, but about their (literal and metaphorical) lightweight nature, their lack of up-market sophistication and her own self-classification as 'articulate, witty and urbane' (46).

Thus although Justine and Tiger Miao may agree to a surprising extent on the parameters of 'authentic' sexual perversion, they do so from different starting points: Miao condemns the Lovecuffs from the position of the 'authentically' perverted, Justine condemns the chain from that of the 'authentically' un-perverted. The apparently anomalous fact that Justine did nevertheless order the nipple chain, and then clearly spent some time seriously weighing up its effectiveness or otherwise during a real sexual encounter, betrays her ambivalence about her own status as 'un-perverted', and the extent to which this boundary between the perverted and the un-perverted is policed. Despite her claims to the contrary there is a strong suspicion that Justine has at least considered and/or fantasised about using an 'authentic' nipple chain herself, and that this is the basis for her disappointment in the Ann Summers version – but she is unable to admit this in the homosocial contexts of her parties or her interview (and perhaps even to herself).

Important distinctions are also drawn between Ann Summers and the 'real' sex industry. These interview quotes are chosen from many:

> I don't think of it as being part of the sex industry because it's not seedy. And I think a lot of people view the sex industry as being, like, really seedy, you know. Like, and I – oh, it's been ages since I've been into one of the Ann Summers shops, but they're all, like, really bright and lit and, you know, they're – they're – it's no different than walking into Top Shop sort of thing, you know. (Lucy)

> I mean, 'cause a lot of – a lot of women, you get women that are – are married and they're settled down and they're reasonably well off and they're in jobs, they don't necessarily want to go into Soho into the sex – the proper sex shops, because it's going to be embarrassing for them. Go to an Ann Summers party, it's fun, you're with your friends, you can have a laugh, they play games, there's a raffle, you've got someone that talks about it in a friendly environment. (Joy)

> [Merl: So do you think that Ann Summers is part of the sex industry?] Um. Er, I think so, yeah. But more, um – ooh, I don't know. Not as hard core, obviously, as what you'd get Soho, up London, in, you know, loads of seedy shops. It's more accepted. Um, and it's not necessarily, you know, tacky or – or seedy like the shops are. And where you can order it from your own home, you don't feel as though, you know, you're some sort of pervert going into a shop. Because, you know, you can do that. (Justine)

In spite of the opportunities available at Ann Summers parties for 'girls' with 'kinky' tastes, Ann Summers remains respectable because it is not the real sex industry. Lucy's and Joy's comments epitomise the class and gender stakes in such respectability: the acceptability of Ann Summer shops is marked by their resemblance to a mass-market fashion chain;

'real' sex shops are unsuitable places for respectable married women. Moreover, as Justine's comments suggest, Ann Summers is not the urban location of the 'real' sex industry: it takes place in women's own living rooms. This renders both Ann Summers itself and its customers respectable because it renders them domestic.

Eroticism/domesticity

The ambiguity between eroticism and domesticity is one of the most intense focuses of negotiation *within* Ann Summers settings, especially parties. On the one hand Ann Summers lingerie is clearly chosen and bought on the basis of its erotic meanings: as Cathy simply puts it, 'Why do people buy, like, sexy underwear? Because they want to feel sexy'. On the other hand, it is taken for granted by party-goers and party organisers alike that this eroticism must somehow be reconciled with a heterosexual division of labour in which the home is both the site of everyday erotic practices and the site of women's unpaid domestic labour (cf. Juffer 1998). As we saw in Chapter 1, the sexual inequality of familial-domestic gender régimes is supported rather than challenged by Ann Summers: the post-feminist discourse that 'men are useless but we love them anyway' naturalises an unequal division of domestic labour, while the pay and employment structure of the party plan itself presupposes that party organisers will be both financially and practically supported by a male partner. This familial-domestic gender régime is so naturalised that in many ways it cuts across social classes: housework is 'women's work' whether one is middle-class or working-class (Oakley 1974, Malos 1995). But the contemporary politics of housework *is* a class politics. The recent growth in the domestic service sector has seen increasing numbers of middle-class professional women employing working-class and/or migrant women to perform some or all of their domestic work – an arrangement in which middle-class women's relative equality with middle-class men in the professions is under-written by their increasing inequality with the women who clean their houses (Lutz 2002). Not only are the women who organise and go to Ann Summers parties extremely unlikely to be able to afford such domestic help; they are also extremely unlikely to want it. Even paid baby-sitters are anathema: Cathy told me that 'I'm not prepared to pay for a baby-sitter, I'd had child-minders before and I – you know, I don't know, it just causes problems I think, you know, a nosy child-minder looking round your house and things'. Doing one's own housework and childcare (or inducing one's female friends and relatives to do unpaid childcare as a favour) marks one out as both responsible (unlike women who pay other people to do it) and respectable (unlike nosy, trouble-causing women who take payment) (cf. Skeggs 1997).

Homosocial negotiations around 'sexy underwear', as class and gender negotiations, therefore *accommodate* domestic inequality. Indeed one of the most interesting aspects of the eroticism/domesticity nexus is that party-goers do not simply choose one term over the other: homosocial talk and representations actually eroticise the domestic, and domesticate the erotic. This process is not confined to lingerie, but also extends to sex toys. During participant observation and interviews alike I heard countless jokes linking sex toys with domestic appliances: vibrators sound like lawnmowers or vacuum cleaners; rotating sex toys can be used as food processors; duo balls can be worn to make vacuum cleaning a more interesting domestic chore; aphrodisiacs can give you an energy boost to get the ironing done in double-quick time. Some party organisers fondly remembered a now obsolete vibrator which had suction cups on the bottom so that it could be attached to the washing machine while it was on the spin cycle. In the case of lingerie, the domestic-erotic infusion often takes place around laundry. It is taken for granted that laundry is primarily women's responsibility, and that at best men can only be trusted to do the simpler kinds of machine washing: party-goers would sometimes greet handwash-only items with the comment that 'you wouldn't be able to leave that one to your boyfriend'. Party organisers frequently make a point of talking about laundry care as part of their kit demonstration of particular items. In some cases comments about laundry care are also sexualised: for example, both Beth and Cathy make regular jokes to this effect about items with G-strings or thongs, where the eroticism of the lingerie is complemented by the ease of laundry care:

> I do make quite a few jokes and things about items of clothing, like, you know, like if it's got a G-string you say, like, um, 'This one is good, you haven't got to wash it, all you've got to do is scrape the bits off', and if you get a laugh you know they're going to be up for it. (Beth)

As Beth's comments demonstrate, whether one 'gets' this kind of domestic joke is an important test of homosociality ('if you get a laugh you know they're going to be up for it'). Homosocial identifications are made around the recognition of women's 'natural' responsibility for domestic chores as well as their 'natural' erotic desire for men. Cathy particularly likes to make this joke about Fifi (Figure 5.6).

Figure 5.6 Fifi maid's outfit, from the Ann Summers catalogue autumn/winter 1999

The maid's outfits Fifi and Wench are among the most popular items in the Ann Summers range; *as* maid's outfits they clearly eroticise women's domestic labour as a service performed for men. However, party organisers and party-goers rarely if ever acknowledge this in their comments and jokes about either item. Instead they are likely to joke about, for example, making their male partners wear the apron. This forms part of a pattern of joking about men, domestic labour and domestic inequality in which men are placed in a position of domestic service and sexual submission. At a party in North London, for example, party-goers joked of the Leather Plaited Whip that you could use it to whip your partner while he did the washing up. Clearly such jokes and comments are congruent with the discourses of the erogenous body analysed in Chapter 4, in which heterosexual women are always represented as 'on top' and sexually dominant. They are also congruent with the aggression and revenge against men discussed in Chapters 3 and 4. Just as those discourses are about homosocial identification between partygoers, so these jokes about men's submission are homosocial fantasies of men's submission.

Insofar as they make no challenge to actual domestic inequalities in women's everyday lives, they are also *post-feminist* fantasies. I became acutely aware of this during a party organised by Melanie in Essex. Melanie offered the Leather Plaited Whip as one of the raffle prizes, and it was greeted enthusiastically by two party-goers in particular, one of whom indeed won it. What was she going to do with it? She was going to display it on the back seat of her car. The woman who had wanted and failed to win it said that she would buy one for herself at the next Ann Summers party so that she could 'scare' her fiancé with it. The two women joked together that they could share it and take it to the pub when they and their respective boyfriends all went out together. This is the epitome of Ann Summers homosociality as a post-feminist dynamic which forges gender identifications around images of 'useless' men and liberated women, but leaves material realities of sexual inequality not just intact but in important ways even unacknowledged.

Summary and Conclusion

Homosocial identifications in Ann Summers settings are not just gender and ethnic identifications, but also involve identifications and distinctions of class. Taste functions as one of the most important media for such identifications and distinctions which, for the working-class and lower middle-class women who predominate in Ann Summers settings, revolve around the classification of oneself, one's peers and one's purchases as respectable or sleazy, normal or perverted, tasteful or tasteless, tacky or serious. The negotiation of these binary pairs is not simply (or not always) about aligning oneself on the 'correct' side of the line, but can also involve a more complex interplay of identification and dis-identification. This is particularly so in relation to categories of the 'normal', 'kinky' or 'perverted', because the commercial context of Ann Summers, in which party organisers strive to turn party-goers' preferences into purchases, tends to frame women's choices for particular sexual products or practices as questions of taste rather than morality. In particular the classification of some of Ann Summers bdsm-related products (such as plastic chains and handcuffs) as 'kinky' but not 'perverted' can produce highly ambivalent negotiations around the notion of 'authentic perversion', the exclusion of which from the Ann Summers product range may be variously read as respectable, normal or tacky. But this framework of 'consumer choice' and 'sexual liberation' is fractured by homosocial conflict, defensiveness, and aggressive policing of oneself and others, especially in relation to the class and gender dynamics of sexual respectability and the stigma of the 'slag'. In this sense negotiations of taste in Ann Summers settings embody one of the central contradictions of post-feminism: it offers a vision of 'sexual liberation' without challenging forms of distinction which are not just un-liberated, but actively serve the class and sexual subordination of working-class and lower middle-class women.

six

Conclusion

M y aim in this book has been to bring female homosociality to the centre of the analysis of gender and sexuality. Heterosexuality is not just something that happens between men and women; it is also something that happens among women themselves. The ways in which heterosexual women and men 'do' their gender homosocially are at least as important as cross-sex dynamics in the construction of heterosexual femininities and masculinities; indeed in some contexts they may be more so. Gender, as Connell (1987, 1995) points out, is a *collective practice*:

> Collective practice is not reducible to a sum of individual practices. In a strict sense there is no such thing as 'individual practice' at all; the phrase is an abstraction from a tissue of relational conduct. [. . .A] personal life is a path through a field of practices which are following a range of collective logics, and are responding to a range of structural conditions which routinely intersect and often contradict each other. (Connell 1987: 222)

Homosociality is one of the key forms of such collectivity, and the processes of homosocial identification and dis-identification one of the key forms of such collective practice. In particular, the 'collective logic' of homosocial identifications involves the construction of heterosexual gender as a particular type of *naturalised difference*: women are constructed as similar to each other but different from men (and vice versa), and heterosexuality is a fundamental law of nature because 'opposites attract'. This notion of heterosexuality as 'natural difference', as Dyer (1997) and others have argued, is absolutely central to the ideology of heterosexuality as 'natural' and 'normal', and hence to the ideology that any other form of sexuality is 'unnatural' and 'abnormal'. Homosociality is thus a crucial site in which the dominance of heterosexuality

219

is maintained. It is also a crucial site in which masculinity and femininity are differentially constructed such that the latter is subordinated to the former – even (or perhaps especially) in female homosocial contexts where men are being condemned for their failures to live up to women's masculine ideals.

This is why Ann Summers parties have a significance which goes far beyond a few hours of fun on a Friday night. The point here is not simply that many women spend considerable proportions of their waking hours under homosocial gender régimes, in both workplaces and leisure settings, although that is also true. But the sense of femininity forged through homosocial identifications does not simply evaporate as soon as the party is over, any more than it magically appears out of nowhere when the party begins. Homosocial femininity is one of those collective logics which respond to structural conditions which 'routinely intersect and often contradict each other'. Those structural conditions include gender subordination at the level of the gender order as well as domestic gender inequality, racism and racial privilege, class relations, material poverty or wealth, heterosexual privilege and homophobia, and women's financial dependence on their male partners while bringing up young children at home. For example, heterosexual women's identifications as 'one of the girls' at Ann Summers parties and meetings offer pleasure and fun in the simple fact of being 'a girl', despite all of the structural conditions bearing on women's lives, and also provide a sense of a feminine 'self' which is both informed by and carried back to other settings. Thus when a married or cohabiting woman with children leaves an Ann Summers party and returns to the familial-domestic gender régime of her home, the notion that 'men are useless but we love them anyway' may continue to shape her sense of herself as the one who takes care of an adult man as well as the children – and indeed her sense of the adult man in question as someone who allows her to go out in the evening by 'baby-sitting' his own children. Conversely, her perception that he 'needs' looking after shapes her recognition of and identification with the 'men are useless' discourse and thus sustains her homosocial identifications, at Ann Summers parties and elsewhere.

Social categories and social identities are unstable, fluid, constantly in process and under negotiation. They are also stubborn, tenacious, slow to change and difficult to escape. This paradox is one of the core themes of social theory in general and feminist theory in particular. This book has explored in depth the ways in which homosocial femininity is an active construction, but its significance also lies in its extraordinary durability, and in the ways in which femininity may provide a 'path' through at least some of the different gender régimes between which women move in the course of a day or a lifetime. Derek McGhee (1998), in his discussion of the armed forces, has used the term 'homosocial habitus' to describe both a set of informal rules and a form of masculinity actively implanted and fostered by male homosocial institutions. The term 'habitus' comes from the work of Bourdieu (1977), and refers to a set of 'dispositions' or habits of thought, dress, body, posture, taste and attitude, which constitute 'the ability to function effectively within a given social field, an ability which cannot necessarily be articulated as conscious knowledge: "knowing how" rather than "knowing that"' (Lovell 2000: 12). McGhee argues that male homosocial institutions such as the armed forces both require and enforce a kind of 'know-how', such that the characteristics of male homosociality described by Sedgwick (and discussed at length in Chapter 2) are the taken-for-granted, informal rules of 'how to be a man'. Bourdieu himself, without using the term 'homosociality' as such, has argued even more strongly that:

> [M]asculine *habitus* is only constituted or achieved in relation to a reserve space in which serious competitive games are played *between men*, games of honour of which the limit case is that of war, or games which, in differentiated societies, offer to the desire for domination, under all its forms, economic, political, religious, artistic, scientific, etc., possible fields of action. (Bourdieu cit. Lovell 2000: 28 n.3)

If homosocial power games between men constitute the space in which masculine habitus is constructed – where men acquire the 'know-how' to be masculine – then homosocial 'games' (both literally and metaphorically) between women of the kind dissected in this book can be understood as the space in which feminine habitus is formed and where women acquire the 'know-how' to be feminine. The point about habitus is precisely that it is durable: it constitutes a set of *bodily* as well as social and psychological 'dispositions' that cling to the subject as s/he moves through different social settings and points in the lifecourse. In saying that masculine habitus can *only* be acquired this way Bourdieu may be overstating the case. The only way to find out whether female homosocial gender régimes are the primary or even the only kind in which feminine habitus can be acquired is to conduct further research on different female homosocial spaces – from primary school games to practices of geriatric care.

The specific case of Ann Summers as a female homosocial space is distinctly *post-feminist* in ways discussed throughout this book. As discussed in Chapter 2, the particular version of post-feminism discussed here may be peculiar to Ann Summers, especially in its sexual explicitness and its overt concern with 'willies'. It is self-evident that in many other female homosocial settings the terms of gender identification are not post-feminist at all, or are post-feminist in different ways and with different emphases and nuances. Here again, further research is required before comparisons can be made and conclusions drawn.

While I have been researching and writing this book my friends and colleagues have often asked me whether I think Ann Summers 'a good thing or a bad thing'. I hope that it is clear by now that this question is too narrow and too simplistic to encompass the complexities of either female homosociality in general or Ann Summers in particular. During my fieldwork, while I was spending my days and evenings with party organisers and party-goers, they all made it abundantly clear to me in word and deed that they were there 'to have a laugh' above all else. Ann Summers *is* a space in which 'the girls' can take pleasure in the simple fact of being heterosexual women. What I have been trying to show throughout this book is in that the different types 'games' being played in Ann Summers, from power games to orgasm bingo, women can have a lot of fun. The problem is that they can have their fun only on the condition that they are willing and able to follow the rules – which, after all, is not a bad metaphor for women's pleasure in heterosexuality more generally. Only when those rules have been overturned will gender equality and sexual liberation have become anything more than a post-feminist fantasy.

References

Bernheimer, Charles (1992), 'Penile reference in phallic theory', *differences* 4 (1): 116–32.

Biggart, Nicole Woolsey (1989), *Charismatic Capitalism: Direct Selling Organizations in America*, London and Chicago: University of Chicago Press.

Bird, Sharon R. (1996), 'Welcome to the men's club: homosociality and the maintenance of hegemonic masculinity', *Gender and Society* 10 (2): 120–32.

Blank, Joani (1989 [1982]), *Good Vibrations: the Complete Guide to Vibrators*, San Francisco: Down There Press.

Bourdieu, Pierre (1977), *Outline of a Theory of Practice*, Cambridge: Cambridge University Press.

Bourdieu, Pierre (1984 [1979]), *Distinction: A Social Critique of the Judgement of Taste*, Cambridge, Mass.: Harvard University Press.

Britton, Dana M. (1990), 'Homophobia and homosociality: an analysis of boundary maintenance', *Sociological Quarterly* 31 (3): 423–39.

Butler, Judith (1990), *Gender Trouble: Feminism and the Subversion of Identity*, London & New York: Routledge.

Butler, Judith (1993), *Bodies that Matter: On the Discursive Limits of 'Sex'*, London & New York: Routledge.

Castle, Terry (1993), *The Apparitional Lesbian: Female Homosexuality and Modern Culture*, New York: Columbia University Press.

Clarke, Alison J. (1999), *Tupperware: the Promise of Plastic in 1950s America*, Washington and London: Smithsonian Institution Press.

Coates, Jennifer (1996), *Women Talk: Conversation Between Women Friends*, Oxford: Blackwell.

Collins, Patricia Hill (1991), *Black Feminist Thought: Knowledge, Consciousness, and the Politics of Empowerment*, London & New York: Routledge.

Connell, R. W. (1987), *Gender and Power*, Oxford: Polity Press.

Connell, R. W. (1995), *Masculinities*, Oxford: Polity Press.

Coward, Rosalind (1984), *Female Desire: Women's Sexuality Today*, London: Paladin.

Craik, Jennifer (1994), *The Face of Fashion: Cultural Studies in Fashion*, London and New York: Routledge.

Crawford, John C. and Garland, Barbara C. (1988), 'A profile of a party plan sales force', *Akron Business and Economic Review* 19 (4): 23–37.

Davis, J. (1973), 'Forms and norms: the economy of social relations', *Man* 8 (2): 159–76.

Direct Selling Association UK (2000), http://www.dsa.org.uk, downloaded 23rd January 2002.

Direct Selling Association USA (2001), http://www.dsa.org/research/numbrs.htm, downloaded 17th May 2002.

Doane, Mary Ann (1987), *The Desire to Desire: the Woman's Film of the 1940s*, Bloomington: Indiana University Press.

Du Gay, Paul (1996), *Consumption and Identity at Work*, London: Sage.

Duncombe, Jean and Marsden, Dennis (1996), 'Whose orgasm is this anyway? "Sex work" in long-term heterosexual couple relationships', in Jeffrey Weeks and Janet Holland (eds), *Sexual Cultures: Communities, Values and Intimacy*, London: Macmillan.

Dyer, Richard (1997), 'Heterosexuality', in Andy Medhurst and Sally R. Munt (eds), *Lesbian and Gay Studies: A Critical Introduction*, London: Cassell.

Edwards, Tim (2000), *Contradictions of Consumption: Concepts, Practices and Politics in Consumer Society*, Buckingham: Open University Press.

Erikson, David John and Tewksbury, Richard (2000), 'The "gentlemen" in the club: a typology of strip club patrons', *Deviant Behavior* 21 (3): 271–93.

Falk, Pasi (1994), *The Consuming Body*, London: Sage.

Faludi, Susan (1991), *Backlash: the Undeclared War Against American Women*, New York: Doubleday.

Findlay, Heather (1992), 'Freud's "Fetishism" and the lesbian dildo debates', *Feminist Studies* 18 (3): 563–79.

Foucault, Michel (1984 [1976]), *The History of Sexuality: an Introduction*, London: Peregrine.

Frankenburg, Ruth (1993), *White Women, Race Matters: the Social Construction of Whiteness*, London and New York: Routledge.

Friese, Susanne (2001), 'The wedding dress: from use value to sacred object', in Ali Guy, Eileen Green and Maura Banim (eds), *Through the Wardrobe: Women's Relationships with Their Clothes*, Oxford and New York: Berg Press.

Frith, Hannah (2000), 'Focusing on sex: using focus groups in sex research', *Sexualities* 3 (3): 275–97.

Fuss, Diana (1995), *Identification Papers*, London and New York: Routledge.

Gagnon, John H. and Simon, William (1967), *Sexual Deviance*, New York: Harper & Row.

Gainer, Brenda and Fischer, Eileen (1991), 'To buy or not to buy? That is not the question: female ritual in home shopping parties', *Advances in Consumer Research* 18: 597–602.

Gamman, Lorraine and Makinen, Merja (1994), *Female Fetishism: a New Look*, London: Lawrence & Wishart.

Gilfoyle, Jackie, Wilson, Jonathan and Brown (1992), 'Sex, organs and audiotape: a discourse analytic approach to talking about heterosexual sex and relationships', *Feminism and Psychology* 2 (2): 209–30.

Gimlin, Debra (1996), 'Pamela's Place: power and negotiation in the hair salon', *Gender and Society* 10 (5): 505–26.

Goffman, Erving (1990 [1959]), *The Presentation of Self in Everyday Life*, London: Penguin.

Gold, Jacqueline (1995), *Good Vibrations: the True Story of Ann Summers: the Autobiography of Jacqueline Gold*, London: Pavilion.

Gronow, Jukka (1997), *The Sociology of Taste*, London and New York: Routledge.

Grosz, Elizabeth (1990), *Jacques Lacan: a Feminist Introduction*, London & New York: Routledge.

Harrison, Kaeren (1998), 'Rich friendships, affluent friends: middle-class practices of friendship', in Rebecca G. Adams and Graham Allan (eds), *Placing Friendship in Context*, Cambridge, New York & Melbourne: Cambridge University Press.

Heath, Stephen (1982), *The Sexual Fix*, London: Macmillan.

Hochschild, Arlie Russell (1983), *The Managed Heart: Commercialization of Human Feeling*, Berkeley and London: University of California Press.

Holland, Janet, Ramazanoglu, Caroline, Sharpe, Sue and Thomson, Rachel (1998), *The Male in the Head: Young People, Heterosexuality and Power*, London: Tufnell Press.

Hollway, Wendy (1984), 'Gender difference and the production of subjectivity', in Julian Henriques, et al. (eds), *Changing the Subject: Psychology, Social Regulation and Subjectivity*, London: Methuen.

Hutchins, Brett and Mikosza, Janine (1998), 'Australian rugby league and violence 1970 to 1995: a case study in the maintenance of masculine hegemony', *Journal of Sociology* 34 (3): 246–63.

Ingraham, Chrys (1999), *White Weddings: Romancing Heterosexuality in Popular Culture*, London and New York: Routledge.

Jackson, Stevi (1999), *Heterosexuality in Question*, London: Sage.

Jackson, Stevi and Scott, Sue (2000), 'Faking like a woman: towards an interpretive theorisation of sexual pleasure', paper delivered at ESRC seminar series *Sexuality: Representation and Lived Experience*, University of York.

Jones, Deborah (1990 [1980]), 'Gossip: notes on women's oral culture', in Deborah Cameron (ed.), *The Feminist Critique of Language: a Reader*, London & New York: Routledge.

Juffer, Jane (1998), *At Home with Pornography: Women, Sex, and Everyday Life*, New York and London: New York University Press.

Lacan, Jacques (1989 [1977]), *Ecrits: A Selection*, London and New York: Routledge.

Laqueur, Thomas (1992 [1990]), *Making Sex: Body and Gender from the Greeks to Freud*, Cambridge, Mass & London: Harvard University Press.

De Lauretis, Teresa (1994), *The Practice of Love: Lesbian Sexuality and Perverse Desire*, Bloomington & Indianapolis: Indiana University Press.

Lees, Sue (1986), *Losing Out: Sexuality and Adolescent Girls*, London: Hutchinson.

Lees, Sue (1993), *Sugar and Spice: Sexuality and Adolescent Girls*, London: Penguin.

Lipman-Blumen, Jean (1976), 'Toward a homosocial theory of sex roles: an explanation of the sex segregation of social institutions', *Signs* 1(3): 15–31.

Lovell, Terry (2000), 'Thinking feminism with and against Bourdieu', *Feminist Theory* 1 (1): 11–32.

Lutz, Helma (2002), '"At your service madam!" The globalization of domestic service', *Feminist Review* 70: 89–104.

Lyman, Peter (1987), 'The fraternal bond as a joking relationship: a case study of the role of sexist jokes in male group bonding', in Michael S. Kimmel (ed.), *New Directions in Research on Men and Masculinity*, London: Sage.

McDowell, Linda (1992), 'Gender divisions in a post-Fordist era: new contradictions or the same old story?', in Linda McDowell and Rosemary Pringle (eds), *Defining Women: Social Institutions and Gender Divisions*, Cambridge: Polity Press.

McGhee, Derek (1998), 'Looking and acting the part: gays in the armed forces – a case of passing masculinity', *Feminist Legal Studies* 6 (2): 205–44.

Mackinnon, Kenneth (1997), *Uneasy Pleasures: the Male as Erotic Object*, London: Cygnus Arts.

Maddison, Stephen (2000), *Fags, Hags and Queer Sisters: Gender Dissent and Heterosocial Bonds in Gay Culture*, London: Macmillan.

Maines, Rachel P. (1999), *The Technology of Orgasm: 'Hysteria', the Vibrator, and Women's Sexual Satisfaction*, Baltimore & London: John Hopkins University Press.

Malos, Ellen (1995 [1980]) ed., *The Politics of Housework*, Cheltenham: New Clarion Press.

Miao, Tiger (1999), 'The word made flesh', *Skin Two* 29: 46–7.

Miller, Daniel (1998), *A Theory of Shopping*, Cambridge: Polity Press.

Millett, Kate (1972), *Sexual Politics*, London: Abacus.

Mitchell, Juliet and Rose, Jacqueline (1982) eds, *Feminine Sexuality: Jacques Lacan and the école freudienne*, London: Macmillan.

Moseley, Rachel (2002), 'Trousers and tiaras: Audrey Hepburn, a woman's star', *Feminist Review* 71: 37–51.

Mulvey, Laura (1975), 'Visual pleasure and narrative cinema', *Screen* 16 (3): 6–18.

Oakley, Ann (1974), *Housewife*, London: Allen Lane.

O'Connor, Pat (1992), *Friendships Between Women*, Hemel Hempstead: Harvester Wheatsheaf.

Oliker, Stacey J. (1989), *Best Friends and Marriage: Exchange Among Women*, Berkeley: University of California Press.

O'Neill, Gilda (1993), *A Night Out with the Girls: Women Having a Good Time*, London: Women's Press.

Pahl, Jan (1989), *Money and Marriage*, London: Macmillan.

Petersen, David M. and Dressel, Paula L. (1982), 'Equal time for women: social notes on the male strip show', *Urban Life* 11 (2): 185–208.

Peven, Dorothy E. (1968), 'The use of religious revival techniques to indoctrinate personnel: the home-party sales organizations', *Sociological Quarterly* 9 (1): 97–106.

Phillips, Angela and Rakusen, Jill (1978), *Our Bodies, Ourselves: a Health Book by and for Women*, London: Penguin.

Phillips, Anne (1987), *Divided Loyalties: Dilemmas of Sex and Class*, London: Virago.

Plummer, Ken (1995), *Telling Sexual Stories: Power, Change and Social Worlds*, London and New York: Routledge.

Probyn, Elspeth (2000), *Carnal Appetites: FoodSexIdentities*, London & New York: Routledge.

Prus, Robert and Frisby, Wendy (1990), 'Persuasion as tactical accomplishment: tactical manoeuverings at home (party plan) shows', *Current Research on Occupations and Professions* 5: 133–62.

Ramazanoglu, Caroline (1995), 'Back to basics: heterosexuality, biology and why men stay on top', in Mary Maynard and June Purvis (eds), *(Hetero)sexual Politics*, London: Taylor & Francis.

Rich, Adrienne (1981 [1980]), *Compulsory Heterosexuality and Lesbian Existence*, London: Onlywomen Press.

Roberts, Celia, Kippax, Susan, Waldby, Catherine and Crawford, June (1995), 'Faking it: the story of "ohh!"', *Women's Studies International Forum* 18 (5–6): 523–32.

Rubin, Gayle (1975), 'The traffic in women: notes on the "political economy" of sex', in Rayna R. Reiter (ed.), *Toward an Anthropology of Women*, New York: Monthly Review Press.

Rubin, Gayle with Butler, Judith (1994), 'Sexual traffic', *differences* 6 (2–3): 62–99.

Sedgwick, Eve Kosofsky (1985), *Between Men: English Literature and Male Homosocial Desire*, New York: Columbia University Press.

Segal, Lynne (1983), 'Sensual uncertainty, or, why the clitoris is not enough', in Sue Cartledge and Joanna Ryan (eds), *Sex and Love: New Thoughts on Old Contradictions*, London: Women's Press.

Segal, Lynne (1994), *Straight Sex: the Politics of Pleasure*, London: Virago.

Skeggs, Beverley (1997), *Formations of Class and Gender*, London: Sage.

Smart, Carol (1996), 'Collusion, collaboration and confession: on moving beyond the heterosexuality debate', in Diane Richardson (ed.), *Theorising Heterosexuality: Telling It Straight*, Buckingham: Open University Press.

Smith, Clarissa (2002), 'Shiny chests and heaving G-strings: a night out with the Chippendales', *Sexualities* 5 (1): 67–89.

Sonnet, Esther (1999), '"Erotic fiction by women for women": the pleasures of post-feminist heterosexuality', *Sexualities* 2 (2): 167–87.

Squire, Corinne (1994), 'Empowering women? *The Oprah Winfrey Show*', *Feminism and Psychology* 4 (1): 63–79.

Steele, Valerie (1985), *Fashion and Eroticism: Ideals of Feminine Beauty from the Victorian Era to the Jazz Age*, New York and Oxford: Oxford University Press.

Storr, Merl (2001), 'New Labour, New Britain, new sexual values?', *Social Epistemology* 15 (2): 113–26.

Sullivan, Oriel (2000), 'The division of domestic labour: twenty years of change?', *Sociology* 34 (3): 437–56.

Taylor, Rex (1978), 'Marilyn's friends and Rita's customers: a study of party-selling as play and as work', *Sociological Review* 26 (3): 573–94.

Thorogood, Nicki (2000), 'Mouthrules and the construction of sexual identities', *Sexualities* 3 (2): 165–82.

Vermeule, Blakey (1991), 'Is there a Sedgwick school for girls?', *Qui Parle* 5 (1): 53–72.

Walkerdine, Valerie (1997), *Daddy's Girl: Young Girls and Popular Culture*, Basingstoke: Macmillan.

Whelehan, Imelda (1994), *Modern Feminist Thought: from the Second Wave to 'Post-Feminism'*, Edinburgh: Edinburgh University Press.

White, Mimi (1992), *Teleadvising: Therapeutic Discourse in American Television*, Chapel Hill: University of North Caroline Press.

Williams, Linda (1989), *Hard-Core: Power, Pleasure, and the 'Frenzy of the Visible'*, Berkeley: University of California Press.

Wilson, Elizabeth (1985), *Adorned in Dreams: Fashion and Modernity*, London: Virago.

Wilson-Kovacs, Dana (2001), 'The fall and rise of erotic lingerie', in William J. F. Keenan (ed.), *Dressed to Impress: Looking the Part*, Oxford and New York: Berg Press.

Winship, Janice (1987), *Inside Women's Magazines*, London: Pandora.

Workman, Nancy V. (1996), 'From Victorian to Victoria's Secret: the foundations of modern erotic wear', *Journal of Popular Culture* 30 (2): 61–73.

Index

age, 13, 14, 19, 21–2, 26, 66, 118, 129, 158, 166, 193
Amway, 3, 9n3, 30
anus, 127n2, 128, 136, 143–5
armpit, 167

Biggart, Nicole Woolsey, 8, 9, 29, 30
Bird, Sharon R., 42
bisexuality, 18, 20, 53, 185, 211
bitching, 70–2, 102, 125, 169, 203–4
body size, 21–2, 71, 154–5, 169–70, 173, 202
bondage-domination/ sadomasochism (bdsm), 124, 136, 208–11, 216, 217
    see also leather, handcuffs
Bordo, Susan, 108–9
Bourdieu, Pierre, 19n5, 177, 182–3, 196, 221
breasts, 145, 146–7, 160, 168, 169, 173, 175–6, 209–12
Britton, Dana M., 40, 43, 47n7
Butler, Judith, 120

Caborn-Waterfield, Kim, 4
Castle, Terry, 84–5
childbirth, 140, 147, 154
children, 24, 25, 26–9, 31, 51, 55, 56–7, 93, 125, 133, 147, 154, 179, 192, 195, 202, 213–14, 220

chocolate, 63, 105, 138, 144, 151–4, 175, 190
class, 13, 14, 19–21, 24, 31, 35, 42, 44–6, 49, 50, 52, 53, 59–62, 63, 66, 93–4, 129, 177–80, 191, 197–9, 213–14
    and taste distinctions, 177, 180–5, 187, 189–92, 195–9, 201–3, 216–17
clitoris, 32, 73, 126–7, 136, 145–6, 148, 149, 167, 168, 173, 175–6
commission, 6–7, 11, 26, 29, 31, 49, 57–62, 192, 195, 199
condoms, 68–9, 95, 104, 106, 142, 160
confessional culture, 32, 125
Connell, R. W., 45–6, 49, 51, 86, 219

Davis, J., 34
direct selling, 3–4, 9, 29, 30, 34–5
    see also Amway, Discovery Toys, Mary Kay, party plan, Pippa Dee, Tupperware
Direct Selling Association, 3
discourse,
    defined, 126–9
    of honesty, 130–2
    of love and relationships, 135
    of male drive, 133, 146
    of male technique, 134–5, 162

of passive vagina, 139–41
permissive, 133
pseudo-reciprocal gift, 134–5
Discovery Toys, 35
diversity, 14–22, 129
domestic labour, 24, 27–9, 31, 32,
    49, 51, 56, 61, 62, 178, 192,
    195–7, 213–15, 220
  see also maid's outfits
Dyer, Richard, 219

Edwards, Tim, 191
emotional labour, 22–6, 31–2
emphasised femininity, 51
erogenous body, defined, 127–30
Essex girl jokes, 62, 63n9
ethnicity, 13, 14, 18–19, 42, 44–6,
    49, 52, 63–7, 115, 129, 177, 216,
    220
  see also whiteness

feminism, 33, 34, 47, 48, 53, 70, 126
  see also post-feminism
fetishism, 124, 209–11
  see also rubber
Fischer, Eileen, 34–5
Frankenburg, Ruth, 19
Freud, Sigmund, 108, 113
friendship
  between men, 42
  between women, 37–8, 47, 53

G-spot, 73, 126–7, 127n2
Gagnon, John, 39n2
Gainer, Brenda, 34–5
Gamman, Lorraine, 153
gay men, see homosexuality
gaze
  female, 102, 104, 168–75
  male, 80, 81, 93–7, 103, 104,
    111–12, 121, 169, 173–5

gender identification, 45, 50, 51, 52,
    53, 63–71, 83, 84, 92, 96, 100,
    101, 110, 118, 123, 124–5, 127,
    128–9, 130, 132, 136, 139, 145,
    147, 149, 152, 154–5, 157, 159,
    162, 164, 169, 174, 187–91, 195,
    199, 216, 220–2
gender order, 45, 49, 51, 52, 53, 62,
    89, 110, 220
gender régime, 45–6, 50, 52, 53, 81,
    89, 93–4, 110, 114, 122, 129, 158,
    213, 220, 221
ghosting, of homosocial by
    erogenous body, 129, 150, 154–6,
    160–1, 165–8, 173–5
Gilfoyle, Jackie, 126, 133–4
Gold, David, 4
Gold, Jacqueline, 5, 11, 30, 37
Gold, Ralph, 4

habitus, 19n5, 221
handcuffs, 208–1, 211, 217
hands, 120, 136, 145, 146, 147, 168
Harrison, Kaeren, 53
hegemonic masculinity, 45–6, 51,
    91–2, 102, 103, 107, 108, 114,
    121
hen nights, 54, 95–6, 103–5, 170
heterosexuality, 14–21, 24, 27, 30,
    34, 35, 37–9, 52, 53, 68, 74, 75,
    78, 86, 90, 143–5, 158, 178,
    184–5, 197, 207, 213, 219–22
  see also homosociality, men,
    penetrative sex, weddings
Hochschild, Arlie Russell, 24
Hollway, Wendy, 133
home shopping parties, see direct
    selling, party plan
homophobia, 20, 40, 41, 43–5, 47–9,
    83, 89, 144n3, 220
  see also lesbophobia

homosexuality, 39–47, 78, 83, 89, 121, 127n2, 128, 143, 144, 144n3, 184–5, 211

homosocial body, defined, 127, 129

homosociality, 39

   female, 35–6, 39, 54–5, 97–8, 110, 114, 119, 121–2, 156, 160, 164, 165, 194, 197, 207, 214, 219–22

      and female bonding, 35, 48, 84–5, 86

      defined, 47–54

      serving interests of men, 48–51, 52, 53, 56–62, 118, 162, 173

      see also hen nights

   male, 39–47, 51, 55, 83–4, 104, 111–12, 121, 221

      and male bonding, 41, 44, 83, 89

      exchange of women, 40–1, 50, 52, 83–4, 86–90, 94

      see also stag nights

Jackson, Stevi, 164

'kinkiness', 201, 207–10, 212, 216–7

   see also bondage-domination/ sadomasochism (bdsm), fetishism, handcuffs, leather, pvc, rubber

kissing, 73, 74, 78, 79, 157, 165

Lacan, Jacques, 107n3, 107n4

Laqueur, Thomas, 127

latex, 116–7

   see also rubber

laughter, 2, 9, 74, 88, 93, 108, 110, 111, 112–13, 116, 118, 120, 124, 129, 133, 143, 158–9, 194, 222

De Lauretis, Teresa, 47–8

leather, 208, 216

   see also bondage-domination/ sadomasochism (bdsm)

lesbian continuum, 48

lesbianism, 18, 47–8, 53, 72, 73–81, 84–5, 110, 118, 120–1, 145, 164, 165, 174, 184–5, 211

lesbophobia, 47–9, 50, 52, 53, 72–80, 89, 123–4, 125, 156, 157, 165, 174, 175

Lévi-Strauss, Claude, 41n3

lingerie, see underwear

Lipman-Blumen, Jean, 39–43, 49, 52, 83

Lovell, Terry, 221

McGhee, Derek, 221

Mackinnon, Kenneth, 109

Maddison, Stephen, 47, 48–9

maid's outfits, 215–6

Makinen, Merja, 153

Marks and Spencer, 205

Mary Kay, 3, 30

masturbation, 120, 130

men, 7, 10, 20, 24, 26–9, 30, 31, 32, 33, 34, 37, 38–46, 53, 54, 55, 63, 66, 70, 71, 75–6, 80–81, 84–5, 107, 109–10, 113–14, 115, 118–21, 127, 128–9, 130, 133, 134–5, 138, 139–40, 141, 142, 143–5, 146, 155, 158, 160–4, 172–5, 178, 191, 192, 195, 196, 201, 204–5, 213, 214, 215–16, 219–20

   as objects of heterosexual desire, 90–2, 97–103

   in uniform, 97–103, 105, 107, 110, 121

   see also friendship, hegemonic masculinity, gaze, homosexuality, penis, strippers

Miao, Tiger, 211

Miller, Daniel, 191
Millett, Kate, 108
Moseley, Rachel, 53
mother-daughter couples at parties,
    67–70
mouth, 136, 141–4, 146, 147, 150–7,
    173, 175

nose, 167

Oliker, Stacey J., 53
oral sex, 78, 120, 136, 141–2, 144,
    154–6, 175
orgasm, 126–7, 129, 134–5, 146,
    149, 160–4, 172, 175, 222
outerwear, 4, 92, 170, 172, 185, 186,
    200

party plan, 3–11, 26, 31, 33, 34–5,
    38, 42, 54, 61
    see also Amway, direct selling,
    Discovery Toys, Mary Kay, Pippa
    Dee, Tupperware
penetrative sex, 120, 127n2, 136,
    137–8, 141, 145–6, 149, 163,
    175
    see also anus, vagina
penis, 104–10, 115–21, 123, 133,
    136–7, 138, 139, 142, 145–6,
    149, 154, 157, 162–3, 176, 194,
    222
    envy, 108
    inflatable plastic, 75, 109, 110–13,
    121
    jelly willy, 105, 113–14, 117, 121
    see also sex toys
personality, 21–4, 158–9, 179
phallus, see penis
Pippa Dee, 5, 66
plastic, 201–11, 217
    see also penis

pornography, 162
post-feminism, 30–4, 63, 66, 86, 110,
    113, 119, 121–2, 124–5, 132,
    133, 135, 136, 139, 149, 162,
    175–6, 203, 213, 216, 217, 222
    see also feminism
pregnancy, 141
psychoanalysis, 107–9, 168
pvc (polyvinyl chloride), 208, 209

race, see ethnicity
racism, 18, 44–6, 64–7, 220
recruitment of party organisers,
    10–11, 66, 67
respectability, 181–2, 185, 201,
    203–7, 212–13, 214
Roberts, Celia, 134–5, 162
Rich, Adrienne, 48
Rubin, Gayle, 41
rubber, 209–10

Scott, Sue, 164
Sedgwick, Eve Kosofsky, 40–5, 47–8,
    53, 83, 84–5, 221
sex industry, 212–13
    see also sex workers
sex toys, 4, 6, 10, 32, 33, 67, 69, 75,
    80, 85, 87, 89, 95, 96, 98, 106,
    109, 111, 114–21, 124, 131, 132,
    136–8, 139–42, 143, 145, 146, 147,
    148, 149, 159–60, 166–8, 176, 190,
    194, 201–5, 214
sex workers, 147
    see also sex industry
sexual experience, 123–4, 131–2,
    158, 201–7
    see also virginity
sexual positions, 135–6
Simon, William, 39n2
Skeggs, Beverley, 24, 50, 179–80,
    185, 201

'slag', *see* sexual experience
Smart, Carol, 108
Smith, Clarissa, 109n5
Sonnet, Esther, 31
stag nights, 103–4
strippers
    female, 103–4
    male, 8, 54, 100–3, 108–10, 159

tactility, 129, 145–7, 157, 164–8, 174
taste, *see* class
Taylor, Rex, 161n6
teasing, 70, 72, 76, 78, 102, 124, 125
Thorogood, Nicki, 156
training of party organisers, 10, 71
transvestites, 9
Tupperware, 3, 30, 34, 35, 54, 161n6

Uhse, Beate, 4
underwear, 4, 10, 22, 71, 80, 88, 89,
    92, 93, 101, 105, 133, 142, 147,

154, 163, 164, 169, 170–5,
185–8, 192–6, 199–201, 203–7,
213–17
and domesticity, 213–16
and luxury, 191–9

vagina, 120, 126–7, 129, 136–41,
142, 145–6, 147, 148, 149, 161,
163, 167, 173, 175–6
Vermeule, Blakey, 47n6
vibrators, *see* sex toys
Victoria's Secret, 2n1
virginity, 123, 130, 143
voice, female, 100–1, 129, 157–64

Walkerdine, Valerie, 53
Warner, Sylvia Townsend, 84
weddings, 103, 180–2, 187
whiteness, 13, 18–19, 35, 49, 63–7,
115, 117, 177, 178
Wilson, Elizabeth, 186